Digital Entrepreneurship

We would like to pay tribute to our families for their unwavering support and encouragement on this project.
Kisito would like to mention in particular Liu Xiaoling, Alexandra Futonge, Athena Liu Futonge, and Mphoweh Jude Nzembayie.
Tony would like to give special mention also to Mairead Harrington Buckley, Paul Buckley, and Shauna Buckley.

Digital Entrepreneurship
Disruption and New Venture Creation

Kisito Futonge Nzembayie

Assistant Professor in Entrepreneurship, Trinity Business School, Trinity College Dublin, Ireland

Anthony Paul Buckley

Assistant Head, School of Marketing and Program Director of MSc in Business and Entrepreneurship, Technological University Dublin, Ireland

Edward Elgar
PUBLISHING

Cheltenham, UK • Northampton, MA, USA

Published by
Edward Elgar Publishing Limited
The Lypiatts
15 Lansdown Road
Cheltenham
Glos GL50 2JA
UK

Edward Elgar Publishing, Inc.
William Pratt House
9 Dewey Court
Northampton
Massachusetts 01060
USA

Paperback edition 2023

A catalogue record for this book
is available from the British Library

Library of Congress Control Number: 2022931035

This book is available electronically in the **Elgar**online
Business subject collection
http://dx.doi.org/10.4337/9781802200584

ISBN 978 1 80220 057 7 (cased)
ISBN 978 1 80220 058 4 (eBook)
ISBN 978 1 0353 1694 6 (paperback)

Printed and bound by CPI Group (UK) Ltd, Croydon, CR0 4YY

Contents

Figures

Tables

Preface

When we began our research on *Digital Entrepreneurship* back in 2016, we were surprised to find no articles written on the subject in the top journals of entrepreneurship – *Entrepreneurship Theory & Practice* (ETP) and *Journal of Business Venturing* (JBV). It made us wonder if we had taken interest in the wrong topic, or were perhaps looking in the wrong place. Some nine months into our study, the discipline finally published its first agenda-setting article in ETP. The article confirmed what we were seeing all along – there was urgent need for research on the subject of digital entrepreneurship. Indeed, *Digital Entrepreneurship*, which represents a distinctive form of entrepreneurship in the digital age, calls for urgent theorizing. However, given the complexity and dynamism of the phenomenon, a cross-disciplinary dialogue and plurality of perspectives is needed to fully appreciate its growing significance.

Pervasive digitization has set in motion a paradigmatic shift in economic value creation. Collectively, digital technology-driven changes create difficulties – both conceptual and practical – for students, educators, practitioners, and policymakers who seek to navigate the 'swampy lowlands' of the digital age. These difficulties become particularly acute when those interested in entrepreneurship consider digitally-driven new venture creation. Hence, a sharp focus on digital entrepreneurship and its transformative and disruptive effects is needed to help advance conceptual clarity. This will then offer guidance for education and practice. As academic researchers, digital entrepreneurial practitioners, and educators working in this domain over several years, we have been well placed to explore and reflect on the intricacies framing this typology of entrepreneurship. Hence, we write this book to offer advanced undergraduate and graduate students, teachers, academics, practitioners, and policymakers a conceptual and pragmatic guide to the subject of 'Digital Entrepreneurship.' All of this is presented in a clear, concise, and action-orientated text.

The material in this book is grounded in our 20 years of academic research in entrepreneurship and over a decade in digital entrepreneurial practice. Our research, which utilized an innovative action design research methodology, resulted in our discovery of new insights into the mechanisms by which a digital entrepreneurial process emerges. More importantly, we identified the fundamental differences between the digital entrepreneurial process versus more traditional entrepreneurial processes. Accepting these differences is the departure point for ensuring that the development of digital new ventures will result in more productive outcomes. Ultimately, we hope that this book will act as a trusted guide for you on your digital entrepreneurship journey.

However, we recognize that we are at the early stages of these exciting new developments in entrepreneurship and thus hope that you build on this text to advance knowledge in the theory and practice of digital new venture creation. Through our collective efforts, knowledge on this disruptive form of economic value creation will continue to percolate down to those who need it most.

Kisito and Anthony
Dublin, Ireland, September 2021

Acknowledgements

Writing a book such as this one is not just a two-person effort. Although it is undoubtedly true that the book would not exist without us, it would indeed not exist in its finished form without the inspiration, help, and support of many people.

We are indebted to Francine O'Sullivan and the editorial board at Edward Elgar Publishing for seeing the potential in this book. The guidance that we received from Francine and her team was instrumental in bringing the project to completion.

We are intellectually indebted to Professor Per Davidsson and Professor Satish Nambisan for their pioneering work in contemporary entrepreneurship thinking and the digital entrepreneurship domain.

A special mention also goes to Professor David Coghlan for his inspirational work in the Action Research field, which shaped our research design and teaching.

We acknowledge the input of our students and colleagues in Technological University Dublin, which constantly reminds us of the value of what we do every day as educators.

Finally, we acknowledge the influence in thinking from the practitioners we regularly engage with in the communities of digital entrepreneurial practice.

1. Digital entrepreneurship: context and conceptualization

1.1 THEORETICAL AND PRACTICAL CONTEXTS

Digitization has ushered in a new era of economic value creation in which soaring cross-border data flows generate more value than traditional flows of traded goods (Manyika et al., 2016). The move to more digital forms of economic value creation has fundamentally altered the rules of innovation and entrepreneurship regarding who participates and how new market offerings are created, and with what consequences (Yoo et al., 2012; Lyytinen et al., 2016). Accordingly, digital entrepreneurship, which refers to the creation and application of digitized and cyber-physical market offerings, has emerged as a subject of significant scholarly and practical interest (Nambisan, 2017). Activities at the micro levels of digital new venture creation have far-reaching consequences, with digital transformation and digital disruption being among the core macro- and micro-level effects on society. The increased centrality of digitization in all forms of value creation motivated veteran industry watcher, investor, and digital entrepreneur, Marc Andreessen, to proclaim figuratively that 'software is eating the world' (Andreessen, 2011).

However, conceptualizing digital entrepreneurship and its effects can become quite challenging, given the nature of complexity and the dynamic environment against which the phenomenon emerges (von Briel et al., 2020). Moreover, the subject lies at the nexus between multiple disciplines with their distinctive interpretations and theoretical emphases. Accordingly, an integrative perspective is needed to fully appreciate the phenomenon and organize scholarship and practice. Hence, this book identifies and integrates relevant theoretical and practical lenses towards a pluralistic and pragmatic explanation of the mechanisms by which a digital entrepreneurial process emerges. It also examines how such emergence upends some widely held assumptions of entrepreneurship and value creation. At an abstract level, entrepreneurship is a complex phenomenon revolving around the discovery and exploitation of opportunity to create new economic value (Shane and Venkataraman, 2000; Wiklund et al., 2011). More current developments in the entrepreneurship discipline define entrepreneurial opportunity more precisely as two interrelated sub-constructs – New Venture Ideas and External Enablers (Davidsson, 2015). Following these developments, technology change is an opportunity; which means it can act as an external enabler that triggers new venture ideas by individuals, which then centrally drives the entrepreneurial process.

Accordingly, the interrelationship between digital technologies, such as digital artifacts and digital platforms, and underlying digital infrastructures, such as cloud computing and internet connectivity, is central to unpacking the complexity of digital entrepreneurship. These complementary, ubiquitous, and often standardized technologies enable entrepreneurship by promoting near-costless communications and transactions, which allow individuals to network, organize, and co-create value with an ever-changing cast of collectives dispersed across geographical regions. Hence, today's digital new ventures can easily become micro-multinationals and born globals in compressed time frames, compared to their traditional counterparts (Bell and Loane, 2010). Moreover, their often agile and stealthy emergence means they can creep up on unsuspecting incumbents, consequently disrupting or transforming entire industries and value chains as a consequence. For instance, outcomes of digital entrepreneurship such as Uber and Airbnb more recently appeared with business models that have proven disruptive to the taxi transportation and hospitality industries – which had remained relatively stable over recent centuries. Hence, Tapscott (2014, p. xxiv) cautions that in an age of networked intelligence, punishment is swift for organizations, industries, and societies that fall behind.

The velocity, scope, and systems impact of change brought about by digitization have led to the assertion that we are on the cusp of a Fourth Industrial Revolution (Schwab, 2017) or the Second Machine Age. This age is believed to have already begun and is accelerating into a future defined by the 'digitization of just about everything' (Brynjolfsson and McAfee, 2014, pp. 57–70). The digitization of virtually everything will continuously result in the merging of digital, biological, and physical spheres into ever more powerful 'new combinations' (Schumpeter, 1942). Accordingly, in 2016, McKinsey reported that some 50 percent of digitizable services had already been digitized (Manyika et al., 2016). Likewise, Machine-to-Machine (M2M) communication from Internet of Things (IoT) devices hooked up to the cloud continues to accelerate the trend in value creation defined by the generation, collection, harnessing, and monetization of insights from big data (UNCTAD, 2019). Furthermore, the application of Artificial Intelligence (AI) and machine learning algorithms on big data is poised to become prevalent and ever more mainstream (McAfee and Brynjolfsson, 2017). Hence, digital and cyber-physical products/service offerings reshape industry structures and alter the mechanisms through which firms create and sustain a competitive edge (Porter and Heppelmann, 2014, 2015).

Consequently, ubiquitous digitization of value creation equally challenges widely accepted theoretical assumptions about entrepreneurship and innovation (Nambisan et al., 2017). New knowledge is therefore required to advance new hypotheses and theories and guide sound policy implementation and practice. As Storey and Greene (2010, p. 208) maintain, nurturing the growth of gazelles (young fast-growth firms) should be essential in any enterprise policy development initiatives. Digital gazelles have indeed had a transformational impact on global economies in just under 30 years. To put it into perspective, by 2017, four digital technology-based firms (Apple, Google, Amazon, and Facebook) had a market capitalization roughly the GDP of the Indian economy at over $2.3 trillion (Galloway, 2017, p. 1). Likewise, there was only one digital technology-based firm (Microsoft) among the top five global companies by market capitalization in 2006. However, by 2020 the trend had been completely reversed, with Saudi Aramco being the only non-digital technology company among the top five – with Apple and Microsoft reaching combined capitalizations of nearly $4 trillion (PricewaterhouseCoopers, 2021). Additionally, relatively newer digital ventures in the sharing economy, such as Uber and Airbnb, have emerged and disrupted entire industry structures with innovative business models. These digital disruptors question what it means to create and capture value in the digital age.

Yet, despite its contemporary significance, the field of entrepreneurship has largely neglected the role of digital technologies in the entrepreneurial process. Remarkably, digital entrepreneurship only very recently received agenda-setting entries in leading journals of entrepreneurship (Nambisan, 2017; Kraus et al., 2018). Earlier and current attempts at describing and understanding the phenomenon had mainly been undertaken by MIS (Management Information Systems) scholars (Hull et al., 2007; Davidson and Vaast, 2010). As the relatively scant but rapidly growing literature on digital entrepreneurship indicates, digitization challenges the degree to which existing theories can inform on the varied issues surrounding digital new venture creation and value creation in the digital age. To underscore the point, Benner and Tushman (2015, p. 498), in reflecting on their decade-old award-winning article in the *Academy of Management Review* noted that digitization has resulted in a 'shift in the locus of innovation,' thereby challenging some of our core organization axioms and the state of organizational scholarship.

The disruptiveness of digitization on extant assumptions of innovation and entrepreneurship appears to be particularly visible in purer forms of digital entrepreneurship, where digital artifacts and digital platforms form the core of new venture ideas, resulting in intangible but highly valuable market offerings (Nzembayie et al., 2019). Purer forms of digital entrepreneurship have spurred new forms of economic value creation based on the digitization, processing, and commercialization of information as new market offerings (Giones and Brem, 2017). They operate in the context of what is commonly termed 'economics of bits,' characterized by the production of non-rival digitized offerings, with 'close to zero marginal cost of reproduction' (Brynjolfsson and McAfee, 2014, p. 62). Digitized non-rival products and services can be consumed by many people simultaneously without being depleted. Accordingly, Shapiro and Varian (1998) argue that digitized information may be costly to produce but relatively less expensive to replicate and maintain. Owing to these characteristics, the economics of pure digital new venture creation often upends some of the more traditional assumptions of entrepreneurship and value creation, rooted in the creation of physical and tactile market offerings.

1.2   CONCEPTUALIZING DIGITAL ENTREPRENEURSHIP (PURE AND HYBRID)

Conceptualizing digital entrepreneurship begins with the understanding that it refers to two main typologies – pure and hybrid. We define Pure Digital Entrepreneurship (PDE) as entrepreneurship in which digital artifacts and digital platforms are solely the new venture ideas and new market offerings, which are cultivated on top of and distributed via external enabling digital infrastructures (Nzembayie et al., 2019). Current examples of PDE market offerings are digital services such as Uber, which is a taxi-hailing service; Apple App Store and Google Play which are mobile app distribution platforms; Netflix, which is a digital movie streaming platform service; Facebook and Twitter, which are social media platforms; and Shopify which is a Software as a Service (SaaS) platform for developing an e-commerce venture.

However, when digital new venture creation is based on creating tightly coupled cyber-physical systems as market offerings, a hybrid form of digital entrepreneurship is distinguishable. Thus, we define Hybrid Digital Entrepreneurship (HDE) as the tight coupling and layering of digital artifacts and digital platforms with physical artifacts and processes, resulting in mutual dependencies of cyber-physical systems as market offerings. Two classifications of outcomes are possible under this typology of entrepreneurship. Fitbit and Garmin are smartwatches that make good examples under the first classification. Smart devices are made smart by the tight coupling of digital software artifacts with microprocessors and networking technologies into a layered, modular, and mutually dependent cyber-physical product/service combination (Lyytinen et al., 2016). In the example, a watch, which is traditionally 'a single function device,' becomes transformed and augmented into a multi-purpose device. Meanwhile, in the second classification of HDE offerings, the tight coupling of a purely digital service with a purely traditional service as market offering results in outcomes such as Deliveroo and Just Eat. Such cyber-physical services combine a purely digital artifact (app) and digital platform with the purely physical and traditional service of takeout food delivery.

There are significant implications for entrepreneurial processes when new venture ideas and market offerings fall under either pure or hybrid typologies of digital entrepreneurship, which we explore in greater depth in Chapter 3. For instance, it is reasonable to assume that HDE is generally more challenging to realize than PDE because of spatial and temporal constraints. Thus processes may combine traditional discrete value chain models with the fluidity and weightlessness of the pure digital value chain. Given its hybrid nature, theories of innovation and entrepreneurship with assumptions of spatiotemporal boundedness may retain some of their explanatory power under an HDE typology but less so under PDE. Therefore, with significant differences in processes and outcomes, it is necessary to distinguish between digital entrepreneurship typologies and more traditional typologies of entrepreneurship in the digital age.

However, owing to the increased blurring of lines between digital and traditional forms of entrepreneurship, we argue that entrepreneurship in the digital age is best conceptualized as a continuum between the extremes of PDE and Pure Traditional Entrepreneurship (PTE) with two hybrid typologies in between. Figure 1.1 illustrates how the typologies of digital and traditional entrepreneurship are differentiated along this continuum based on the centrality or peripherality of digital artifacts and digital platforms in new venture ideas and market offerings (Fiss, 2011). We expand on this conceptualization in Chapter 3, following a grounding in traditional theories of entrepreneurship in Chapter 2.

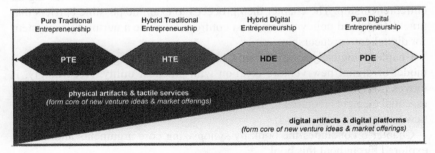

Figure 1.1   Typologies of entrepreneurship in the digital age

1.3   ROADMAP OF THE BOOK

The following structure has been developed to guide the reader throughout this book. It is divided into five main thematic chapters and a synoptic final chapter. The current chapter has provided a general introduction to digital entrepreneurship, which will be discussed in greater depth in subsequent chapters.

Chapter 2 provides a general background to entrepreneurship scholarship and state-of-the-art theories of the entrepreneurial process. It identifies and reviews established theories and concepts which explain entrepreneurial decision-making and action. Consequently, an integrative traditional model of the entrepreneurial process is developed, around which a holistic narrative of new venture emergence can be woven. The model also serves as an analytical tool for examining how the digital entrepreneurial process both intersects with and differs from traditional assumptions of entrepreneurship in Chapter 3.

Chapter 3 builds on Chapter 2 in defining digital entrepreneurship and unbundling its distinctive technological basis. It examines the fundamental similarities and differences between digital and traditional assumptions of entrepreneurship at an advanced theoretical and practical level. In examining the distinctive technological basis of digital entrepreneurship, the chapter also explores the generative mechanisms of digital technologies which interact to drive digital new venture creation in distinct ways. In the end, it develops a framework that explains the causal mechanisms driving the digital entrepreneurial process.

Chapter 4 examines the dynamic landscape in which digital entrepreneurship and entrepreneurship in the digital age currently emerges. As such, it highlights the enabling technological changes currently happening that shape current and future forms of digital entrepreneurship. Centrally, it elucidates how the convergence of four critical technologies – cloud computing, big data, machine learning and AI, and IoT are shaping the next wave of digital entrepreneurship. The chapter then proceeds to examine possible barriers that practitioners and policymakers must confront to create a nurturing ecosystem for digital entrepreneurship.

Chapter 5 logically follows from Chapter 4 in providing an evidence-based model of digital new venture creation with practical utility. Accordingly, it moves from theory to practice in offering fine-grained steps that highlight the essential elements required to increase the odds of building a successful digital new venture.

Chapter 6 concludes the book by synopsizing core arguments and themes explored throughout this book.

2. Theories of the entrepreneurial process

2.1 INTRODUCTION

Entrepreneurship is a complex, multidimensional process of emergence leading to new economic activity (Wiklund et al., 2011). Hence, this chapter critically examines established theories, constructs, and assumptions that explain the entrepreneurial process. It is a necessary precursor to explaining key differences between traditional and digital entrepreneurship in subsequent chapters. Initially, it summarizes the evolution of entrepreneurship thought since its inception while showing its co-evolution with economic thought. Furthermore, it synthesizes an eclectic mix of relevant concepts and constructs to arrive at a conceptual model for explaining the entrepreneurial process. Central to this model is the *opportunity* construct, which current developments decompose into two sub-constructs – external enablers (EE) and new venture ideas (NVIs), which form the processual basis of new venture creation (Davidsson, 2015). Underlying this process model are theories and explanations of the causal mechanisms driving action and performance at various stages in the process. Thus, the model provides a summative conceptualization of the entrepreneurial process, around which causal narratives of the drivers of new venture creation are usually woven.

2.2 EVOLUTION OF CONTEMPORARY ENTREPRENEURSHIP THOUGHT

Entrepreneurship scholarship has long co-evolved with economic thought (Murphy et al., 2005; Pittaway, 2012, p. 9). The field traces its origins in the works of Irish-born French economist Richard Cantillon (1732 [1931]), who first coined the term 'entrepreneur' to describe a risk-taking individual in an economic system. Hence, *risk* and *uncertainty* were among the earliest developments in our understanding of entrepreneurship.

French Classical School: Owing to the French etymology of the word entrepreneur, it is hardly surprising that early thinkers of entrepreneurship were French economists. Thus, following Cantillon, Jean Baptiste Say (1816) constructed a theory of production and distribution based on three agents – human industry, capital, and land. He gave prominence to the entrepreneur by arguing that while land and capital were essential for production, it was human industry that was indispensable to production (Barreto, 1989). Human industry, according to Say, was comprised of effort, knowledge, and the applications of the entrepreneur (Koolman, 1971, p. 271).

British Classical and the Neoclassical Schools: Meanwhile, British economists such as Adam Smith (1904) and Stuart Mill (1909) were late in explicitly appreciating the role played by entrepreneurs in the economy (Pittaway, 2012). Koolman (1971) suggests that British economists were perhaps more preoccupied with macroeconomic thought, while French economists were concerned with microeconomic connections. Given the differences in theoretical focus, British economists arguably offered little contribution to entrepreneurship thought at the agent level. The popularity of British economic thought led to an *entrepreneurship winter* which further worsened under the arrival and dominance of neoclassical economics (Kirzner, 1980). Neoclassical economics advanced an equilibrium theory of capitalism which argued that production, rational choice, and perfect information did not warrant an entrepreneurial function (Barreto, 1989).

Austrian and Neo-Austrian Schools: However, it was economists from the Austrian, neo-Austrian, and Chicago schools who subsequently revived entrepreneurship thought. They did so by parting ways with neoclassical thinking, arguing from a disequilibrium theory of capitalist markets. They asserted that risk and uncertainty are important aspects of economic systems that allowed entrepreneurs to make a profit. For example, economist Frank Knight (1921) argues that supply and demand cannot be in equilibrium because other forces shaped the conditions of markets. Since markets must be in a constant state of disequilibrium, entrepreneurship represents a type of decision-making that demands action in the face of uncertain future occurrences. Knight's work enshrines the idea of *uncertainty* as a cornerstone of most contemporary entrepreneurship theories and differentiates uncertainty from risk. Kirzner (1979) built on the contribution to focus on the opportunities for profit created by uncertainty and imperfect knowledge. Entrepreneurial opportunity was seen to arise from imperfect distribution of information and knowledge in an economy (Hayek, 1945). This state of imperfect knowledge presents opportunities for exploitation by 'alert entrepreneurs' (Kirzner, 1979, p. 38).

Schumpeterian Thought, Mark 1 & 2: Accordingly, Joseph Schumpeter (1942, 1963) argues that 'creative destruction' was the entrepreneur's function, whom he described as an innovator that creates 'new combinations' of products, processes, and new markets while disrupting existing markets and systems. Schumpeter, however, did not expatiate on the characteristics that distinguished the entrepreneurial agent from ordinary individuals, leading to a subsequent dominance in psychology-based theories.

Consequently, from the 1960s to the 1990s, entrepreneurship scholarship was dominated by psychological, sociological, behavioral, and cognitive theories (Pittaway, 2012). These theories sought to explain entrepreneurial process mechanisms by making the agent the centerpiece of investigation. Thus, they made contributions to our understanding of the potential psychological composition of the individuals who initiate and drive new venture creation.

Personality Traits Theories: Personality theories came to inform earlier attempts at understanding the entrepreneurial agent. McClelland (1961) suggested that an individual's high 'achievement motive' predisposes them to act entrepreneurially. Meanwhile, Rotter (1966) proposed the 'locus of control' theory by arguing that some individuals believe the achievement of their goals is strictly based on their actions. As such, entrepreneurs were those who believed they could control their destinies. Brockhaus (1980) focused on the risk-taking propensity of entrepreneurs.

However, the problem with personality theories was that they sought to link single traits as causal mechanisms driving entrepreneurial entry and action. However, they were unsuccessful in proving a predictive capability. Furthermore, they wrongly considered entrepreneurs to be a homogeneous group (Delmar and Witte, 2012). Consequently, Aldrich (1999, p. 76) concluded that personality theories of entrepreneurship were 'an empirical dead end.'

Sociological Perspective: The failure of personality theories to yield valuable insights prompted a shift in focus towards sociological theories. Accordingly, Kets de Vries (1977) and Shapero (1975) suggested that entrepreneurs were displaced and socially marginalized individuals who had been forced into an entrepreneurial way of life by circumstances. Negative factors were considered a dominant motivational explanation for the mechanisms driving entrepreneurial entry and action. This perspective on the entrepreneurial individual made contributions to sub-themes in entrepreneurship research such as minority, immigrant, and ethnic entrepreneurship.

However, in a seminal piece, Gartner (1988) challenges the emphasis of scholarship on the entrepreneurial agent by stating that 'Who is an entrepreneur?' was the wrong question for entrepreneurship. Hence, he helped refocus studies on entrepreneurial action and the role of uncertainty which is central to current studies of entrepreneurship.

2.3   ENTREPRENEURSHIP AS PROCESS: PHENOMENON AND DOMAIN

The economic significance of the entrepreneurship phenomenon has resulted in the rapid growth of entrepreneurship as a domain of scholarship. Hence, this section examines definitions of the entrepreneurship phenomenon and the conceptual framework that unifies current scholarship in entrepreneurship.

2.3.1   Entrepreneurship – Phenomenon and the Multitude of Definitions

Entrepreneurship is a 'slippery concept' that has been historically difficult to conceptualize (Penrose, 1959) – hence the multitude of definitions. To offer guidance, Davidsson (2016) synopsizes the themes embedded in various definitions, subsequently underscoring the need to separate a definition of entrepreneurship as a societal phenomenon from entrepreneurship as a domain of scholarship.

Recurrent in most definitions of the phenomenon are the following concepts: new venture creation, process and opportunity, risk and uncertainty, and value creation. For instance, Lumpkin and Dess (1996) define entrepreneurship as *new* entry into markets with new or existing goods and services. Similarly, Low and MacMillan (1988) conceptualize entrepreneurship as the creation of a *new* enterprise or organization. Other definitions emphasize the process of *new* venture creation – alternatively conceptualized as the pursuit of opportunity. Among them, Stevenson and Jarillo (1990) define entrepreneurship as the *process* through which individuals, either on their own or inside an organization, pursue *opportunities* without regard to the resources which they currently control. Likewise, Hisrich et al. (2008) define entrepreneurship as the *process* of creating something of value by committing time and effort while assuming different kinds of risks and reaping the rewards. The risk–reward view of the phenomenon is equally echoed in definitions by Kihlstrom and Laffont (1979). Gartner (1990) also finds that the entrepreneur, innovation, organizational creation, value creation, profit, and growth were prevalent themes in the definitional literature. Ultimately, what the multiple definitions suggest is that entrepreneurship is a multifaceted phenomenon. Therefore, the themes in various definitions are but conceptual lenses for examining the complex process of entrepreneurial emergence.

2.3.2 Holistic Definition of Phenomenon and Domain

Kirzner's (1973, pp. 19–20) many reflections on the entrepreneurship phenomenon contribute towards providing a concise and holistic definition of entrepreneurship as a phenomenon and an area of scholarship. He defines entrepreneurship as 'the competitive behaviors that drive the market process.' Subsequently, Kirzner (1997) states that entrepreneurship is a mechanism through which temporal and spatial inefficiencies in an economy are discovered and mitigated. Kirzner's conceptualization of entrepreneurship is often lauded because it successfully depicts entrepreneurship as a micro-level phenomenon that has macro-level implications. Furthermore, he situates entrepreneurship within a market context (Davidsson, 2016, pp. 6–7). However, while the Kirznerian definition advances scholarly examination of the phenomenon, it is arguably broad and lacks a concrete scholarly demarcation. As a result, it does little to resolve the contention that entrepreneurship lacks distinctiveness and legitimacy as a domain of scholarship (Low, 2001).

To demarcate a scholarly domain, Venkataraman (1997) argues that the problem with entrepreneurship scholarship is that it involves a nexus of two phenomena – the presence of lucrative opportunities and the presence of enterprising individuals. Therefore, merely focusing on the individual makes the search for an integrative framework elusive. To carve out a distinctive field of scholarship, Shane and Venkataraman (2000), in their agenda-setting paper in the *Academy of Management Review*, proposed a conceptual framework that has proven pivotal in organizing the current state of entrepreneurship research. Consequently, the entrepreneurship domain is framed as 'the scholarly examination of how, by whom and with what effects opportunities to create future goods and services are discovered, evaluated, and exploited' (Shane and Venkataraman, 2000, p. 218). Hence, scholarship has since focused on the process by which agents discover and exploit opportunities (Shane, 2003) – succinctly described as the Individual-Opportunity (IO) nexus, discussed subsequently.

2.3.3 Entrepreneurial Opportunity – Discovery versus Creation Impasse

The IO nexus has helped to organize scholarship on the entrepreneurship phenomenon. However, it has ignited a contentious debate regarding entrepreneurial *opportunity* – that is: *Is opportunity created or discovered?* The contention is rooted in two main philosophical assumptions. The first assumption holds that opportunity is an objective phenomenon, independent of the entrepreneur's knowledge (Eckhardt and Shane, 2003, 2013), while the second sees opportunity as the subjective constructions of the entrepreneur (Alvarez and Barney, 2007, 2013). If opportunities are discovered, it would suggest they exist objectively, thereby leaving little room for a constructivist worldview that sees opportunity as created by agents.

Opportunity Discovery Theory: From an objectivist stance, entrepreneurial opportunity is defined as a chance to profitably introduce new goods, services, raw materials, and organizational methods to the market (Casson, 1982; Eckhardt and Shane, 2003). This stance depicts opportunities as existing in the environment independent of the knowledge of the entrepreneur. Therefore, it can only be discussed as a speculative idea that can be fully articulated and explained retrospectively (Dimov, 2011). Kirzner (1979) explains that opportunities are discovered by 'alert entrepreneurs,' and they follow intuitively from political, economic, and technological change (Schumpeter, 1963), imperfect information and knowledge (Hayek, 1945), as well as changes in values and preferences (Davidsson, 2003). Klein (2008) argues that these assumptions can be perceived as external structures and generative mechanisms, giving rise to entrepreneurial action.

Opportunity Creation Theory: From a subjectivist stance, opportunities are created internally by the actions of entrepreneurs (Alvarez and Barney, 2007, 2013) and represent a stream of continuously modified and developed ideas (Davidsson, 2003; Dimov, 2007). As such, opportunity cannot be separated from the individual, as it is interwoven with the entrepreneur's beliefs, cognitions, motivations (McMullen and Shepherd, 2006), and prior knowledge (Shane, 2000). Thus, it exists only in the entrepreneur's imagination (Klein, 2008) and constitutes an organizing vision. This subjectivist worldview favors a focus on motivation, knowledge, cognitive, and learning abilities in examining drivers of the entrepreneurial process (Dimov, 2012, p. 133). McMullen and Shepherd (2006) describe this view as *first-person* opportunity.

The contrasting views of opportunity are best contextualized within the broader philosophical wrestling that tends to create an impasse in management disciplines. This tension has been criticized for adding little value in terms of understanding societal phenomena. As a result, Bygrave (2007) laments that the entrepreneurship paradigm was becoming increasingly aloof from any nexus with practical utility. Accordingly, recent developments have called for the complete 'ditching' of the opportunity creation versus discovery theories while refocusing on the process of emergence of new economic activity centered around new venture creation (Davidsson, 2021).

2.3.4   Entrepreneurial Opportunity – Beyond the Impasse

Recent, novel perspectives on how to re-conceptualize entrepreneurial opportunity have emerged from the debates to move the discipline beyond the philosophical impasse. For instance, Dimov (2011) suggests a substantive focus, while Garud and Giuliani (2013) offer a narrative perspective. Likewise, by arguing that entrepreneurship is a science of the artificial, several scholars propose a new nexus for entrepreneurship scholarship revolving around action and interaction.

Opportunity in Substantive Terms: A substantive approach proposed by Dimov (2011) presents the following three different tangible premises for studying opportunity: *opportunity as happening*, with the NVI as the unit of observation, *opportunity as expressed in actions*, with entrepreneurial action being the unit of observation, and *opportunity as instituted in market structures* – whereby market interaction becomes the unit of observation. Dimov (2011) further argues that opportunities occur through the generation and modification of NVIs. Research, he maintains, should dwell on the circumstances through which this process occurs. Likewise, if one can observe actions as already taken by certain individuals, there is hardly a need to focus on why the actions occur, but rather why they occur in a certain way. This argument is particularly relevant in the context of this book as it seeks to differentiate digital entrepreneurship by the composition of NVIs and the distinctive ways in which they shape action.

Narrative Perspective – Opportunity as Meaning-Making: Meanwhile, Garud and Giuliani (2013) adopt a narrative perspective in order to move beyond the opportunity impasse. They explain that 'meaning-making' associated with opportunities is a continuous process which occurs through non-stop interaction between actors and artifacts (Garud et al., 2014). Drawing from actor-network theory (ANT), a narrative perspective considers actors to be part of a synergistic ecology between social and material elements (Latour, 2005) – which provide the basis for entrepreneurial narratives. ANT is premised on a relational ontology, which interprets opportunity as emerging from the interweaving and recombining of social and material elements – consequently enabling and constraining the orientation and possibilities of agents in dynamic ways (Garud et al., 2010). Agency is distributed and emergent, while discovery and creation are interwoven in dynamic ways as the entrepreneurial journey unfolds. Seeing opportunity as a relational interaction between actors and artifacts offers insights into the role of digital artifacts in shaping and differentiating a digital entrepreneurial process – further explored in the next chapter.

Furthermore, the narrative perspective adopts a temporal dimension of the entrepreneurial process, which endogenizes time. This means entrepreneurial narratives enable actors to look back into the past to understand what occurred and imagine a future accomplishment of a venture. It implies a different notion of time in which the past, present, and future are intertwined. The interaction between the relational and temporal elements of a narrative perspective translates into meaning – whereby meaning-making is not objectively given or subjectively constructed but unfolds in a continuous relational process. Thus, entrepreneurial opportunity emerges and develops from plotting social and materials elements from the past, present, and future, into a comprehensive narrative. Accordingly, Garud and Giuliani (2013, p. 159) conclude that 'entrepreneurial journeys are dynamic processes requiring continual adjustments by actors.'

Entrepreneurship as Action and Interaction in Artifact Creation: Relatedly, Venkataraman et al. (2012) sought to move beyond the opportunity impasse by arguing for a new nexus of entrepreneurship scholarship revolving around action and interaction. Accordingly, they draw from Herbert Simon's philosophy to recast entrepreneurship as a *science of the artificial* (Simon, 1996; Sarasvathy, 2003), which holds that human artifacts are 'objects and phenomena in which human purpose, as well as natural laws, are embodied' (Simon, 1981, p. 6). Thus, artifacts arising from entrepreneurial action and interactions are but manifestations of knowledge combined with use in ways that transform the extant world (Venkataraman et al., 2012, p. 30). Therefore, a focus on the actions and relationships that result in new artifacts should represent a prime concern of scholarship.

Consequently, Selden and Fletcher (2015, p. 605) re-conceptualize the entrepreneurial process as an *emergent hierarchical system of artifact-creating processes*, a view which is relevant in the context of this book. Six subsystems are identifiable in this hierarchy. The first level is the sense-making subsystem (Weick, 1995) involving the creation of an NVI (an artifact). The NVI is then functional at the second level, which is the entrepreneur-stakeholder interaction subsystem that results in the birth of an operational business model (artifact). Further up, the business model is functional at the third level in the emergence of firm capabilities and marketable commodities (artifacts). Meanwhile, at the fourth level, the marketing of commodities is functional to the emergence of a Kirznerian or Schumpeterian market system. Further up the hierarchy at the fifth level, the market subsystem is functional to the formation of clusters and regional relationships (artifacts). Finally, at the sixth level, a combination of levels 1–5 becomes functional to the society as culture, discourses, and practices.

Selden and Fletcher distinguish between the lower hierarchy of levels 1–3, which constitutes the emergence of an entrepreneurial journey (McMullen and Dimov, 2013), and levels 4–6, which are patterns of emergence in higher-level populations. Levels 1–3 appear consistent with the entrepreneurial process as delimited by this book – since it involves the new venture creation stages of converting an NVI into a codified business model and usable market form.

2.4   EXTERNAL ENABLERS (EE), NEW VENTURE IDEA (NVI) AND ACTION

A seminal development in the entrepreneurship discipline appears to have resolved the opportunity impasse, enabling a more pragmatic examination of processes and mechanisms driving new venture emergence. It is based on the award-winning paper by Davidsson (2015) and its subsequent developments (Davidsson, 2016, pp. 235–41; Davidsson et al., 2020). In this seminal development, Davidsson proposes a re-conceptualization of the opportunity construct and the entrepreneurship nexus by arguing that the problem with the opportunity construct is that it bundles within it multiple sub-constructs. Deconstructing these constructs enables an empirical investigation into the entrepreneurial process with practical utility. Accordingly, a new framework is advanced that decomposes the opportunity construct into three individual sub-constructs – *External Enablers*, *New Venture Ideas*, and *Opportunity Confidence*. Building on these developments, Davidsson (2021) further argues that new venture creation is the processual core of entrepreneurship, involving actions taken to realize NVIs, which are usually externally enabled and continuously sustained by varied EEs along the way. Consequently, the opportunity discovery versus creation impasse can be forever eschewed and wholly ditched. We find this theoretical contribution quite compelling and thus build on its core axioms in examining the digital entrepreneurial process in subsequent chapters.

The interrelationships between EEs and NVIs become central subjects that explain how action unfolds in new venture creation. NVIs are metaphors for new market offerings which influence the setting up of new business activities. Hence, Davidsson (2012) earlier defines the entrepreneurial process practically as the setting up of a new business activity resulting in a new market offer. This process can occur in a start-up or within an established organizational context. The new market offer may be innovative or simply imitative. Imitative offers have been found to outnumber 'innovative' ones (Reynolds et al., 2003). This process could begin as a proactive, reactive, or fortuitous search (Davidsson, 2012). Hence, while it is typical for entrepreneurs to begin with an NVI, this is not always the case.

The nature of EEs and NVIs can help explain action and performance in various typologies of entrepreneurship. By examining EE, one can focus on the actor-independent mechanisms that differentiate action and performance in one form of entrepreneurship over the other. By mechanism, we mean 'a cause or causal pathway, or an explanation without explicit theorizing about the nature of the mechanism' (Ylikoski, 2018, p. 3). Alternatively, they are described as intermediate causes which tell us how a cause produces an effect by describing the process by which it happens. They can be distinguished from more superficial causal claims that only identify what makes a difference to the outcome. By exploring the composition of NVIs and their corresponding market offerings, one can also explain the mechanisms by which ideas result in actor-derived mechanisms. Subsequently, actor-derived social mechanisms help explain action in the entrepreneurial process (Gross, 2009).

2.4.1   External Enablers (EEs) – Characteristics, Mechanisms, and Roles

An EE is an aggregate-level occurrence, defined as 'a distinct external circumstance, which has the potential of playing an essential role in eliciting and/or enabling a variety of entrepreneurial endeavors by several (potential) agents' (Davidsson, 2015, p. 683). Examples of EEs include changes in technology, demographics, culture, human needs and wants, macroeconomic conditions, institutional framework conditions, and the natural environment. Furthermore, Davidsson et al. (2020) argue that it is much more useful and defensible to reserve the EE concept to instances of significant change to the business environment, assuming the starting point is a reasonably functioning society and economy.

Moreover, agents neither need to be aware, have strategic intent, or assess EEs correctly to benefit from them. This argument eschews the need for measurement, which is typical of an objectivist stance on entrepreneurial opportunity. Davidsson et al. (2020) identify several mechanisms and roles detailing the specific benefits that EEs can bestow on new ventures – summarized in Table 2.1. Subsequently they offer a framework which describes types of enablers, their characteristics, mechanisms, and roles in new venture creation.

Characteristics of EEs are objective facts about them which do not vary by process across stages or agents within a spatiotemporal context (Davidsson et al., 2020). They are defined by their scope and onset. Scope is a spatiotemporal concept which refers to geographical areas, industries, and people affected over a duration of time. Meanwhile, onset is a concept which describes how sudden or gradual an EE is, with gradual suggesting predictability.

Mechanisms refer to the specific ways in which EEs facilitate the initiation, development, and performance of new ventures – or how they are helpful. They also vary in terms of being obvious to obscure, requiring varying levels of knowledge, skills, and creativity – that is, agency-intensity (Ramoglou and Tsang, 2016). Entrepreneurial agents may have limited knowledge or perfect ability to identify EE and their mechanisms correctly.

It is useful to point out that an EE can generate multiple mechanisms. Likewise, one mechanism can reside in two or more EEs. Therefore, EEs

Table 2.1   *Mechanisms of external enablers*

Mechanisms	Definition
Compression	Reduction in the amount of time required to perform an activity
Conservation	Reduction in the amount of resources needed to perform an activity
Resource Expansion	Increase in the amount of resources that are accessible
Resource Substitution	Replacement of one resource with another
Combination	Coupling with external artifacts or resources to provide functionality
Generation	Allowing the creation of new artifacts
Uncertainty Reduction	Reduction of the perceived uncertainty of any business decision of buyers or sellers
Legitimation	Psychological/socio-cultural acceptability of the venture or its offerings
Demand Expansion	Increase in demand at a given price and functionality
Enclosing	Increase in a venture's ability to capture the loyalty of buyers and the value it creates

Source: Davidsson et al. (2020).

interrelate with each other, with circumstances and with agents producing actor-derived mechanisms that drive new venture emergence.

Meanwhile, roles refer to the effects of EEs and mechanisms at various phases of new venture creation. They describe where and how enablers influence new venture creation. Roles can also influence the process without strategic intent. For example, anticipated mechanisms of an EE may be used to shape the new venture's market offerings, design, business model, or process of creation. Accordingly, three broad types of roles are identified – triggering, shaping, and driving success or outcome-enhancing. The triggering role of EEs examines how they entice entrepreneurial agents to act. The shaping role is three-pronged and examines how EEs influence the offering, venture, and process. The shaping role places emphasis on events, progress, and changes in the process. It allows for the combination of objective external factors with dynamic process perspectives on new venture creation. Finally, the driving success role focuses on how EEs and their mechanisms can be correlated to new venture success or how they enhance outcomes. Conversely, a role can be explained by imagining how the absence of an EE would influence outcomes. Outcome-enhancing can occur without intent and awareness.

EEs and their corresponding mechanisms, as well as the higher-order roles they play, are essential ingredients in developing a comprehensive narrative of the new venture creation process. However, the ways in which entrepreneurial agents interpret EEs to generate derived mechanisms that drive new venture creation indicate that explanations also need to be found at the micro-agentic levels for a process narrative to be comprehensive. Hence, Davidsson (2015) suggests NVI and Opportunity Confidence (OC) as constructs that can organize thought around this area.

2.4.2   New Venture Ideas (NVIs) as Internal Drivers of Action

In defining the domain of entrepreneurship scholarship, Shane and Venkataraman (2000) suggest that what entrepreneurs act on is an important source of variance in entrepreneurial processes. More recently, Davidsson (2015) offers the NVI construct as an important subject in the study of the entrepreneurial process. He defines the NVI as 'an imagined future venture.' It is more concretely conceived as an imaginary combination of product and service offerings, markets, as well as the means of bringing these offerings into existence. Alternatively, it can be thought of as an imaginary and formative business model, which acts as an organizing vision or non-human driver of the entrepreneurial process at micro levels.

Being imaginary implies that determining its roles in the entrepreneurial process demands the use of cognitive theories derived from psychology. The NVI is not a manifest venture idea or business model, and it is not necessarily well articulated or complete. NVIs also include theoretical ideas that never get acted on. Furthermore, there may or may not be a direct link between the NVI and an EE. NVIs are usually the result of an entrepreneur's cognitive processes and sense-making, mainly using prior knowledge, education, and personal characteristics (Shane, 2000). However, the NVI construct does not assume favorability. NVIs are cognitions which are not separable from the individual. They can, however, be shared or formulated for the purpose of communication to stakeholders.

Aspiring entrepreneurs do not search randomly for NVIs but draw from their relevant prior knowledge such as work experience or hobbies (Shane, 2000). Gartner and Carter (2003) found that NVIs were the result of both systematic and fortuitous searches. When NVIs and EEs are subsequently evaluated by entrepreneurial agents, they result in what Davidsson (2015) describes as Opportunity Confidence (OC). OC is the result of an agent's evaluation of EEs and the NVI, and the degree to which it offers a sound basis for new venture creation. Confidence could range from extremely high to extremely low. Evaluation to determine OC draws on the entrepreneurial agent's cognition, prior knowledge, and motivation, which are among the micro-level explanations of mechanisms driving the new venture creation process (Baron, 1998). Therefore, focal agents, together with their decision-making processes, represent avenues for explaining the cognitive mechanisms that translate into actions that influence the new venture creation process.

2.4.3 New Venture Idea Assessment (NVIA) and Typology of Innovation

Additionally, Davidsson (2016) argues that new venture performance, coupled with the behaviors of actors may also be explained by the characteristics of the NVI. Evaluating characteristics of the NVI may be one way in which entrepreneurial agents arrive at OC and subsequently act to realize it.

Venture Idea Assessment (VIA) Framework and OC: Accordingly, the VIA framework has been developed as a conceptual tool for evaluating NVIs (Davidsson et al., 2021). VIA is a tool for determining the degree of OC an individual has in a venture idea in and of itself as the basis for action. It is divorced from the perceived qualities of an entrepreneurial agent with whom the idea may be associated. Thus, it is a subjective assessment framework which may be utilized by entrepreneurs and external stakeholders in assessing the viability of an idea.

For the entrepreneur, it departs from the self-efficacy-related self-assessment question – *How confident am I in my capabilities as an entrepreneur?* Next, it proceeds to a third-person question – *Is this idea, objectively speaking, a sound basis for a new venture?* It returns to a first-person question – *How should I act? Precisely, is this idea an opportunity for me to pursue?* Based on this assessment, an entrepreneur arrives at a combination of product/service offerings, markets, and means of bringing these offerings into existence.

For external assessors such as venture capitalists, employers, and investors, it begins with subjective and intersubjective questions: *How competent is this agent as an entrepreneur?* Next, the question is asked: *How should I act, based on their competence?* Then other questions follow, such as *Does this agent have what it takes to pursue the idea?* Furthermore, it asks: *How should I act based on the fit between agent and idea?* Finally, the external assessor moves to more objective third-person questions that ask: *Is this idea a sound basis for action? How should I act, based on the merits of this idea?* Similarly, the external assessor arrives at a combination of product/service offerings, markets, and means of bringing them to existence. The VIA framework is a subjective and intersubjective framework which should not ignore the multiple contexts that frame new venture creation.

Ideas – Sustaining, Incremental, Disruptive, and Radical Innovations: For an objective examination of NVIs, typologies of innovation may offer some guidance – sustaining, incremental, disruptive, or radical (Christensen, 2013). One approach is by examining the degree to which ideas are new and their potential market impact. Ideas classed as sustaining innovation represent significant improvements in products and services with the aim of maintaining their existing market position. In the context of this book, digitalization may result in sustaining innovations for established organizations along the Hybrid

Traditional Entrepreneurship (HTE) and Hybrid Digital Entrepreneurship (HDE) continuum. Meanwhile, incremental innovation is the gradual and continuous improvement of existing products and services. This may very well describe laggards in a Pure Traditional Entrepreneurship (PTE) context who digitalize more slowly. Overall, the market impact of sustaining and incremental innovations tends to be low, with incremental innovation at times creating no new markets at all. Likewise, technological newness is equally low.

However, it is disruptive and radical innovations which tend to have a high market impact. Disruptive innovations, according to Christensen (2013), begin at the low end of the market and chip away at the dominance of unsuspecting incumbents. Firms such as Netflix developed ideas which moved from the low end to the mainstream market, in the process resulting in the eventual disruption of Blockbuster's DVD rental model. Meanwhile, radical innovation is based on technological breakthroughs which transform entire industries and create new markets. The internet represents an example of a radical departure in how we telecommunicate and conduct business, resulting in new forms of entrepreneurship and value creation.

Idea Performance and Diffusion of Innovation (DOI): The success of an idea depends on its ability to spread. According to the Diffusion of Innovation theory, the diffusion of NVIs is defined as the process by which it is communicated through certain channels over time among the members of a social system (Rogers, 1995). Members of a social system are classified according to the level of innovativeness. At the initial stages of adoption, there are the innovators who represent a very small but influential subsection of the market, followed by a larger early adopter subsection. In the middle, the early and late majority make up the largest chunk of the social system, while laggards close the bell-shaped curve as late adopters.

Rogers (1995) goes on to identify five main characteristics of ideas which successfully diffuse through a social system. They are relative advantage, compatibility with existing values and practices, simplicity or ease of use, trialability, and observability. With reference to technological ideas, Moore (1999) complements Rogers by explaining that some ventures fail because they cannot 'cross the chasm' from early adopters to early majority. One reason for failure reverts to the characteristics of the original NVI – that is, it does not meet Rogers's characteristics of successful ideas that can spread.

However, critics of DOI are not convinced by some of its core assumptions. For instance, the supposition that technologies move in a discrete package from an independent innovator through a diffusion area is questionable in a digital entrepreneurial context. In a network-centric context, the notion that innovation has separate, distinguishable, and objective features, which are easily recognizable by interested parties is also challenged. Also, while the characteristics of successful NVIs proposed by DOI offer guidance, there are limitations to the degree to which they help new venture performance in the network-centric context in which digital entrepreneurship occurs. Explaining performance solely through the characteristics of the NVI, as defined by DOI, could therefore be misplaced.

2.4.4 Contextual Embeddedness and New Venture Creation

Since entrepreneurship is shaped by the multiple contexts in which actors are embedded, context has emerged as an important consideration in entrepreneurial process theorizing (Welter, 2011). Hence, Davidsson et al. (2020) argue that context has a moderating influence on EEs and their characteristics, mechanisms, and roles, as well as agents engaged in new venture creation. Thus, new venture creation and the entrepreneurs who affect change cannot be fully understood without consideration of the nested contexts in which they occur. As Baumol (1996) argues, the rules of entrepreneurship 'have varied dramatically from one time and place to another,' making the spatiotemporal context of the entrepreneur an important consideration. Consequently, a contextual view of entrepreneurship enhances understanding of the generative structures and mechanisms driving the process of new venture creation and venture performance.

Contextual *embeddedness* presents a useful framework for explaining the concrete and unfolding ecology that enable entrepreneurs to identify, create, and act on NVIs. Moreover, it has been described as a key moderator of success or failure in the entrepreneurial process (Garud et al., 2014). However, context, like other concepts, can be used to mean very different things. Often, it is conceptualized as spatiotemporal circumstances external to the entrepreneur which influence the entrepreneurial process (Davidsson, 2015). It is also described as situational opportunities and constraints on behavior. Accordingly, it can be divided into substantive (context individuals or groups face) versus methodological (detailed information about the research study) contexts. In substantive terms, it is further subdivided into omnibus (broad) and discrete (specific) contextual dimensions (Welter, 2011).

Likewise, Zahra and Wright (2011) present four dimensions for the examination of context in entrepreneurship research – spatial, temporal, social, and institutional. The spatial dimension of context refers to a physical setting or location of events or network of relationships, while the temporal dimension refers to the sequence of events concerning other events. Meanwhile, the social dimension refers to relationships that develop among multiple groups and stakeholders in society (Welter, 2011). Finally, the institutional dimension considers the effects of different institutional contexts, such as characteristics of the external environment in which new ventures are created. To fully identify the influence of context on decision-making and action that drive new venture performance, a relational perspective is recommended. Taking a relational perspective allows researchers to identify how situational factors more clearly enable and constrain decision-making and action under uncertainty.

2.5   ENTREPRENEURIAL AGENCY

At this stage, it is evident that entrepreneurial agents and their characteristics play a crucial input role in shaping the entrepreneurial process and new venture outcomes. Hence, Casson (1982, p. 20) defines the entrepreneurial agent as 'someone who specializes in making judgmental decisions about the coordination of scarce resources.' Although entrepreneurship is hardly a solitary activity, focal entrepreneurial agents are considered essential in leading the process (Cooney, 2005). These agents, according to Drucker (1985, p. 32), are individuals who search for change, respond, and exploit it as an opportunity. Therefore, determining why certain individuals respond to situational cues, initiate, act upon and succeed in pursuing NVIs remains a crucial avenue for examining the social mechanisms driving the process of new venture emergence.

2.5.1   Cognition and Motivation Mechanisms of Agents

Cognitive and motivation models provide useful frameworks for explaining decision-making which results in behaviors that drive new venture creation and performance. Given that cognition and motivation are so intricately linked, McMullen and Shepherd (2006) argue that they can hardly be discussed as separate concepts. Cognition and motivation theories are deemed useful because they possess better explanatory power than single traits theories (Delmar and Witte, 2012).

According to Baron (2004), they can generally be separated into three main lines of inquiry. First, why do some individuals and not others initiate and act on NVIs? Second, what leads certain individuals to identify and combine EEs to form NVIs? Finally, why do some individuals perform better than others? Ultimately, these questions search for answers to the 'entrepreneurial mindset' – that is, the ability to rapidly sense, act, and mobilize under conditions of uncertainty (Haynie et al., 2010). Recurrent in the established entrepreneurship literature are three distinct categories of cognitive mechanisms which purport to explain the cognitive mechanisms driving new venture emergence and performance at an individual level – attitude-based models, achievement context models, and ability models.

Attitude-Based Models: Eagly and Chaiken (1993, 2007) state that attitude-based models are focused on the evaluation of an object or concept and the degree to which it is judged as good or bad. Attitude models of cognition hold that individuals carefully assess information they have about a given situation and then use their knowledge to form beliefs or attitudes. These attitudes become proximal and critical determinants of behavior (Ajzen, 2005, p. 94). Ajzen's (1991) theory of planned behavior is an attitude model that explains entrepreneurship entry and NVI initiation, performance, and business growth (Kolvereid and Bullvag, 1996; Wiklund et al., 2003). It suggests that individuals enter the entrepreneurial process if they have enough information and knowledge to make a judgment. If their perceived uncertainty is favorable, they will be driven to start a new venture (McMullen and Shepherd, 2006). A fundamental shortcoming of attitude models, however, stems from the observation that the correlation between attitude and actual behavior is still a 'black box' (Thompson, 2009). Additionally, the lack of clarity about how attitudes translate into actions and outcomes is a key limitation (Delmar and Witte, 2012, p. 171).

Achievement Context Models: Another category of cognitive models of entrepreneurial behavior relates to motivation in achievement contexts. It explores why and how entrepreneurs engage in situations with risk and uncertainty. It is dominated by two models – perceived self-efficacy and intrinsic motivation (Delmar and Witte, 2012). Perceived self-efficacy is similar to the locus of control theory (Rotter, 1966). However, it differs in terms of its focus on an entrepreneur's belief in their ability to muster the motivation, cognitive abilities, and plan of action essential to control events in their life (Bandura, 2012). A higher level of perceived self-efficacy has been positively correlated with initiating and persisting in new venture creation processes (Wood and Bandura, 1989; Krueger et al., 2000). Therefore, it may explain venture performance as survival. Presumably, a high level of perceived self-efficacy enables an entrepreneur to approach difficult tasks as challenges to be mastered, as opposed to problems to be avoided (Bandura and Locke, 2003). Hence, it has been used to explain differences in entrepreneurial performance and the evolution of process.

Meanwhile, intrinsic motivation refers to motivation that is coming from what the entrepreneur finds self-fulfilling and enjoyable – that is, it requires no reward except for the activity itself (Delmar and Witte, 2012, p. 174). Intrinsic motivation is contrasted with extrinsic motivation – which is the result of an external controlling variable such as rewards or punishments, as perceived by the acting individual. The model assumes that entrepreneurs who are intrinsically motivated display better decision-making and enjoy a higher level of performance. The main reason for this stems from the fact that interest is necessary for creativity since creativity demands a high level of devotion (DeTienne and Chandler, 2004; Delmar and Witte, 2012, p. 175).

Ability Models: In a similar vein, ability models explain new venture performance as the collection of skills and motivation of agents. Basic intelligence and interest are considered the necessary ingredients driving entrepreneurial agents to develop the skills needed to be successful. It is argued that successful entrepreneurs need to possess relevant knowledge and cognitive ability, mastery of relevant skills, as well as persistence over long periods (McCloy et al., 1994).

Among these skills, social competence, which is the ability to interact effectively with others based on discrete skills, is also deemed necessary for entrepreneurial pursuits. A study by Baron and Markman (2003) in the cosmetic and high-tech industries found that social adaptability (ability to adapt in a wide range of social situations) and expressiveness (ability to express oneself clearly to generate interest) were important qualities needed by entrepreneurs to drive new venture performance. Such expressiveness may attract stakeholders who contribute in co-creating NVIs.

Cognitive Biases: Relatedly, behavioral psychologists argue that human cognition is often plagued by biases and errors in judgment (Baron, 1998). Thus, the cognitive mechanisms explaining behavior are prone to error of perception with implications for new venture emergence. Cognitive theories of entrepreneurial decision-making have often developed along with the assumption that individuals possess limited knowledge of the world due to an oversupply of information. Entrepreneurs are believed to operate under conditions that overload their information processing capacities. These situations are defined by high levels of uncertainty, novelty, strong emotions, time pressures, and fatigue. As such, agents tend to select and interpret information based on prior knowledge (Shane, 2000), cognitive biases, and multiple fallacies (Khaneman, 2011). Consequently, individuals are bound to have different perceptions and motivations towards the same situation, with consequences for the entrepreneurial process (Baron and Ensley, 2006; Grégoire et al., 2010).

Counterfactual thinking is a cognitive mechanism relevant to explaining biases which result in NVI initiation (Baron, 1998, p. 289). It works by making individuals imagine what might have been in each given situation (Roese, 1994). It is assumed that missed opportunities may lead to intense feelings of regret and magnification of lost potential benefits of acting. Meanwhile, a *planning fallacy* is another bias which explains the tendency for most people to underestimate the time required to complete various projects – or overestimate how much they can accomplish in each given period (Lovallo and Kahneman, 2003). A planning fallacy results in a tendency to set unrealistic timelines for completing various tasks. It can be beneficial because it prompts action, which is sometimes necessary to enable entrepreneurs to learn by doing along the journey.

However, Baron (1998) notes that entrepreneurs are more prone to planning fallacies, which contribute towards an *escalation of commitment* and *self-justification* that negatively affect new venture emergence. Such fallacies enable human agents to continue investing time and resources in failing courses of action due to an initial commitment. Likewise, there exists a tendency to justify the initial choice and decision to escalate commitment. Since entrepreneurs are believed to be more susceptible to escalation of commitment and self-justification biases, they may find themselves learning the hard way by committing to ventures that are potentially doomed to fail.

2.5.2   New Venture Co-creation and Focal Agent Leadership

Cognitive and behavioral research that overemphasize the entrepreneur's beliefs and cognitive abilities often tend to lionize focal agents (Shaver and Scott, 1991; Chandler and Hanks, 1994; Hmieleski and Baron, 2009; Fauchart and Gruber, 2011). However, research on entrepreneurial teams (Harper, 2008) suggests that new venture creation and performance are often the result of collaborations between agents. The main argument stems from the view that a single individual hardly possesses all the skills and motivation needed to drive the process of new venture emergence with optimal results (Cooney, 2005; Aldrich and Kim, 2007). As such, entrepreneurial teams are most effective in collectively driving new venture success. Therefore, the justification for emphasizing the entrepreneurial mindset of focal agents may reside in identifying the kind of leadership which assists in combining the skills, motivations, and abilities of multiple actors to drive new venture creation and performance. Therefore, entrepreneurial leadership is conceptualized as leadership that creates visionary scenarios used to organize and mobilize a 'supporting cast' of co-creators committed in realizing a new venture (Gupta et al., 2004; Kuratko, 2016). Accordingly, the role of focal agents is to provide the vision and leadership that attracts and manages a team or founding collaborators in new venture co-creation (Kim and Aldrich, 2017).

Focal entrepreneurial agents are, therefore, 'individuals who, through an understanding of themselves and the contexts in which they work, act on and shape opportunities that create value for their organizations, their stakeholders, and the wider society' (Greenberg et al., 2011, p. 2). As such, a framework has been developed with three interrelated mechanisms which explains the key drivers of successful process leadership. The framework depicts entrepreneurial leadership as resting on a tripod of *Cognitive Ambidexterity*, *SEERS* (Social, Environmental, and Economic Responsibility and Sustainability) and *SSA* (Self and Social Awareness). Cognitive Ambidexterity refers to the idea of engaging prediction reasoning when an entity's future goals and circumstances mirror the past; and creation logic when the future is unknowable due to the absence of a past reference (Fixson and Rao, 2011).

Meanwhile, SEERS relates to the desire to simultaneously and responsibly seek socio-economic value that does not translate in environmental or societal degradation. Finally, SSA deals with how the actions of entrepreneurial leaders are directed by a deep and metacognitive knowledge of themselves and their social contexts. Accordingly, high metacognition, an awareness of the environment, and management of relationships with collaborators are essential leadership qualities needed to drive new venture creation and performance.

2.6   MECHANISMS OF DECISION MAKING AND ACTION UNDER UNCERTAINTY

The actions of focal agents are pivotal in deciding how an entrepreneurial process emerges. Without action, the entrepreneurial process may reside in the realms of idle imaginings. Action is often a product of the amount of uncertainty perceived and the willingness to bear uncertainty (McMullen and Shepherd, 2006). Hence, new venture enactment under uncertainty forms the core of the entrepreneurial process. Enactment refers to acting out ideas, which in turn leads to feedback loops that result in adjustments to the original idea, as well as levels of OC (Garud and Giuliani, 2013). As indicated above, the decision-making that results in actions driving new venture performance is a function of the judgmental decisions agents make in the face of uncertainty (Casson, 1982). Hence, entrepreneurial decision-making is defined as a process of 'choosing between alternative courses of action that take place in an uncertain future' (McMullen and Shepherd, 2006, p. 134).

Milliken (1987, p. 136) describes uncertainty as the 'perceived inability to predict something accurately' when making decisions. Alternatively, uncertainty is a sense of doubt that blocks or delays action (Lipshitz and Strauss, 1997, p. 150). The ability to interpret and respond to uncertainty is often a deciding factor in new venture performance (McKelvie et al., 2011). Also, uncertainty manifests in three forms – state, effect, and response (Milliken, 1987). *State* uncertainty is the inability to predict how the components of the environment are changing. This type of uncertainty appears to have attracted the bulk of scholarship – this is not the case with effect and response uncertainty. *Effect* uncertainty describes the inability to predict how environmental changes will influence new venture creation. Finally, *response* uncertainty describes a lack of insight into response options against a changing environment, as well as the inability to predict the likely consequences of a response choice.

Consequently, McMullen and Shepherd (2006, p. 136) conclude that entrepreneurial action is the result of the amount of uncertainty perceived and the willingness to bear uncertainty. In addition, an agent's expertise serves to moderate the relationship between uncertainty and action in unexpected ways. Surprisingly, expertise appears to moderate the relationship between uncertainty and action only in the case of effect uncertainty (McKelvie et al.,

2011). Perhaps, experts downplay the significance of predicting the future but focus more on creating it. Alternatively, they could be overconfident in their ability to deal with an uncertain future. Depending on the levels of perceived uncertainty, entrepreneurial agents may choose different approaches to new venture enactment.

2.6.1 Causal Mechanisms and Low Levels of Perceived Uncertainty

Choosing causation or a linear process of new venture creation is associated with traditional assumptions of the entrepreneurial process. With causal reasoning, an individual decides on predetermined goals and selects the means to achieve them (Sarasvathy, 2001). The outcome is believed to be given, and entrepreneurs simply select a variety of means to achieve it. The causation mechanism is, therefore, a linear process in which entrepreneurial volition results in gestational and planning activities (Baker et al., 2003, p. 256). Thus, intentionality, objective opportunity identification and evaluation, planning and resource acquisition, and the deliberate exploitation of the objective opportunity are its hallmarks (Bhave, 1994; Shah and Tripsas, 2007; Fisher, 2012). Causation develops from decision theory which holds that decision-makers dealing with a measurable or predictable future will systematically gather information and conduct analysis within certain bounds. The idea that the future is measurable or predictable stems from low levels of perceived uncertainty. For instance, an entrepreneur may adopt this approach if demand uncertainty for a product or service is perceived to be low. Under such circumstances, they may simply develop a business plan, gain stakeholder commitment, and execute.

Sequence of Causal Events: Delmar and Shane (2003) found evidence to suggest that the following sequence of behaviors may be common in new ventures adopting a causal approach. First, the entrepreneur writes a business plan accompanied by market research which sizes potential demand. Next, they make financial projections and establish a legal entity. After that, they proceed to obtain licenses and secure intellectual property. Finally, they seek finance, initiate marketing, and acquire inputs. These sequences of events assume that the future is knowable or at least marked by low levels of uncertainty. It draws from rational decision-making models derived from neoclassical economic thought. While findings by Delmar and Shane (2003) illustrate the value of such a causal approach, others particularly question the usefulness of writing a static business plan in the often uncertain and dynamic environments in which today's ventures operate (Blank, 2013).

In defense of a written business plan and formal planning, Delmar and Shane suggest that they are useful for a number of reasons. First, it represents an analytical tool for articulating the strengths, weaknesses, opportunities, and threats to the new venture, as well as a gauge for the external environment. Second, it is a communication tool to aid external stakeholders such as lenders, investors, and governmental agencies to understand the business. Third, business plans may increase the entrepreneur's commitment to the realization of the NVI (Klofsten, 1994), as well as reduce the likelihood of the venture disbanding. Fourth, it represents an action guide.

Davidsson (2012, p. 99) summarizes the following arguments against the business plan and its blind use as a guide to action. First, it may be less productive to spend time planning rather than acting. Acting out NVIs is ultimately considered more important. Second, a focus on business plans may blindfold founders to emergent threats and opportunities along the way. Finally, commitment to business plans may lead to what psychologists describe as *escalation of commitment*, which is related to the concept of a *sunk cost fallacy* (DeTienne et al., 2008) – that is, persisting in what is possibly a doomed path, rather than staying flexible, failing early, and responding to changing circumstances. Brinckmann et al. (2010) find that there is only a mild degree of success when new venture creation was planned for established small businesses, and less so for start-ups. While planning and writing a business plan may be useful, staying flexible and responsive is deemed more critical in today's VUCA (Volatile, Uncertain, Complex, and Ambiguous) environment. Accordingly, emerging practitioner theories such as the Lean Start-up (discussed in the next chapter) blame the failure of start-ups on the allure of a good business plan and the adoption of a causal approach to new venture creation (Ries, 2011; Blank, 2013). Ultimately, agile planning which is continuous, as opposed to static, may be more beneficial to the entrepreneur and new venture success. In summing up the arguments against a causal approach, Liao et al. (2005, p. 13) conclude that 'firm gestation is a complex process that includes more than simple, unitary progressive paths.' It involves a process where developmental stages are hardly identifiable, and events seldom go according to plan.

2.6.2   Effectual Mechanisms and High Levels of Perceived Uncertainty

Sarasvathy (2001) offers effectual logic as an alternative to causation logic. By contrasting a causal approach against an effectual approach, Sarasvathy argues that effectual entrepreneurs begin with given means and focus on selecting the possible effects that can be created with them. Effectuation is, therefore, unlike causation which defines an objective and systematically searches for opportunities within developed industries which can meet that objective.

In keeping with an effectual logic, the entrepreneur's available means dictate the possible effects which can be created. As such, 'effectuators' start with available means, such as who they are, what they have, and whom they know – the *bird-in-hand principle*. Unlike causal entrepreneurs, effectuators adopt an *affordable loss* mindset as opposed to expected returns. This principle has also been described as a 'risk little, fail cheap' strategy. Meanwhile, the *lemonade principle* explains that effectual entrepreneurs remain flexible, leverage contingencies, and take advantage of surprises along the way.

To further reduce uncertainty and increase resources, effectuators form partnerships with self-selecting actors who bring new means and expand the range of possibilities which shape the entrepreneurial process – known as the *crazy quilt principle*. Thus, unlike a causal approach, effectual logic advocates focusing on strategic alliances rather than competitive analysis, adapting to changing circumstances rather than sticking to business plans; and controlling the future rather than trying to predict it. By focusing on activities within their control, effectual entrepreneurs know their actions will produce desired outcomes in a principle known as *pilot in the plane*.

In a validation study, Chandler et al. (2011) find that effectuation is a formative multidimensional construct associated with three sub-dimensions – experimentation, affordable loss, and flexibility. They also find that unlike causation, effectuation is well suited to situations of high uncertainty. In addition, they recommend that entrepreneurs and firms develop frameworks that allow them to identify as well as remain responsive to environmental cues (Dew et al., 2009). While effectuation has been cast as a viable alternative to causal entrepreneurial decision-making theory, its critics take a positivist stance in arguing that it lacks originality (Arend et al., 2015). In its defense, proponents of effectuation point out that it is a pragmatic theory that is ill-suited to positivist theory evaluation, thereby making criticisms invalid (Read et al., 2016). Garud and Gehman (2016) concur by adding that positivist theory evaluation techniques used to criticize effectuation theory are more suited to phenomena with assumptions of linearity thereby making them a poor instrument. However, Perry et al. (2012) note that effectuation is at an intermediate state of development, requiring the testing of suggestive models. The combination of bricolage and effectuation provides a more comprehensive explanatory framework for decision-making and action under uncertainty.

2.6.3 Bricolage Mechanisms, Uncertainty, and Resource Scarcity

Bricolage is premised on the assumption that new ventures are often resource-constrained and therefore need to find clever and frugal ways of moving forward (Garud and Karnøe, 2003; Baker and Nelson, 2005). The bricolage approach to navigating uncertainty and resource constraints is closely related to the concept of financial bootstrapping (Winborg and Landström, 2001). It generally refers to *resourcefulness* in the ways in which entrepreneurs develop their ideas without substantial resource commitment. Furthermore, bricolage has the added benefit of being hard to replicate by large competitors. Baker and Nelson further explain that bricolage consists of three elements – *making do* (i.e., finding workable rather than perfect solutions), use of *resources at hand* (involves seeing value in something others would miss) and *recombination of resources for new purposes* (reimagining new uses for surrounding things). As such, it represents a pragmatic approach to new venture creation under conditions of uncertainty and extreme resource scarcity (Fisher, 2012).

Bricolage has been positively associated with innovativeness in start-ups with limited resources (Senyard et al., 2011). While its actionable mechanisms may be deemed resourceful, Baker and Nelson caution that if overused, bricolage msy become a stumbling block to further development of a new venture. As such, bricolage, like effectuation, is not offered as a universal theory of the entrepreneurial process, but rather as a mechanism-based explanation describing how processes might unfold in different contexts. Hence, it can be combined with other process theories to offer explanations for the actionable mechanisms which drive new venture enactment under uncertainty. Like effectuation, however, its contribution to the domain currently lies in the realms of description rather than prescription.

2.6.4 Bricolage and Effectuation as Complementary Mechanisms

At the core, bricolage and effectuation are united by a shared focus on existing resources as a source of opportunity. As a result, they are complementary. Furthermore, they view action as a way of discovering opportunities that may be embedded along an entrepreneurial journey, and community engagement as a mechanism for overcoming resource constraints and scarcity (Fisher, 2012). Both theories extol the virtues of flexibility and experimentation, which is fundamental to the uncertain process of entrepreneurial emergence (Chandler et al., 2011; Kerr et al., 2014; Manso, 2016). Thus, effectuation and bricolage deviate from traditional rational goal-driven decision-making theories. As such, they both take a more realistic view of the focal actor at the center of the theories – moving from the limiting 'economic or rational man' at the center of traditional theories to the more accurate 'predictably irrational' person of today's behavioral economists (Ariely and Jones, 2008).

Fisher (2012) identifies four dimensions that are shared by effectuation and bricolage models of decision-making. First, both theories assume that existing resources serve as a source of entrepreneurial opportunity. Second, 'taking action' is a mechanism for overcoming resource constraints. Third, 'community' is a catalyst for new venture emergence and growth. Finally, resource constraints are, in themselves, a source of creativity and innovation. Fisher does point out that when effectuation and bricolage are described as processes of new venture creation, it becomes difficult to understand and interpret the essence of the theories. However, when they are conceptualized as a series of behavioral mechanisms, their value is much better appreciated in the new venture creation process.

As findings from the field of behavioral economics suggest, human actors are not as rational as previously thought (Ariely and Jones, 2008; Kahneman, 2011; Thaler, 2015). Thus, effectuation and bricolage present alternatives to explaining social mechanisms of the entrepreneurial process which depart from the overly rational decision-making and action, consistent with a causal approach. Notably, the bird-in-hand principle of effectuation may very well be an operationalization of the 'endowment effect' (Kahneman et al., 1991). The endowment effect attributes more value to what is already owned, as opposed to valuing resources or profits with no certainty of ownership or control. It partly informs the stance of effectuation and bricolage, which are based on starting and developing new ventures by valuing means already in possession or those which emerge because of taking action.

2.6.5 New Venture Idea (NVI), Environment, Stage, and Decision-Making Hypotheses

To determine the factors that may drive entrepreneurs to adopt either an experimental approach to new venture creation such as effectuation and bricolage, versus a causal approach, Davidsson (2012) proposes four hypotheses. These hypotheses hinge on characteristics of the NVI, the environment, the stage of development of the venture, and the entrepreneur.

Hypothesis 1 – NVI and Cost/Value Structure: Depending on the new venture's potential for incremental and experimental exploitation (determined by the cost of development versus value for the buyer), decision-making and action may follow a particular pattern. First, if the product is costly to produce and each unit has high value to the buyer, the entrepreneur may adopt a causal approach. In addition, high value to the buyer suggests room for strategic alliances; thus, making it possible for small actors to play a vital role. Second, some NVIs are difficult to exploit with small funds and an incremental strategy. Under these circumstances, huge upfront costs are required to produce the first unit, yet value to the customer is low. Such NVIs will often be undertaken by large corporations or require huge investments. They may leave little room for an effectual or experimental approach.

Third, when the NVI is economical to create and the value per unit is low, producers and customers can afford to experiment. This situation, according to Davidsson, is the best space for independent start-ups to use an experimental and incremental strategy, given that risk levels are acceptable and the possibility for profit exists. Fourth, a NVI with low cost of realization may provide room for incremental strategies, especially if the idea is based on specialized knowledge, with high value to the customer. The problem with this quadrant is that an established firm's presence may present high barriers to new entrants. The second problem is that given the potential for high margins, a small actor approaching the market incrementally may easily be overrun by a larger later entrant.

Hypothesis 2 – NVI and Degree of Uncertainty: Another characteristic of the NVI is based on the level of uncertainty perceived. Sarasvathy et al. (2003) identify three types of opportunities. First, opportunity recognition with low uncertainty is one where supply and demand are apparent. Secondly, opportunity discovery with medium uncertainty is one in which one side of either demand or supply is evident. For instance, the supply of a vaccine or treatment for a menacing virus such as Covid-19 may be uncertain, but demand is more certain. Finally, opportunity creation with the highest uncertainty is one in which demand, or supply, is not obvious. An example would be radical innovations which may or may not create new markets. This echoes Knight's (1921) assertion that uncertainty arises from the level of novelty involved in the NVI. Under high levels of uncertainty, the entrepreneurial process may lend itself to experimentation. Likewise, cognitive psychological research on expertise suggests that analytical rationality only functions best in situations of low uncertainty (Gustafsson, 2006).

Hypothesis 3 – Characteristics of the Environment: The literature on dynamic capabilities suggests that improvization and trial-and-error learning are recommended in turbulent environments (Zahra et al., 2006; Teece, 2012). However, depending on the stage of industry and new venture development, causal and flexible approaches may be needed less or more. As the level of uncertainty decreases due to knowledge acquired in the new venture process, there may be less need for incremental experimentation and more of causal approaches. Thus, entrepreneurs may begin with an experimental approach that jump-starts a generative process of learning, which results in new knowledge that reduces uncertainty – thereby prompting a switch to a more causal approach at subsequent phases.

Hypothesis 4 – Characteristics of the Individual: The individual behind the NVI is also a factor in determining what kind of process is adopted. Research has highlighted the need for a fit between the entrepreneur and the NVI. It could, therefore, be assumed that new venture creation processes will align with the type of idea and entrepreneur. Davidsson (2012) notes that while some individuals thrive on chaos, others prefer a systematic, planned approach. Thus, although a particular approach may be recommended under certain circumstances, individual motivation influences decision-making.

The above-explored hypotheses offer a useful guiding framework for understanding the circumstances under which causal or experimental decision-making mechanisms may be most appropriate in driving action and venture performance.

2.7   NEW VENTURE GROWTH: SURVIVING AND SCALING

Two main approaches are adopted in evaluating performance in the entrepreneurial process. Among them, survival and success are seen as more reliable and generic (Chrisman et al., 1998). Survival depends on the ability of the venture to continue on a self-sustaining trajectory. Meanwhile, venture success is a relative measure which occurs when the venture creates value for its customers or users in a sustainable and economically efficient manner (Schumpeter, 1942, 1963). A venture is considered new if it has not reached a phase where it could be considered a mature business. The time it takes for a new venture to become mature varies depending on industry, resources, strategy, and a host of other factors. It may take several years for some ventures to become profitable – reasonably assumed to be around three to five years on average and up to 12 years in certain cases (Kazanjian and Drazin, 1990). Thus, a survival approach to conceptualizing venture performance assumes that ventures that survive have a higher chance of growing into profitable and mature ventures at some point in the future. Therefore, survival is the prime concern of early developments of the entrepreneurial process.

As venture performance is determined by survival and success (Chrisman et al., 1998), the actions which influence them can be described as a *growth process*. Thus, it is no wonder growth is a central assumption in entrepreneurial process studies (Davidsson et al., 2006). Moreover, the statement 'growth is the very essence of entrepreneurship' is enshrined in the literature (Sexton et al., 1997). However, growth, like everything in entrepreneurship, is a multifaceted construct. Predominantly, it is conceptualized as the differential outcome between two points in time.

Traditional assumptions of the mechanisms by which new ventures grow are traced back to Penrose's (1959) *Theory of the Growth of the Firm*, in which growth is defined as an 'internal process of development' as well as 'increase in amount.' While the 'outcome' literature has mainly focused on 'increase in amount,' the process by which new ventures grow has largely been neglected. As Penrose argues, the ability of a business venture to grow is contingent on how well it can exercise judgment in applying its resources. Thus, it is a firm-centric perspective on growth. Additionally, Penrose identifies organic growth and growth by acquisition as the two main modes of growth, with corresponding limitations.

Organic growth occurs when a new venture expands naturally. When it expands, its potential resource combination expands with it. Thus, organic growth will lead to the development of new resources that are similar, not complementary. Yet, it is complementary resources, not similarities, which create value (Harrison et al., 2001) – meaning, firms cannot rely solely on organic growth. As such, acquisition presents an option as 'a means of obtaining the productive services and knowledge that are necessary for a firm to establish itself in a new field' (Penrose, 1959, p. 126). The problem with acquisition, however, is that it brings new managerial challenges with relation to integrating newly acquired resources. Also, acquiring other firms is arguably not a realistic scenario for resource-constrained new ventures.

Hence, the venture growth literature has been described as 'tilting at windmills' – an observation of the many years of fragmented and inconclusive research on growth (Leitch et al., 2010). Indeed, following a review of the growth literature, Storey and Greene (2010, pp. 215–16) conclude that only four 'stylized facts' can be trusted to explain new venture growth. First, new ventures that have grown are more likely to survive subsequently. Second, fast business growth is highly unusual. Third, growth is discontinuous – meaning, growth at one point does not necessarily translate into growth at another point in time (Delmar et al., 2003). Finally, with due consideration for survivor bias, younger and smaller ventures were tend to grow faster than older and larger ones.

McKelvie and Wiklund (2010) blame the lack of progress in understanding growth on a premature concern with the question 'how much' firms grow, as opposed to 'how' they grow. Similarly, Dobbs and Hamilton (2007) note that research on venture growth has mostly indicated change in size, when in reality, growth is a process. Meanwhile, *growth as an outcome* is the object of concern in much of the literature. However, Shepherd and Wiklund (2009) argue that simply observing increments in amounts over time only yields partial insights which ignore a host of factors such as differences in the motivation to grow or venture characteristics (Delmar and Wiklund, 2008).

A second stream of research has been focused on the *outcomes of growth*. This group treats growth as an independent variable. It examines the changes which occur within a new venture, by emphasizing managerial challenges (Greiner, 1972). However, it has been heavily criticized for being too deterministic because it assumes that all ventures pass through biological phases of growth and decline. A substantial number of new ventures do not grow, and those that survive never grow beyond a small size (Coad, 2007). Consequently, *growth as a process* has been deemed a more fruitful approach to conceptualizing growth in the entrepreneurial process.

However, Davidsson et al. (2009) argue that growth as a process does not simply happen for growth sake, but it is ultimately geared towards value creation and profitability as an outcome at some stage. Using a Resource-Based View (RBV) of the firm, they contend that growth is not direct evidence of effective value creation and appropriation. Therefore, it is not always a measure of venture success – that is, there is such a thing as unprofitable growth. Based on their research findings, Davidsson et al. (2009) hypothesize that ventures which show high profitability at low growth are more likely to attain a state of high growth in subsequent periods. On the contrary, ventures which show high growth at low profitability are more likely to reach a state of low growth and low profitability in subsequent periods. However, this may be different from one industry to another. Relatedly, growth and exit appear to be two sides of the same coin, with exit being an equally multifaceted phenomenon that both explains new venture failure and success.

2.8   ENTREPRENEURIAL EXIT AND STRATEGIES

Irrespective of how we conceptualize growth, early phases of the entrepreneurial process are critical to any discussion on growth as a process or growth as an outcome. Ideally, early phases of the entrepreneurial process 'end' with the validation of a scalable, repeatable business model and new market offering (Ries, 2011; Blank, 2013). However, focal agents leading the entrepreneurial process may also choose to exit it for one reason or another. Hence, knowledge of the entrepreneurial process is incomplete without knowledge of entrepreneurial exit.

Exit: DeTienne (2010) defines entrepreneurial exit as 'the process by which the founders of privately held firms leave the firm they helped to create; thereby removing themselves, in varying degree, from the primary ownership and decision-making structure of the firm' (p. 204). This outcome is not the same thing as entrepreneurial failure or success. Entrepreneurial exit can occur when ventures are in financial distress, as well as under conditions of good financial performance (Wennberg et al., 2010). Equity and psychological ownership affect the decision to exit. Exit is considered a liquidity event which allows entrepreneurs to take advantage of other opportunities. However, taking the dimension of exit as a process, the context may vary at different phases of the entrepreneurial process (Wennberg and DeTienne, 2014).

Exit Strategies: To offer some clarity, DeTienne et al. (2015) build on prior literature to develop a typology of entrepreneurial exit strategies which includes three higher-level exit categories – financial harvest (Mason and Harrison, 2006), stewardship, and voluntary cessation. These typologies are further tied to the entrepreneur's perceived innovativeness of their opportunity, motivations, decision-making approach, founding team and firm size. Financial harvest strategies such as IPO (Initial Public Offering) or acquisitions by another firm result in substantial value which accrue to the entrepreneur (Cumming, 2008). Meanwhile, stewardship strategies such as family succession, employee buyout, or sale to an individual allow founders to influence the long-term viability of the organization. Finally, voluntary cessation strategies such as liquidation and discontinuance allow founders to disband a venture when the main activity ends or changes, or when the firm fulfills the purpose for which it was formed. Voluntary cessation may also be linked to failure, which has 'many faces' (Khelil, 2016).

In linking exit strategies to founder characteristics and motivation, DeTienne and Cardon (2012) found that entrepreneurial experience positively correlates to IPO and acquisition but negatively correlates to independent sale and liquidation intentions. Furthermore, entrepreneurial education positively correlates to IPO and acquisition intentions but negatively relates to family succession. However, Fauchart and Gruber (2011) caution that there was too much variance in entrepreneurial motivation and characteristics to accurately decipher the reasons behind individual exit strategies. Nevertheless, Shepherd and DeTienne (2005) suggest that entrepreneurs who saw financial rewards as primary motivation were more likely to seek opportunities that provided financial harvest in exiting. Exit strategies also vary depending on the characteristics of the venture and its founding decisions.

Kunkel (2001) distinguishes between low- and high-growth ventures. Within the low-growth category, a further distinction between income substitution, income supplementation, and lifestyle firms is identified. Low-growth firms are more likely to be small, owned, and managed by a self-employed individual and are likely to close once the need for which they were created had been achieved. For this reason, voluntary cessation is less likely to be formalized. Meanwhile, financial harvest as an exit strategy was often correlated with firms that had larger founding teams, higher levels of innovation (Cefis and Marsili, 2012), and planning-based approaches in general. By contrast, stewardship exit strategies often correlated with smaller founding teams due to a desire for autonomy and a strong locus of control. Such firms were less likely to have formalized exit strategies (Wennberg and DeTienne, 2014).

The entrepreneurial exit literature indicates possible areas where outcomes of the early stages or lower hierarchies of the entrepreneurial process (Selden and Fletcher, 2015) may be delineated. With exit, adjustments and scalable business model validation suggesting 'end phases' of new venture emergence, the building blocks for a conceptual process model, may be assembled.

2.9 EXTANT MODELS OF THE ENTREPRENEURIAL PROCESS

First, Moroz and Hindle (2012) conducted a comprehensive critique of some 32 process models in the entrepreneurship literature. Following Phan (2004), they taxonomize them into stage models, static frameworks, process dynamics models, and quantification sequences. Using these categories, they find that most entrepreneurial process models are static frameworks that do not capture sequence dynamics. Additionally, they find that stage models are quite fragmented. Consequently, only four process models are seen as converging on conceptualizing the entrepreneurial process as being both generic and distinct. Hence, Moroz and Hindle echo criticisms of entrepreneurial process models by Van de Ven and Engleman (2004) as lacking in a fundamental understanding of what process theory development entails – a problem possibly attributed to the overwhelming adoption of a variance approach to process research as opposed to a process approach to theory development (Mohr, 1982).

2.9.1　Criticisms of Extant Process Models – Good, Bad, and Ugly

Beginning with Gartner's (1985) model, Moroz and Hindle lauded its simplicity but were critical of its inability to successfully incorporate a temporality and innovation dimension. Gartner's model is further criticized for its limited focus on entrepreneurial outcomes as being mainly profits. Meanwhile, Bruyat and Julien's (2001) model of the entrepreneurial process did address the issue of temporality but appeared too simplistic and only partially accounted for innovation. Next, the dynamic model of effectuation was credited for having a direct practical focus. Finally, Shane's (2003, p. 18) model of the entrepreneurial process, around which the IO nexus revolves, was described as an opportunity-driven, means-ends framework.

Based on their review, Moroz and Hindle (2012, p. 811) arrive at six good points of convergence. First, the relationship between individuals and opportunities is crucial in all models. Second, the need to critically assess the transformative and disruptive value of knowledge is both explicit and implicit in every model. Third, there is a shared emphasis on the entrepreneurial process as having an evaluation of ways to create value for stakeholders through creating new business models. Fourth, time matters in entrepreneurship, making a temporal dimension of process important. Fifth, action matters – without action, formulating and evaluating an NVI remains mostly theoretical. The sixth and final good observation is that the socio-spatial and spatiotemporal dimensions of context are just as important.

However, Moroz and Hindle (2012, p. 811) offer several criticisms ranging from 'bad, worse and ugly.' In relation to the *bad*, no model seems to accommodate multiple perspectives. Instead, each model compels its users to adhere a priori to a prescribed philosophical perspective. None of the models synthesize multiple viewpoints into a pragmatic whole. Worse still, many of them are simply artifacts unsupported by systematic evidence. For this reason, Moroz and Hindle (2012) arrive at the conclusion that 'the field of entrepreneurship needs a new, comprehensive, evidence-based model of the entrepreneurial process that is consistent with a strong theoretical and philosophical appreciation of process' (p. 811). They are unequivocal in their criticism that 'for all superficial use of the phrase *entrepreneurial process* all we really have to date is a hodgepodge of different perspectives, using a variety of different multidisciplinary theories that investigate entrepreneurship in narrowly themed contexts' (p. 810).

What is suggested by these criticisms is that the development of a harmonizing model of the entrepreneurial process hinges on an inclusive pragmatist stance. A pragmatist stance is paradigm agnostic and considers truth to be that which is useful. As such, it values concepts that support action in more concrete terms, as opposed to abstract philosophical debates that increasingly become detached from the phenomenon under study (Bygrave, 2007). To arrive at a comprehensive process model of new venture creation, Moroz and Hindle suggest following some of the methodologic guidelines proposed by Van de Ven and Engleman (2004).

2.9.2   Process Model Development and Methodological Considerations

Mohr (1982) identifies two theories of change that have generally been used to develop process models in entrepreneurship – a variance and process theory approach. A variance approach is based on static connections of variables, while a process theory approach uses a narrative method that describes how things develop and change using mechanism-based theorizing (Ylikoski, 2018). According to Langley (1999), variance models deliver simplistic, potentially high generality with modest accuracy of results. In addition, a variance approach, with its deterministic approach to providing causal explanations, is described as a limiting way to conceptualize change and development.

However, a variance approach appears to have informed the development of most models of the entrepreneurial process, thereby attracting the above-discussed criticisms. Van de Ven and Engelman (2004) contend that variance theory remains 'causally shallow,' thereby making critical a 'temporal sequence' of events a much better approach to process model development.

Taking these guidelines into consideration, we extract key building blocks for a process model from the literature to develop a parsimonious, yet comprehensive model of the entrepreneurial process. The model serves as an underlying analytical framework around which mechanism-based explanations can offer a departure point for differentiating various typologies of entrepreneurship in the digital age.

2.10 COMPREHENSIVE ENTREPRENEURIAL PROCESS MODEL

Figure 2.1 visually captures our model. Being a process, it is directional in nature; but this should not be misconstrued as being a linear process.

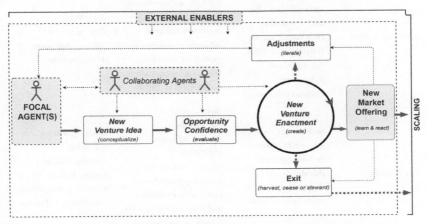

Figure 2.1   *Comprehensive conceptual model of the entrepreneurial process*

It emphasizes the critical early phases of an entrepreneurial process prior to new venture scaling (Selden and Fletcher, 2015) – reason being, scaling changes the meaning of the process. Key constructs such as EEs, NVIs, and entrepreneurial agency provide basic building blocks. EEs, focal and collaborating agents, are targets for examining the actor-driven and actor-independent mechanisms that trigger an NVI which subsequently gets acted upon. Thus, the process itself initially follows in the order of NVI conceptualization, evaluation to gain OC, enactment described as new venture co-creation, and various outcomes – adjustments, new market offerings, scaling, and a potential exit of focal agents.

In critical realist terms, the model is a general empirical framework which says little about the deeper layers which distinguish between various typologies of entrepreneurial processes in the digital age. These differences are best highlighted through mechanism-based explanations which trace the generative structures giving rise to distinctive mechanisms that shape observable events differently across typologies of entrepreneurship. Thus, we extracted and

Table 2.2   *Input factors of an entrepreneurial process*

INPUT FACTORS

Factors	Definition	Mechanisms	Typical Events
External Enablers	distinct actor-independent *external stimuli* that elicit a response from human agents (Davidsson, 2015); key macro and industry-level influences on process	*Actor-independent mechanisms:* compression, conservation, resource expansion, resource substitution, combination, generation, uncertainty reduction, legitimation, etc. (von Briel et al., 2020)	triggering, shaping process, outcome-enhancing/ driving success
Focal Agent(s)	leading human agent(s) whose role is critical in driving process (McMullen and Shepherd, 2006); key micro-level influences on process	*Actor-dependent mechanisms:* relevant cognition, motivation, decision-making and leadership capabilities, effort, prior knowledge and skills, means, network, behavioral mechanisms, etc.	initiating, steering, evaluating, enacting, shaping process, bearing uncertainty, calculating, strategizing, and taking risks
Collaborating Agents	individuals who enter or self-select into the entrepreneurial process (Sarasvathy, 2001); micro-level influences on process and performance	*Actor-dependent mechanisms:* means expansion, relevant cognition and motivation, prior knowledge and skills, behavioral mechanisms, etc.	co-creating, making adjustments and shaping, influencing venture success, leading specific tasks, expanding possibilities

summarized essential building blocks from the above distilled theories of the entrepreneurial process in Tables 2.2 and Table 2.3.

In Table 2.2, enabling factors are agents and their actor-dependent mechanisms, and EEs with their actor-independent mechanisms which cumulatively shape the entrepreneurial process through the different inputs they bring.

Meanwhile, Table 2.3 subsequently captures the central thematic subjects and the critical sequence of events that they prompt in the entrepreneurial process. Accordingly, the *NVI* is an initiating subject that drives an entrepreneurial process towards various outcomes. Multiple *outcomes* are possible. Since experimental models suggest that entrepreneurship is often a non-linear process involving several feedback loops, *adjustments* are the outcomes which continuously happen along the entrepreneurial journey. At 'end'

Table 2.3   *Entrepreneurial process and outcome components*

PROCESS		
Subject	Definition	Key Events
New Venture Idea	conceptual envisioning of a future market offering, business model and/or new organization (Dimov, 2011; Davidsson, 2015)	initiation, conceptualization and adjustments
Opportunity Confidence	evaluation that determines high-level favorability for pursuing new venture idea; articulates a business model and results in a reduction in perceived uncertainty (Amit and Zott, 2001; McMullen and Shepherd, 2006; Davidsson, 2015)	idea evaluation, market sizing, business model articulation, re-evaluation and adjustments
New Venture Enactment	a series of actions and gestational behaviors central to turning new venture ideas into new market offerings	product and service development and related gestational activities
OUTCOMES		
Type	Definition	Key Events
Adjustments	continual adjustments are changes coming from new knowledge and means acquired in the process of emergence (Sarasvathy, 2001; Baker and Nelson, 2005; Ries, 2011; Garud and Giuliani, 2013)	iterating idea, process, offerings, or business model
New Market Offering	products and services that create value for consumers, underpinned by a business model that may form the basis of a new organization	distributing a functional market offering to audiences as all or part of the value proposition which triggers a feedback loop
Exit	potential departure of focal agent(s) with or without venture disbanding	deciding prior and choosing between exit strategies – harvest, voluntary cessation, and stewardship
Scaling	a potential outcome which entails efforts towards reaching a larger audience, while formalizing operations based on lessons learned at earlier phases of the entrepreneurial process	investing in the scaling of new venture ideas that have evolved into a validated business model (Ries, 2011)

phases, critical outcomes are *new market offerings* embodied in products and services for consumers. *Exit* for various reasons is another potential outcome. Meanwhile, *scaling* is a potential outcome which entails efforts geared towards reaching a larger audience, while formalizing operations based on lessons learned. At scaling phases, the NVI and market offerings have been tested, and a validated business model can easily be deciphered (Ries, 2011).

Based on the model and its theoretical frameworks, the next chapter will unbundle the deep layers and mechanisms which differentiate digital entrepreneurship from other typologies of entrepreneurship in the digital age.

2.11   CONCLUSION

This chapter has explored a comprehensive range of theories, concepts, and constructs, to explain the multidimensional phenomenon of entrepreneurship. It shows that entrepreneurship is a process of emergence, leading to new economic activity. To understand this process in its broadest form, the chapter began by stepping back into history to trace the origins of contemporary entrepreneurship thought. It therefore prepares the reader to appreciate why digitization represents a transition point in the evolution of entrepreneurship thought in Chapter 3.

To provide an overarching analytical framework, this chapter synthesizes multiple theoretical lenses into a comprehensive, yet parsimonious conceptual model that unifies explanations of the entrepreneurial process. The model supports the more recent arguments that 'opportunity' can be more accurately described using the sub-constructs of EEs, NVIs, and OC. Based on these developments, the entrepreneurial process is unified around the interrelationship between the generativity of the environment which offers EEs, and individual cognitions which result in NVIs. These ideas are then evaluated and acted upon by reflective and motivated agents, leading to various outcomes. Relatedly, uncertainty is a cornerstone for understanding action as it influences how and why entrepreneurs act to realize NVIs.

The chapter further identifies various mechanisms which are critical in explaining how and why entrepreneurial processes may unfold differently across various cases and contexts. These mechanisms are grouped together as actor-dependent and actor-independent. Mechanisms and their related generating structures are seen as critical to differentiating various typologies of entrepreneurship. The next chapter examines the distinctiveness of digital entrepreneurship and its causal mechanisms in detail.

3. Conceptualizing the digital entrepreneurial process

3.1 INTRODUCTION

This chapter builds on the previous one by focusing on key concepts, constructs, and theories that explain the structures and mechanisms that differentiate the digital entrepreneurial process. As noted in Chapter 1, digital entrepreneurship is a unique form of entrepreneurship that comes in two varieties – pure and hybrid. Its uniqueness derives from its distinctive technological basis. It is entrepreneurship in which digital artifacts and digital platforms form the core of New Venture Ideas (NVIs) and new market offerings (Nambisan, 2017; Nzembayie et al., 2019). It is the pursuit of 'opportunity' in which digital technologies play a dual role as external enablers and internal drivers of the process leading to new economic activity. In this chapter, we dissect the role of various digital technologies and the mechanisms by which they interact with digital entrepreneurial actors to shape digital new venture creation differently. Thus, we distill this form of entrepreneurship down to its very essence and elucidate the degree to which it upends established assumptions of innovation and entrepreneurship.

3.2 DIGITAL ENTREPRENEURSHIP: EVOLUTION AND DEFINITION

Digital entrepreneurship lies at the intersection between two main disciplines – Entrepreneurship and Management Information Systems (MIS) (Davidson and Vaast, 2010; Huang et al., 2017; Nambisan, 2017). Thus, it is not a subject that lends itself to disciplinary silos (Nambisan et al., 2019). It represents a highly distinctive form of technology entrepreneurship needing cross-disciplinary examination (Giones and Brem, 2017). Only recently have agenda-setting publications and special issues in academic journals begun to tackle the subject of digital entrepreneurship. Prior research on technology entrepreneurship has, by and large, focused on entrepreneurship in technology-intensive industries (including digital), in which technology is often portrayed merely as a context for empirical work (Beckman et al., 2012). The past tendency to bundle digital entrepreneurship with other forms of technology entrepreneurship and entrepreneurship in the digital age is partly to blame for the subject's lack of visibility and distinctiveness. It was unclear where it sits on the technology entrepreneurship continuum. Not surprisingly, some scholars remain skeptical about referring to this form of entrepreneurship as distinctive (von Briel et al., 2020).

3.2.1   Digital Entrepreneurship and the Evolution of ICT

Digital entrepreneurship has indeed proven elusive to conceptualize. Its evolution is inextricably linked to changes in Information and Communications Technology (ICT), which infrastructurally enable it. The multi-layered internet architecture, in particular, and the changes happening within are central to understanding the phenomenon. The internet is a physically and wirelessly connected global network of computers that uses standardized protocols to talk to each other. Meanwhile, the web is the main application that operates the internet at the topmost tier – it is what users interact with. Lying between the internet and the web are other infrastructural technologies such as the Internet Protocol (IP) and Transmission Control Protocol (TCP) which are standardized transport services. There are also middleware infrastructural services such as cloud storage, security, and file systems (Laudon and Traver, 2019, p. 119) – more on this in Chapter 4. Changes in various layers of the internet technology infrastructure such as 5G networks and cloud computing are external enablers of all forms of entrepreneurship in the digital age. They are often distal external enablers. Technology is a distal enabler when it becomes infrastructural and fades from our consciousness. It is so taken for granted that we only notice the technology when it is absent. For instance, we tend to notice electricity only when there is a power outage. However, changes in the upper layers of internet technologies such as the web and cloud computing are more critical and proximal in tracking the evolution of digital entrepreneurship. They are proximal because we interact with them more closely in everyday value creation.

First-Wave Digital: Web and internet technologies have become pivotal platforms for innovation and entrepreneurship. In their turbulent early years, the infamous dot.com bubble crash of the late 1990s to early 2000s may have contributed to skepticism in referring to digital entrepreneurship as a paradigm-shifting mode of value creation. The crash was partly due to flawed business assumptions and an underdeveloped Web 1.0 architecture (O'Reilly, 2007). Given the hype that first-wave digital businesses were game-changers, there was a temptation to ignore fundamental business principles. While web technologies were applied in earlier transformation of business processes, change was rather incremental. As O'Reilly explains, the problem lay with the architecture of Web 1.0, which was a static one. Thus, first-wave 'digital' businesses developed on Web 1.0 technology tended to be 'mere equivalents of existing analog functionality,' built and organized along the lines of existing social and technical infrastructures (Tilson et al., 2010). It was a server-centric and tightly integrated architecture with synchronous and page-centric experiences mainly involving static HTML (HyperText Markup Language) and navigations through web browsers and hyperlinks. Users were primarily limited to surfing and downloading documents. Capabilities for transacting and personalizing experiences were somewhat limited. Likewise, content creation applications tended to be tightly coupled with personal computers due to the underdeveloped infrastructure, which did not allow for richer online experiences based on user-generated content.

Second and Third-Wave Digital: However, from the early 2000s, an interactive Web 2.0 architecture emerged with profound implications for value creation in the digital age. Together with the increased speed of internet connectivity, several digital services began to take root. For instance, the emergence of prominent digital services such as Facebook, Wikipedia, Twitter, and YouTube, which depend on interaction for their business models (BMs), emerged in the wake of Web 2.0. Likewise, many first-wave digital technology firms such as Amazon and eBay, which were built on Web 1.0 architecture, survived the dot.com bubble crash and subsequently grew exponentially under the enabling architecture of Web 2.0 (O'Reilly, 2009).

Unlike Web 1.0, Web 2.0 was loosely integrated, service-centric, and driven by open standards. Loose integration made it easy to decouple software from hardware and form from function while allowing for asynchronous and application-centric experiences. The dynamic architecture created a culture of collaboration, community, sharing, and participation. Additionally, changes in other ICT such as the arrival of Apple's iPhone in 2007, further accelerated and expanded participation by extending the consumption of digital services from the personal computer which was the dominant client, to smartphones and tablets. Simultaneously, the speed of computer processors and increased chip miniaturization doubled in keeping with Moore's Law. The convergence of these enabling technologies would eventually spawn a paradigm shift in value creation, unlike anything that came before.

Given the volumes of portable data generated from user interaction in a Web 2.0 environment, some argue that we are at the early stages of Web 3.0 – a third-generation web architecture which will define the next wave of digital new venture creation. While not fully defined, Web 3.0 is assumed to focus on machine-based understanding of big data, resulting in an AI (Artificial Intelligence) renaissance. It is a more intelligent web with connected and distributed systems hosted on cloud-based infrastructure. Hence, some describe it as a semantic web with significant implications for value creation across entire industries.

The paradigm shift ushered in by the convergence and maturation of ICT, and their transformative economic impact, has made it dangerous to assume that traditional assumptions of innovation and entrepreneurship were still fully equipped to explain this new context (Benner and Tushman, 2015, p. 498). In sum, digital entrepreneurship is a relatively novel form of entrepreneurship that is both externally enabled and internally driven by evolved ICT. With rapidly changing ICT, several scholars began to draw attention to the differences in emerging BMs (Amit and Zott, 2001; Walker, 2006).

Traditionally, scholars interested in digital entrepreneurship are challenged by the fact that rapid advances in digital technology endanger the timeliness and relevance of academic pursuit of analysis and prediction (von Briel et al., 2018). Thus, there is need to re-evaluate existing knowledge constantly in the wake of disruptive change. Not surprisingly, some earlier conceptualizations and nomenclatures of digital entrepreneurship have become redundant. Concepts such as cyber entrepreneurship (Carrier et al., 2004), internet entrepreneurship, and e-entrepreneurship (Matlay, 2004; Kollmann, 2006) were earlier attempts at conceptualizing digital entrepreneurship.

Likewise, e-business and e-commerce, which appeared frequently in earlier literature, often did so alongside e-entrepreneurship. As Chaffey (2015, pp. 13–14) explains, the term e-business was first coined by IBM in 1997 to refer to the transformation of key business processes through ICT. Meanwhile, e-commerce was used more narrowly to refer to the buying and selling of goods online. However, *digital* business and digital commerce appear to be today's preferred industry terminologies, which are superseding the use of the terms e-entrepreneurship, e-business, and e-commerce. Digital entrepreneurship is now a preferred conceptualization because the technological scope of internet-driven entrepreneurship has become broader.

3.2.2   Digital Entrepreneurship and Entrepreneurship in the Digital Age

Davidson and Vaast (2010, p. 2) defined digital entrepreneurship as 'the pursuit of opportunities based on the use of digital media and other information and communication technologies.' This definition is a comendable earlier attempt, but lacks focus because it suggests that any use of digital media and ICT in the entrepreneurial process may somehow be classified as digital entrepreneurship. However, in an age of pervasive digitization, we argue that a more specific definition is required to differentiate digital entrepreneurship from other forms of entrepreneurship in the digital age. The definition is also a victim of an ill-defined *opportunity* construct which, as seen in the previous chapter, has been the source of an impasse in the entrepreneurship discipline.

Therefore, building on new developments in the discipline, we define digital entrepreneurship more narrowly as entrepreneurship in which digital artifacts and digital platforms form the core of NVIs and new market offerings, which are cultivated and distributed via external enabling digital infrastructures (Giones and Brem, 2017; Nambisan, 2017; von Briel et al., 2018; Nzembayie et al., 2019). Our proposed conceptualization places an explicit theoretical focus on the role of digital artifacts and digital platforms as NVIs in the entrepreneurial process, and digital infrastructures which mainly play the role of external enablers of all forms of entrepreneurship in the digital age.

The rationale for our conceptualization is also linked to an earlier and often overlooked attempt at defining digital entrepreneurship, which defines it as entrepreneurship in which some or all of what would be physical in a traditional organization has been digitized (Hull et al., 2007). The authors of this definition argue that digital entrepreneurship exists in mild, medium, and extreme forms. One of the merits of this earlier definition is its recognition that not all digital technology applications in entrepreneurship can be considered equal. Likewise, it proposes physicality and digitization as the basis for differentiating digital entrepreneurship from traditional entrepreneurship. There is great value in this thinking which we adopt in developing our conceptualization and typologies of entrepreneurship in the digital age. Since our definition highlights the centrality of digitization in digital entrepreneurship, it is helpful to unpack and contrast the term with digitalization before progressing any further. The two constructs are critical in understanding entrepreneurship in the digital age, yet they are often the source of great misunderstanding and misuse. Conventional dictionaries are not very helpful either, as they tend to define the two terms as mere synonyms.

Digitization: It is the *technical* process of converting or representing analog information in digital format where it is stored as numeral bits of data – or ones and zeroes. It means that once information is digitized, it exists as lines of digitally coded data. Thus, it takes on a new life form, mainly manifested in digital artifacts and digital platforms. As noted in Chapter 1, value creation based on 'economics of bits' is fundamentally different from that defined by physicality, such as in manufacturing and distribution models. Since digital artifacts and digital platforms technically exist as digitized bits of data, we can begin to see why the digital entrepreneurial process resides in this context. An illustrative example of digitization of information is the scanning of a physical photo (analog artifact) onto the computer, where it becomes a digital artifact. The digitized photo then becomes a 'quasi-object' (Ekbia, 2009) with very distinct properties from its analog twin. The process of creating new ventures based on digitizing information forms the core of digital entrepreneurship.

Digitalization: Meanwhile, digitalization refers to a '*sociotechnical* process of applying digitizing techniques to broader social and institutional contexts that render digital technologies infrastructural' (Tilson et al., 2010, p. 749). It involves the structuring of many and diverse areas of social life around digital media and communication technologies. It is the use of digital technologies to change, enable, or transform BMs and value creation processes. It is the effects of digital entrepreneurship on all forms of societal value creation. Therefore, entrepreneurship in the digital age is a catch-all for the role of digitization and digitalization in entrepreneurship. As noted in Chapter 2, the domain of entrepreneurship scholarship studies 'how' (process) and 'with what effects' (consequences) opportunities to create future goods and services are discovered and exploited. From this viewpoint, digitization is a concept that assists in explaining *how* the digital entrepreneurial process emerges at a technical and relational level.

Meanwhile, digitalization is largely concerned with examining the effects of digitization on society. These societal effects are often viewed through the conceptual lenses of digital transformation and digital disruption. To illustrate the point, Uber's ride-hailing service is a digital platform offering, which was created largely through a technical and relational process of digitization. However, when applied to society, it digitalizes a traditional system of value creation by a socio-technical process that transforms ride-hailing into a more efficient activity for its consumers. Ultimately, the example illustrates that actions taken at the micro levels of the digital entrepreneurial process have significant macro-level implications for societies and industries, thereby making digital entrepreneurship disruptive and paradigm-shifting.

Typologies: As noted in Chapter 1, the term digital entrepreneurship more accurately describes pure and hybrid typologies of the phenomenon. Typologies are unique forms of theories in which complex webs of cause-effect relationships are woven into a coherent, typified, and easy-to-remember profile. The rationale for our proposed typologies is rooted in the argument that although value chains in most industries have been digitalized, physicality and tactility of processes and market offerings remain core differentiating features of traditional entrepreneurial processes. Hence, entrepreneurship in the digital age is best conceptualized as a broader phenomenon that swings between the extremes of Pure Digital Entrepreneurship (PDE) to Pure Traditional Entrepreneurship (PTE) with two hybrid typologies in between (Figure 3.1).

PDE and HDE (Pure/Hybrid Digital Entrepreneurship): With PDE, the core of NVIs, the process of realizing them, and the resulting new market offerings are defined by digitization. Hence, market offerings are usually intangible information-based products and services. The opposite is true for PTE, where physicality defines the core of NVIs, processes, and outcomes. Given the differences, entrepreneurial processes are bound to emerge differ-

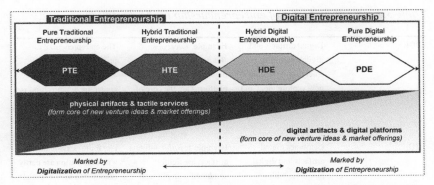

Figure 3.1   Digital entrepreneurship and entrepreneurship in the digital age

ently under each typology. For instance, spatial and temporal inefficiencies are considerably minimized in PDE but amplified in PTE. Therefore, PDE processes can emerge at a highly rapid and dynamic velocity compared to PTE processes.

However, these distinctions are not so clear-cut. Thus, hybrid forms of digital and traditional entrepreneurship integrate digital technologies in ways that render them core or peripheral to new venture creation. HDE combines digital artifacts and digital platforms with physical artifacts and tactile services, which jointly form the core of NVIs, processes, and new market offerings. Therefore, market offerings come together to form complex, layered, and modular cyber-physical systems (Lyytinen et al., 2016). HDE may also represent a growth strategy for established digital firms. For instance, Microsoft, which began as a pure digital venture providing software, has expanded its portfolio with physical products such as the Xbox gaming console and the Surface portfolio of computers. The Xbox product/service offering combines digital artifacts and a digital cloud-based platform into a cyber-physical market offering, involving mutual dependencies of pure digital and physical technologies. We hypothesize that this complex relationship of physicality and digitization is potentially more challenging to realize, but may represent a pathway to creating a defensible and sustainable advantage in the digital age (Porter and Heppelmann, 2014, 2015).

HTE and PTE (Hybrid/Pure Traditional Entrepreneurship): Meanwhile, HTE (Hybrid Traditional Entrepreneurship) is differentiated from HDE by the peripheral but significant role of digital artifacts and digital platforms in processes and outcomes. Examples of HTE outcomes include smart cars such as the Tesla car models. While digital artifacts and digital platforms are applied to greatly enhance the functionality of Tesla's core market offerings, they remain

Table 3.1   *Typologies of entrepreneurship in the digital age*

PDE	Digital artifacts and digital platforms solely form the core of new venture ideas and new market offerings	Example: *Facebook*, *WhatsApp*,and *Shopify* – digital artifacts and digital platforms are the core of idea/offering	The entrepreneurial process is less spatially and temporally constrained; innovation is network-centric, dynamic, fluid, and rapid; outcomes infinitely expansible
HDE	Combines digital artifacts and digital platforms with physical artifacts and tactile services, which jointly form the core of new venture ideas, processes, and new market offerings	Example 1: *Fitbit* – digital artifacts are tightly combined with physical artifacts in cyber-physical market offerings Example 2: *Deliveroo* and *Just Eat* – digital services are tightly coupled with tactile services such as food pick-up and delivery	Flexibilities associated with digitization are partly constrained by the spatial and temporal boundedness of physical artifacts and tactile services
HTE	Physical and tactile services form the core of new venture ideas and new market offerings, but they are enhanced by the peripheral but significant application of digital artifacts and digital platforms	Example: *Tesla* – the physical car is the core market offering but greatly enhanced by the layering of digital artifacts and digital platforms in a complex cyber-physical offering – digital technologies are peripheral – i.e., without them, the core product can still exist	Entrepreneurial processes remain largely bounded in terms of their temporal and spatial structures; agency is largely centralized, and innovation tends to be firm-centric
PTE	Physical artifacts and tactile services form the core of new venture ideas and new market offerings; however, value creation is sparsely digitalized	Example: Restaurant – food and dining remain core, but the sparse application of digital services is adopted to facilitate customer service and business operations	Entrepreneurial processes remain largely bounded in terms of their temporal and spatial structures; agency is centralized, and innovation is firm-centric

peripheral to the core product, which is automobile transportation. Likewise, while digital artifacts such as machine learning algorithms have been applied in transforming Tesla's manufacturing processes through automation, it is still constrained by the spatiotemporal boundedness of a traditional manufacturing process. Thus, fundamental research interests under HTE typically explore the digital transformation and disruption of traditional value creation across industries. The automobile industry provides a good example of how the digitalization of entrepreneurship is transforming several industries.

In primarily service-dominant industries (Vargo and Lusch, 2017), HTE often manifests as the digitalization of an aspect of the value chain or service offering, while the core process and offering remain physical or tactile. For instance, in the banking industry, banks have created internal digital platforms and digital artifacts to deliver operational efficiencies for themselves through value co-creation with customers. Thus, *digital intrapreneurship* and *corporate digital entrepreneurship*, which are manifestations of digital entrepreneurship within traditional and established organizations, are themes to be explored under HTE. Consequently, one of the transformative impacts of digital entrepreneurship is that it can become a targeted innovation activity within an established traditional firm. While market offerings and processes remain largely physical and therefore traditional, critical areas of a firm's value chain are transformed through the application of digital technologies – digitalization. In certain instances, the role of digital entrepreneurship transforms entire industries and firms from pure traditional value creation to purely digital value creation. For example, the application of digital technologies in the news media industry has seen certain newspaper organizations completely transform over time from PTE to PDE processes. These newspapers have wholly gone digital, reserving physical print artifacts to a niche segment of the market. Such information-based industries are particularly susceptible to pure digital transformation.

Therefore, the four typologies of entrepreneurship should not be viewed as static categorizations of entrepreneurship in the digital age but rather a conceptual framework for analyzing entrepreneurial activity in context. For instance, Netflix first began as a traditional venture offering physical DVD sales and rentals. However, over time, it leveraged new technologies and morphed into a purely digital video streaming service. Information-based industries are particularly susceptible to such radical forms of digital transformation from purely traditional to purely digital entrepreneurial ventures.

3.3   DIGITAL TECHNOLOGIES AS EXTERNAL ENABLERS AND DRIVERS

Since digital technologies play varying roles in entrepreneurship, unpacking them is critical to differentiating the digital entrepreneurial process. Nambisan (2013) makes a crucial distinction between two roles of digital technologies in entrepreneurship – as an *operant* and *operand* resource. When digital technologies trigger action, they function as an operant resource; whereas when they indirectly enable entrepreneurship, they assume the role of an operand resource. By initiating action, it means they are the basis of NVIs which entrepreneurial agents act on – an operant resource. Accordingly, digital artifacts and digital platforms are the NVIs in digital entrepreneurship (operant resource), while digital infrastructures are external enablers supporting new venture creation (operand resource). As previously noted, digital technologies enable entrepreneurship by producing actor-independent mechanisms which influence the process of emergence. Actors, using their cognitions, translate these mechanisms into social mechanisms that ultimately drive the entrepreneurial process. Figure 3.2 provides a conceptual framework for explaining the interrelationships between technology, actors, mechanisms, and the effects on entrepreneurial processes and outcomes.

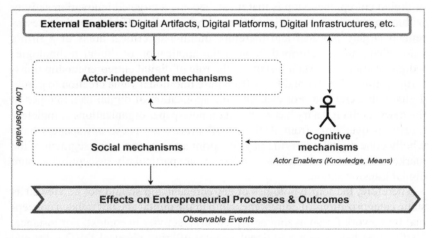

Figure 3.2   Framework for explaining relationships between external enablers, actors, and processes

3.3.1   Digital Technology Affordances and Actor-Independent Mechanisms

Technology Affordances and Constraints Theory (TACT) is a relational theory that offers useful theoretical constructs for deconstructing the role of technology in entrepreneurship (Gibson, 1977). Affordances are the action potential of technology as distinct from its features. While features of a technology are often easily observable, affordances are less observable. For instance, the technical features of a smartphone may include its high-definition camera and fast processor. However, it does not explain how and why one actor might use it to create a documentary while another does not see the same potential. Constraints are the opposite of affordances because they limit what actors can do with technology (Majchrzak and Markus, 2012).

When human actors interact with technology, they bring along their prior knowledge, cognitions, and motivations, which allow them to see different possibilities in the technology. Thus, two actors will interpret the same technology differently and with varied consequences. Therefore, technology is not deterministic. Actors have the capacity to shape technological outcomes. For instance, when Google opened up its mapping Application Programming Interface (API) to the public, it did not realize the hidden potential for ride-sharing and many *uberized* digital services such as Uber and Airbnb. Since affordances tend to be less observable, they are often theorized backward from their effects but not always – some are relatively obvious.

The affordance construct is therefore a useful theoretical lens for discerning the actor-independent mechanisms or potentialities of digital technologies which entrepreneurs translate into NVIs, processes, and outcomes (Bygstad et al., 2016). Digital technology affordances enable entrepreneurship by creating an environment marked by openness, hyper-connectivity, convergence, and generativity (Yoo et al., 2012; Lyytinen et al., 2016; Autio et al., 2018). The exploitation of digital technology affordances by digital entrepreneurs is critical to differentiating the digital entrepreneurial process.

3.3.2 Digital Artifacts, Affordances, and New Venture Creation

Given the centrality of digital artifacts in digital entrepreneurship, examining its features and mechanisms contributes towards our understanding of the digital entrepreneurial process. Digital artifacts are 'quasi-objects' (Ekbia, 2009), distinguished from physical objects that constitute traditional value creation. They are applications, components, or digital media content that form all or part of a new market offering and add value to end-users by offering a specific functionality or service. Being digitized objects, they technically exist as lines of code. Mobile apps, software, digital media content such as video and audio, as well as websites, make good examples of digital artifacts. While physical objects are constrained by spatial and temporal limitations, digital artifacts offer the potential for minimizing such limitations.

Space is traditionally viewed from an economic perspective as an impediment that increases transaction costs – such as cost of storage, transportation, distribution, and much more – hence the expression, 'the tyranny of space' (Lyytinen et al., 2016). Likewise, space is also strongly linked with temporal inefficiencies – that is, it takes time to move things across space resulting in added costs. The inertia of physical artifacts, coupled with temporal inefficiencies of movement across space, constrains the speed at which new venture creation can occur. However, digital artifacts have the opposite effect on the entrepreneurial process since they operate in the more efficient cyberspace. When combined with related digital technologies, they offer great potential in terms of extreme agility and flexibility, as well as a different definition of new venture performance (Leonardi, 2011). Not surprisingly, digital entrepreneurs have operationalized the agile affordances of digital artifacts by codifying them into social mechanisms embodied in process models such as *Scrum* – an agile software development methodology (Cervone, 2011; Ghezzi and Cavallo, 2020). Scrum aims to ship software functionalities early and often in rapid iterations called *sprints*.

Thus, digital artifacts provide agile affordances. Agile affordances are defined as potentialities for extremely rapid, dynamic, and continuous emergence. The agile affordances of digital artifacts enable actors to begin the digital entrepreneurial process early by creating and deploying Minimum Viable Products (MVP) geared towards eliciting user feedback and the incremental reduction in outcome uncertainty. Hence, agile methodologies such as the *Lean Start-up* (discussed in more detail subsequently) have been adopted by practitioners as guidelines for the creation and scaling of digital new ventures (Ries, 2011). These methodologies incorporate digital artifacts in their frameworks but do not explicitly establish causal linkages (Ghezzi and Cavallo, 2020). To establish these linkages, it is essential to review the characteristics of digital artifacts and the reasons they differentiate digital entrepreneurship accordingly.

Modifiability, Re-combinability, Decomposability, and Agility: Digital artifacts are extremely granular, modular, standardized, and therefore highly modifiable technologies (Kallinikos et al., 2013). As such, they are *editable* and thus pliable, which makes it possible to change and continuously update them at will. Editability is a less complex process of modifying digital artifacts and includes actions such as deleting, rearranging, cutting, and pasting. For instance, a digital video artifact can simply be edited by deleting, copy-pasting, and cutting scenes. More importantly, digital artifacts are *reprogrammable* in terms of being modifiable by skilled actors such as computer programmers. They are also reprogrammable by software artifacts. For instance, software can be programmed to find and fix bugs in the code of other software or update them entirely.

Relatedly, the granular, modular, and standardized characteristics of digital artifacts contribute towards their *re-combinability*. Digital modularity comprises units that are designed independently but still function as an integrated unit due to standardized or shared communication protocols. Re-combinability allows digital artifacts to merge effortlessly into a final product or service. Furthermore, digital artifacts can also be recombined with non-digital artifacts. Since combination is an identified actor-independent mechanism which allows two artifacts to merge into an augmented new product, the re-combinability of digital artifacts alludes to this mechanism (Davidsson et al., 2020). Hence, re-combinability equally drives hybrid forms of entrepreneurship in the digital age, where digital artifacts are increasingly merged with physical product and service offerings (Yoo et al., 2012).

Additionally, the extreme modularity and granularity of digital artifacts, as well as their standardized protocols, contribute to their *decomposability*. Decomposability allows digital artifacts to be broken down into smaller bits easily. As such, tasks can be split into the smallest possible units for co-creation at varying circumstances that suit the time availability of different actors (Benkler, 2008). Together with re-combinability, decomposability allows outcomes of divided tasks to be merged easily into a finished digital artifact offering. For example, in a digital game creation project that we were involved in, game coding was carried out by a programmer in Spain, while a graphic designer in Brazil created the graphics and fonts for its interface. Meanwhile, digital sound effects were simultaneously being created by talents on work-based platforms. In the end, disparate digital artifacts were combined into a finished HTML5 game that was subsequently embedded on a website for end-user consumption. These activities were only made possible by the highly modular properties of digital artifacts and their standardized protocols, which allowed for re-combinability and decomposability. With multiple actors simultaneously co-creating and recombining digital artifacts, new venture creation can emerge at velocities not typically observed in traditional entrepreneurial processes. Therefore, decomposability and re-combinability underpin the actor-independent mechanisms of *combination*, *generation*, and *compression*, which Davidsson et al. (2020) identify as possible mechanisms by which an external enabler may shape the entrepreneurial process (see the previous chapter).

Interoperability, Openness, Distributedness, and Agility: Moreover, digital artifacts are *interoperable* and *open*, which combines with their modifiable and re-combinable characteristics to render them borderless, incomplete, and subject to infinite expansibility (Faulkner and Runde, 2009; Garud et al., 2009). Modifiability and incompleteness offer the potential for the rapid deployment of an 'incomplete' market offering, which jump-starts a continuous learning process in search of scalable new venture outcomes. Not surprisingly, users have become accustomed to multiple and regular updates of software-based digital artifacts. The open and interoperable characteristics of digital artifacts ensure that code can be continuously modified, repurposed, and expanded to meet changing needs of consumers.

Relatedly, the interoperability and openness of digital artifacts render them *distributed* objects, which are seldom held within a single system. It makes them 'transient assemblies of functions' and components spread over information and internet infrastructures – thereby differentiating them from physical artifacts (Kallinikos et al., 2013, p. 360). *Distributedness* reinforces their borderless characteristics, thereby providing the potential for entrepreneurial actors across geographical time zones to co-create NVIs rapidly. For example, digital artifacts stored on remote cloud-based systems can be simultaneously and collaboratively modified. Hence, digital new venture creation is defined by seamless, decentralized, and location-independent co-creation of market offerings, integrated by cloud-based digital infrastructures.

Interactivity, Traceability, Non-Rivalry, and Agility: Relatedly, digital artifacts are *interactive* – which means actors and software agents can activate or explore functions and arrangements embedded in them without modifying their core structure (Kallinikos et al., 2013). For instance, users can interact with digital games by tapping, dragging, and dropping objects during play without changing the source code. Likewise, software agents such as search engine algorithms can interact to trace digital artifacts across the vast expanse of cyberspace without changing them. Interactivity and *traceability* allow data logs to be analyzed with the purpose of generating insights that reveal patterns of digital artifact usage and journey across cyberspace. Thus, digital artifacts promote data-driven operations that use analytics to study consumer behavior, learn, and reduce uncertainty (Huang et al., 2017). Since uncertainty can stall entrepreneurial action, data-driven operations contribute towards a reduction in action-specific and outcome uncertainty, thereby potentially accelerating the emergence of a digital new venture (McMullen and Shepherd, 2006).

Finally, digital artifacts, unlike physical artifacts, are characterized by *non-rivalry*. Non-rival artifacts may be expensive or inexpensive to create but cheap to replicate (Shapiro and Varian, 1998); and they do not get depleted when consumed (Faulkner and Runde, 2009). For instance, YouTube and the video artifacts hosted on the platform get consumed by billions of users without becoming depleted. It is a consequence of the non-rivalry of digital artifacts. Contrarily, physical artifacts have a tendency to wear out with repeated use, while spatiotemporal constraints limit the number of actors who may consume such artifacts at any given time.

Moreover, several human and material resources are needed to develop, deliver, and maintain physical artifacts. However, the non-rivalry of digital artifacts presents a different type of economics – described as 'economics of bits.' Consequently, different metrics are emphasized in defining digital new venture performance. Among them, positive network effects remain a significant driver of digital new venture success in keeping with Metcalfe's law (Amit and Zott, 2001). For instance, more users consuming a digital service results in ever-larger volumes of data, which can be analyzed and used for targeted advertising, thereby increasing the value of the service from a revenue generation standpoint (Huang et al., 2017).

Owing to the characteristics of digital artifacts explained here, Nambisan (2017) concludes that they render entrepreneurial processes less bounded in terms of their temporal and spatial structures. Similarly, von Briel et al. (2018) hypothesize that ideas based on digital artifacts are differentiated by the potential for rapid emergence of digital entrepreneurial processes. These arguments are linked to the agile affordances of digital artifacts, which work by allowing multiple decentralized actors to readily and dynamically fork, merge, and terminate diverse activities in new venture co-creation. However, we note that while agility and flexibility are evident in traditional new venture creation, physicality curtails the degree to which they occur.

3.3.3 Digital Platforms, Affordances, and New Venture Creation

Meanwhile, a second interrelated technological enabler and trigger of digital entrepreneurship is the digital platform. It also forms the core of NVIs in digital entrepreneurship and shares similar characteristics with digital artifacts, given its digitized existence. A digital platform is defined as a shared, common set of services and architecture that serves to host complementary offerings, including digital artifacts and their components (Parker et al., 2016; Nambisan, 2017, p. 1032). It is technically defined as 'the extensible codebase of a software-based system that provides core functionality shared by the modules that interoperate with it and the interfaces through which they interoperate' (Tiwana et al., 2010, p. 676). Being an extensible codebase implies that digital platform architectures are created using digital artifacts and bits of digital code. Hence, digital platforms and digital artifacts are interrelated because they share the same technological basis. However, they are differentiated by their architecture and purpose, which is to host and transact complementary offerings (Zahra and Nambisan, 2011).

Since all NVIs have the purpose of creating value, digital platforms are best defined in terms of their role. Digital platforms usually create value by providing multisided ecosystems around which two or more actors congregate to conduct a business transaction – typically consumers and producers (Parker et al., 2016). Digital platforms such as *Upwork* and *Fiverr* are work-based platforms which facilitate the transaction of services between producers of those services and consumers who pay for them. Likewise, payment gateways such as *PayPal* and *Stripe* are platforms that secure transactions between merchants and buyers. E-commerce platforms such as *Shopify* and *Amazon* create value by facilitating interactions between buyers and vendors. Not surprisingly, therefore, digital platforms have a more significant economic footprint than digital artifacts alone.

Digital artifacts and digital platforms share similarities in terms of their *interoperability* and *generativity*, which enable the capacity to recombine elements, assemble, extend, and redistribute functionality (Yoo et al., 2010). The generativity of a platform is its ability to produce unprompted change, driven by large, varied, and often uncoordinated audiences (Zittrain, 2006). It can be the result of the digital platform architecture or governance of the ecosystem (Förderer et al., 2014). Activities on digital platforms generate big data footprints which are perfect for data-driven value creation (Huang et al., 2017). Likewise, when digital artifacts are recombined and transacted upon the generative digital platform, the result is a fluid and dynamic process of entrepreneurial emergence (Yoo, 2010, 2012; Nambisan, 2017).

Digital platforms are equally marked by *variability* and *agility* – that is, the ability to rapidly adapt to the changing needs of its users (Tiwana et al., 2010). The properties of digital platforms assume the role of 'shaping the fluid boundaries of entrepreneurial outcomes' (Nambisan, 2017). Thus, new venture creation and outcomes are never complete and remain open, thereby questioning the validity of discrete models of innovation and value creation (Porter, 1985; Utterback, 1994; Ulrich and Eppinger, 2011). Innovation tends to be network-centric as opposed to firm-centric (Nambisan and Sawhney, 2011; Gawer and Cusumano, 2014). Therefore, digital entrepreneural processes more closely align with dynamic problem-solution design pairing models, marked by sporadic, parallel, and heterogeneous co-creation (Nambisan et al., 2017).

Since digital platforms create value by encouraging participation between multiple actors, traditional explanations of new venture creation and performance get upended. Likewise, instead of profitability, growth in employment, and other standard performance metrics, strong network effects largely explain scale and success (Ceccagnoli et al., 2012; Srinivasan and Venkatraman, 2018). For instance, a platform such as *Facebook*, with some 2.7 billion active monthly users as of 2020, largely derives its value from the billions of users who congregate on it. A large user base that meets the need for digital socialization of its consumers further creates a defensible advantage as its users get locked into mutual dependencies facilitated by the platform (Amit and Zott, 2001). Additionally, network effects provide benefits of economies of scale – whereby, the cost of serving additional users drops to near-zero once a tipping point is reached (Parker et al., 2016, p. 25). Thus, digital platforms, unlike their traditional counterparts, can 'scale without mass' (Brynjolfsson et al., 2008). Concurrently, the digital platform's generativity results in the production of copious amounts of data, which can be monetized through targeted advertising services offered to the paying side of the market. Thus, digitization enables BMs which are not realistic in traditional new venture creation.

3.3.4   Digital Infrastructures, Affordances, and New Venture Creation

Digital platforms and digital artifacts are created and cultivated on top of digital infrastructures, which are typically physical computing and network resources that allow multiple actors to orchestrate new venture creation. This view, however, offers a more *technical* definition of digital infrastructures as underlying objective structures of the digital economy. Examples of digital infrastructures include internet technologies such as fiber optic connections, 5G wireless networks, cloud computing, Content Delivery Networks (CDN), open standards such as IEEE 802.11, microprocessors, intelligent sensors, Universal Serial Bus (USB), and physical computing devices such as smart-phones, tablets, and personal computers (PCs). They are tools and systems which support all forms of innovation and entrepreneurship in the digital age – beyond digital entrepreneurship. Furthermore, digital infrastructures are differentiated from other types of infrastructures by their capacity to collect, store, and render available, digital data across several systems and devices. They enable pure and hybrid forms of digital entrepreneurship where data from cyber-physical systems interact with digital software artifacts and digital platforms resulting in efficient and augmented systems and processes. Given that digital artifacts and digital platforms reside and flow through the veins and arteries of digital infrastructures, they are often discussed concomitantly (Constantinides et al., 2018).

Additionally, digital infrastructures can also be defined from a *socio-technical* perspective. It means they are understood in terms of relational sense-making by users and stakeholders (Henfridsson and Bygstad, 2013). It is a subjectivist view that makes it possible to view all forms of digital technologies as being potentially infrastructural. Therefore, digital artifacts and digital platforms can be interpreted as digital infrastructures if they become a foundational framework supporting the activities of several actors. For instance, a digital e-commerce platform such as *Shopify* becomes infrastructural to several businesses which rely heavily on it for their operations. Likewise, a digital artifact such as the *WhatsApp* messaging app becomes infrastructural to its users if a high level of dependency develops from using it as a communication tool. Accordingly, success in digital entrepreneurship may be explained by the degree to which a digital artifact or digital platform offering creates value by locking its users into an infrastructural dependency – that is, positive network effects discussed subsequently.

Technically speaking, digital infrastructures such as cloud computing are scalable and dynamic. By drawing on the scalable and dynamic characteristics of digital infrastructures, digital new ventures can scale at velocities not easily afforded to their traditional counterparts (Huang et al., 2017). For instance, elastic cloud infrastructures result in resource conservation as entrepreneurs need not own all the resources necessary to start new venture creation; but rather, they can rent or lease such services and scale upwards or downwards depending on need. Moreover, digital infrastructures facilitate collaboration and ultimately reduce transaction costs (Amit and Zott, 2001). For instance, cloud computing infrastructure offerings such as *Google Cloud* and *Amazon Web Services* (AWS) have allowed digital entrepreneurs to experiment, build, and cost-effectively scale resource-hungry digital application services with a diverse cast of actors – more on this in Chapter 4.

In some cases, cloud-based infrastructures come preloaded with software tools that make them ideal platforms for digital innovation by actors of all sizes. Hence, they externally enable entrepreneurship by providing possibilities of *resource conservation* and *resource expansion* (Davidsson et al., 2020). Accordingly, a highly flexible and experimental form of effectual digital entrepreneurship and bricolage is possible since enormous upfront costs are often not required by resource-constrained start-ups. Accordingly, digital entrepreneurs can concentrate on new venture enactment rather than expending time on overcoming resource limitations.

Similarly, ubiquitous wireless networks and mobile computing afford location-independent co-creation of value, limiting constraints relating to spatial and temporal anchoring. These technologies promote the democratization of entrepreneurship, whereby actors enter and exit the entrepreneurial process on their own terms (Aldrich, 2014). For instance, digital platforms such as *GitHub* have become infrastructural tools for the co-creation of digital artifacts with independent collectives who often solve coding challenges free of charge. Thus, co-creation is not always team-based (Cooney, 2005). As a result, digital infrastructures enable a new form of organizing that is lean, agile, flexible, and potentially more productive than in traditional forms of value co-creation. Furthermore, with the advent of robust synchronous and asynchronous digital communication and collaboration tools such as *Asana*, *Slack*, and *Zoom*, information asymmetries between decentralized collaborating agents can be significantly reduced.

Finally, pervasive digital infrastructures such as mobile devices ensure that digitized market offerings such as digital artifacts and digital platforms can be instantly distributed and consumed across global customer segments. Tools such as data analytics provide detailed insights on how best to serve customers. Thus, market reach becomes exponentially greater and integrated with the potential for generating insights that result in more personalized services (Evans and Wurster, 1999). With nearly instant feedback from data analytics, customers become heavily involved in value co-creation. The result is the potential for strong performance through exponential growth, strong network effects, and winner-take-all market dynamics. Table 3.2 summarizes the three interrelated digital technologies and their affordances.

Table 3.2   *Interrelated technologies driving digital entrepreneurship*

Digital artifacts	Quasi-objects existing as bits of data (Ekbia, 2009) Components that form all or part of a new product or service offering (Nambisan, 2017) E.g., mobile apps, software, digital media content	Modifiable, extremely modular, interactive, distributable, decomposable, re-combinable, infinitely expansible, interoperable, non-rival, and open (Garud et al., 2009; Yoo et al., 2012; Kallinikos et al., 2013)	Promotes agile and flexible processes and outcomes (Yoo et al., 2012) Lean and iterative processes of experimentation (Ries, 2011; von Briel et al., 2018)
Digital platform	Shared, standard set of services and architecture that serves to host complementary offerings (Parker et al., 2016) The extensible codebase of a software-based system (Tiwana et al., 2010) Provides the governance structure for value creation and appropriation between consumers and producers E.g., Shopify, Amazon, Facebook	Generative, interoperable, defined by variability and agility (Zittrain, 2006; Tiwana et al., 2010)	Unpredictable outcomes due to generativity Sudden and unexpected change Change can be instigated by the platform leader or uncoordinated audiences Generativity adds a level of uncertainty in processes and outcomes (Nambisan, 2017)
Digital infrastructure	Technically the physical infrastructure upon which digital platforms and digital artifacts are cultivated and transacted (Constantinides et al., 2018) E.g., cloud computing providers such as *Amazon Web Services* and *Google Cloud*, the internet, telecommunication networks, personal computers, etc. Socio-technically, any digital technology that provides an underlying framework for the activities of multiple actors	Scalable and dynamic, hence constantly changing; distal and taken for granted (Tilson et al., 2010)	Foster hyper-connectivity and mutual dependencies among actors, organizations, processes, and things – network-centric innovation (Yoo et al., 2012) Reduced transaction costs (Amit and Zott, 2001) Democratization of entrepreneurship (Aldrich, 2014) Greater market reach and potential for rapid scaling Resource conservation and resource expansion make digital entrepreneurial bricolage more feasible

3.3.5   Digital Opportunity Confidence: The Digital Business Model

The NVI, as Davidsson (2016, p. 32) argues, is 'less than a manifest business model.' Consequently, the Opportunity Confidence (OC) construct is the next step in the development of the NVI towards a market offering. To reiterate, OC is the result of an agent's evaluation of the NVI and the degree to which it is deemed favorable or unfavorable prior to enactment. Furthermore, Davidsson explains that an NVI may begin as a rudimentary hunch about a technically possible product or perception of an unsolved problem, for which the market would pay to have. Central to a business model (BM) is the customer value proposition (CVP), which indicates how a new venture plans to solve the customer's problem – that is, create value for the customer (Osterwalder and Pigneur, 2010). Hence, articulating the BM can be interpreted as a sense-making process through which the NVI is evaluated to gain OC (Weick, 1995).

Business Model (BM) Definition: Teece (2010, p. 172) defines the BM as management's hypothesis about 'what customers want, how they want it and what they will pay, and how an enterprise can organize to best meet customer needs and get paid well for doing so.' Similarly, Afuah and Tucci (2003, p. 4) define the BM as: 'the method by which a firm builds and uses its resources to offer its customers better value than its competitors and to make money doing so.' Of particular relevance to the digital entrepreneurial context is the definition of the BM as 'a coherent framework that takes technological characteristics and potentials as inputs and converts them through customers and markets into economic outputs' (Chesbrough and Rosenbloom, 2002, p. 532).

A common thread appears to run throughout the definitions. They identify resource structure, transactive structure, and value structure as primary constituents of a BM (Amit and Zott, 2001, p. 493; George and Bock, 2011). One way in which digital entrepreneurs develop the digital NVI is by articulating it on a nine-section, one-page document called the *Business Model Canvas* (Osterwalder and Pigneur, 2010). This document articulates the hypothesis or NVI as a precursor to action. The value proposition, customer segments and relationships, revenue models, key value-adding activities, partnerships, and cost structures are among the core aspects of the BM, which operationalizes the NVI.

Digital Business Models (BMs): A more fine-grained focus on digital BMs highlights how often they substantially differ from those in traditional industries (Kraus et al., 2018). Digital BMs often emerge and continuously get refined by digital entrepreneurs in a process more consistent with agile and *lean start-up* approaches to new venture creation (Ghezzi and Cavallo, 2020) – discussed subsequently. Maurya (2016, p. 30) identifies three broad types of digital BMs by the number of actors involved and the affordances of digital technologies – direct digital BMs, multisided digital platform models, and digital marketplace models.

Direct business models (BMs) are one-actor models where users are the customers – as is the case with visitors who subscribe to access a website for their own needs. In *multisided* or multi-actor digital platform models, however, users and customers are different segments of the market. With this model, firms create and deliver value to users, but revenue is captured from customers who may not be consumers. For example, Facebook's BM is multisided because it does not directly charge end-users for its services. The derivative currency it gets is user attention, which is then traded on a secondary market to advertisers or other actors, who rent its data-driven services for their own purposes. Digital artifacts and digital platforms are information goods and services, which operate in the context of 'economics of bits' (Brynjolfsson and McAfee, 2014). With *economics of bits*, digital artifacts and components may be expensive to create but can be reproduced at nearly 'zero marginal cost' (Shapiro and Varian, 1998). As such, digital new ventures can afford data-driven BMs which involve distributing digital artifacts gratis, while generating revenue through advertising and the renting of digital data and services. Thus, they enjoy the flexibility of experimenting with multiple revenue streams compared to their traditional counterparts providing physical and tactile offerings.

Finally, *marketplace models* are also multi-actor models but are differentiated by the concurrent bringing together of producers and consumers while charging a percentage for processing transactions and regulating the ecosystem. E-commmerce platforms such as Amazon and Shopify, and FinTech ventures such as PayPal and Stripe, make good use of this model.

Digital Business Model Innovation: Since NVIs captured in BMs are not static, they are themselves artifacts of innovation as the digital entrepreneurial process unfolds (Zott et al., 2011). Business model innovation (BMI) is therefore an ongoing process of change that arises from the continual adjustments actors make during entrepreneurial processes (McGrath, 2010). BMI can sometimes provide more value than the new market offering itself. It is especially true of digital new venture creation where BMI entails unlocking the hidden value potentials embedded in digital technologies (Chesbrough and Rosenbloom, 2002). Unlocking value is not achieved solely through superior technology development or ownership. Hence, Chesbrough (2007, 2010) explains that a mediocre digital technology pursued within a great BM may be more valuable than a great technology exploited via a mediocre BM. Similarly, it is not the best-designed digital product that tends to succeed in the market, but those that are good enough and can spread (Chaffey and Smith, 2017).

BMI, as evident in the sharing economy, illustrates how changing digital BMs can become more transformative than market offerings alone (Kraus et al., 2018). Thus, a *product* in a digital entrepreneurial context is best interpreted from a service-dominant (S-D) logic (Lusch and Nambisan, 2015; Vargo and Lusch, 2017). S-D logic views value co-creation not as the production and offer of tangible or intangible goods but rather as the exchange of services involving the use of skills and knowledge by actors for the benefit of other actors. Consequently, a product is a metaphor for services rather than a finished item that is exchanged (Barrett et al., 2015).

In the network-centric context of digital new venture co-creation, *open innovation* represents an ideal path to designing superior BMs and offerings (Chesbrough, 2006). Openness involves integrating suppliers, partners, distribution channels, and coalitions in extending a new venture's resources. As Amit and Han (2017) argue, generating superior digital BMs centers around the organization of access to resources controlled by other actors. For instance, when dominant digital technology firm such as Google opens its data to other actors through its APIs, it enables firms like Uber to digitally rent access to the data from *Google Maps* for their location-based digital service offerings. Google, in turn, benefits by collecting digital economic rent from its digital data assets, while Uber benefits through resource conservation and expansion.

3.4   DIGITAL NEW VENTURE ENACTMENT AND PERFORMANCE

As explained in the previous chapter, NVI initiation and evaluation resulting in visually represented BMs are of little value unless acted upon. Thus, enactment is central to understanding the entrepreneurial process. As Schumpeter (1942) points out, innovation is the tool which entrepreneurs leverage to exploit change as an opportunity. Hence, new venture enactment is the process of turning ideas into concrete outcomes. Given the fluid boundaries of innovation made possible by digital technologies, the focus of new venture creation is shifted away from linear, discrete, and stable process assumptions to dynamic process mechanisms (Lyytinen et al., 2016). Hence, digital new venture enactment has been described as dynamic problem-solution pairing (Nambisan and Sawhney, 2011), which departs from discrete and bounded innovation process and outcome mechanisms (Von Hippel and Von Krogh, 2015).

Digital new venture creation follows trajectories that are more sporadic and parallel, involving 'the constant initiation, forking, merging, and termination of diverse activities facilitated by digital technologies' (Nambisan, 2017, p. 1034). Consequently, unlike traditional entrepreneurship assumptions, digital new venture creation may 'not necessarily start with a new venture idea or single action to realize this idea but a set of actions that indicate commitment' (von Briel et al., 2018, p. 292). It lends some support to effectual and bricolage entrepreneurial models, which propose that entrepreneurs begin enactment with available means while staying open and responsive to new means that emerge to shape the entrepreneurial journey in dynamic ways.

As Benner and Tushman (2015) argue, many theories governing product/ service innovation were developed for a pre-digital era. A pre-digital era operated under relatively more stable and less complex environments (Child and McGrath, 2001; McGrath, 2013). Hence, dominant theories of product lifecycle (Utterback, 1994), architectural innovation (Henderson and Clark, 1990), and the product innovation process have underlying assumptions of relative stability and well-defined boundaries of process and outcomes. Recently, these innovation models have been challenged in a digital entrepreneurial context (Barrett et al., 2015). When digital artifacts form the core of NVIs and market offerings, they provide metaphors for innovation defined by dynamism, with outcome boundaries becoming porous and fluid. Given the loose coupling and ephemeral embodiment of digital artifacts, they potentially result in ease of initiation, multiple iterative cycles of experimentation, and shorter duration of processes (von Briel et al., 2018). Indeed, the scope, features, and value of digital market offerings continue to evolve long after the initial launch. As noted, digital new market offerings remain 'incomplete by design' (Garud et al., 2009) and subject to infinite expansibility – thereby making it hard to draw clear boundaries between the start and end phases of digital new venture creation.

Additionally, 'nailed' or validated BMs (Furr and Ahlstrom, 2011; Ries, 2011) can be rapidly scaled at unprecedented velocities (Huang et al., 2017). Short and rapid processes stem from the fact that digital artifacts can be tweaked, reprogrammed, recombined, and instantly distributed over cyberspace. Hence, agile and lean start-up process models (discussed below) suggest behaviors and mechanisms that may drive successful digital new venture enactment (Ries, 2011; Blank, 2013). As such, causal decision-making models do not appear workable or of much use in digital innovation (Nambisan, 2017; Nambisan et al., 2017). The modifiable and transient characteristics of digital artifacts indicate that they can be co-created by multiple participating actors across digital value networks (Lyytinen et al., 2016). Accordingly, processes are defined by continual adjustments by actors in multiple, iterative cycles of action (Garud and Giuliani, 2013). Further, processes often have unclear beginning and ending phases. Given the nature of the process, we differentiate digital entrepreneurship as *a process of rapid, dynamic, and continuous emergence.*

Not surprisingly, frustrated by the failures of linear models of innovation such as *Waterfall Methodology* and causal entrepreneurship models, digital entrepreneurs in software-based industries began to develop alternative models of digital new venture creation. These models emphasize agility, flexibility, and dynamism in the face of uncertainty (Berglund et al., 2018). Models such as the Lean Start-up and Design Thinking (DT) have broadly been described as a hypothesis-driven approach to new venture creation (Eisenmann et al., 2013).

3.4.1   Lean Start-up Model of Digital New Venture Enactment

In recognizing the role of uncertainty in entrepreneurship, Eric Ries establishes the basis of the Lean Start-up Methodology (LSM) by defining a start-up as 'a human institution designed to create a new product or service under conditions of extreme uncertainty' (Ries, 2011, p. 27). Besides, a start-up is not a scaled-down version of a large company (Blank, 2013). Therefore, it cannot be managed in the same way as a large or established organization. As such, proponents of the LSM argue that new ventures exist to learn how to build a sustainable BM, while established ones already have their BMs 'nailed' (Furr and Ahlstrom, 2011). New ventures learn by running several experiments geared towards achieving validated learning of multiple hypotheses codified in the BM (Blank, 2013). Experimentation is therefore a critical social mechanism for building and reinforcing OC (Davidsson, 2015).

Unlike traditional models of new venture enactment, which emphasize the business plan and thorough market research as departure points for new venture creation, proponents of the LSM are highly critical of this approach. Instead, they view the allure of a good business plan as a significant contributor to start-up failure. Hence, they argue that sticking to business plans ignores the fact that new ventures often operate under conditions of extreme uncertainty. They do not know who their customers are or what their product should be (Ries, 2011). Therefore, business plans and forecasts are ill-suited to the less stable, complex, and unpredictable contexts in which digital new ventures emerge. This argument appears particularly valid in a digital entrepreneurial context where entrepreneurs cannot be certain that an NVI will gain traction. Accordingly, Ries advances the following five principles of the LSM:

- *Entrepreneurs Are Everywhere:* Ries claims that the LSM can work in any size company, sector, and industry. This assertion is based on its integrative framework, which borrows from lean manufacturing principles developed by Japanese automakers (Blank and Dorf, 2012), and agile development principles developed in software industries.
- *Entrepreneurship Is Management:* Given the extreme nature of uncertainty in which new ventures are created, entrepreneurship is a different kind of management.
- *Validated Learning:* New ventures exist to learn how to build a sustainable BM under uncertainty. As such, learning is best validated by running

frequent experiments to test business hypotheses, with the goal of reducing uncertainty.

- *Build-Measure-Learn:* Experiments begin with the agile process of turning ideas into products and measuring how customers respond. Thus, digital entrepreneurs begin by developing an MVP to elicit customer feedback. Feedback results in the decision to either pivot (make adjustments), persevere, or perish (disband). Thus, innovation processes need to be geared towards accelerating feedback loops of learning.
- *Innovation Accounting:* Finally, the principle of innovation accounting refers to determining how to measure progress by setting up milestones and prioritizing tasks. It involves basing decisions on actionable metrics that emanate from experimentation – for example, funnel metrics, cohort analysis, and conversion rates. An *actionable metric* is one that meets new venture creation goals, while a *vanity metric* is deceptively impressive but does little to advance key business objectives.

3.4.1.1 Steps in the lean start-up process
Based on the above five principles of the LSM and related agile methodologies, Eisenmann et al. (2013) distill concrete steps that summarize how new venture creation may unfold under such an approach.

1. *Vision:* The process begins with the vision or destination in mind. This vision describes how a new venture intends to create and capture value for and from its customers. It is, therefore, another way of conceptualizing the NVI (Davidsson, 2015).
2. *Falsifiable Hypotheses:* Next, the vision is translated into a series of falsifiable hypotheses, represented on a Business Model Canvas (BMC) (Osterwalder and Pigneur, 2010). Unlike a detailed business plan, the BMC is a recommended one-page document with nine components for laying out building blocks of the vision. These nine components begin with the *value proposition* which is at the center of what a new venture offers to its audiences. It is followed by *customer segments*, which identify the target customers the new venture aims to solve problems for.

Customer relationships help to define the types of relationships that will be formed with audiences. In addition, the canvas also indicates *channels*, which are methods by which a firm's services will be delivered. Next, *key partners* represent individuals and organizations who will be instrumental in realizing the vision. While the *cost structure* defines the fixed and variable costs of realizing the vision, the *revenue stream* describes the model by which the venture captures value from customers. The BMC also describes key firm *activities* required to deliver the value proposition, as well as the *resources* needed to realize it.

Blank and Dorf (2012) note that unlike the business plan, the BMC is not a static and finite artifact. Its power lies in the ability to discard and redevelop as new knowledge gets fed back into the process. Indeed, the simplicity of the BMC stands in contrast to a business plan document which may involve months of planning and research, yet 'rarely survives the first contact with customers' (Blank and Dorf, 2012). In more recent years, Maurya (2012) has developed the *Lean Canvas*, which, he argues, serves to make the BMC more actionable by focusing on critical aspects of the BMC at different stages in the entrepreneurial process. The BMC and Lean Canvas are single-page documents because they see business planning as an ongoing process.

3. *Specifying MVP Tests:* This step involves specifying the test of a series of hypotheses indicated in the BMC. To do this, the new venture rapidly puts together ideas for an MVP, which it builds and uses to begin eliciting customer feedback on various aspects of the BM. The MVP is the usable but not full-featured version of a market offering that enables the *Build-Measure-Learn* feedback loop. The focus is on nimbleness and speed by minimizing the total time through the loop. This approach to new venture creation is considered useful for digital start-ups because it speaks to the characteristics of digital artifacts, which are, among others, incomplete by nature and subject to infinite expansibility.

4. *Prioritizing Tests:* At this stage, the entrepreneur prioritizes tests that may help eliminate the most significant risks to the new venture and deliver rapid success.

5. *Learning from MVP Tests:* Next, the entrepreneur evaluates feedback from testing the MVP while watching out for false positives and false negatives.

6. *Pivot, Persevere, or Perish:* After evaluating feedback from MVP tests, the entrepreneur must decide whether to pivot, persevere, or perish. To *pivot* is to correct course or adjust based on feedback. If a test returns positive results, the entrepreneur *perseveres* on course. However, if feedback from customers suggests a resounding negative, the entrepreneur may decide to *perish* by disbanding the new business venture, thereby eliminating further waste.

7. *Scaling:* When the entrepreneur validates all hypotheses, the new venture achieves *product-market fit* (Blank and Dorf, 2012). As the name suggests, the new market offering has found a receptive market. It is usually demonstrated by demand and revenue generated from early adopters or lead users. The BM is 'nailed' and ripe for scaling (Furr and Ahlstrom, 2011; Maurya, 2016). Scaling is the mechanism by which the new market

offering diffuses to larger audiences while remaining sustainable. In line with the *Diffusion of Innovation Theory* (Rogers, 1995), it is the customer acquisition process that helps new market offers to 'cross the chasm' from early adopters to reach an early and late majority (Moore, 1999).

3.4.1.2 Limits of the lean start-up

While the LSM has gained popularity among practitioners as an experimental model of entrepreneurial action, it is not without its fair share of criticisms. Blank (2013, p. 69), a key proponent of the LSM, states that 'while some adherents claim that the lean process can make individual start-ups more successful, I believe that claim is too grandiose.' He is cautious in stating that using the methodology will result in fewer failures than with traditional models. This clarification is necessary as it acknowledges that the lean start-up may not always work for every new venture. Other critics argue that the LSM is more suitable to digital new venture creation, though some of its principles can be applied in a traditional entrepreneurial context. The LSM may very well be an illustration of how digital entrepreneurship is not only transforming our assumptions of entrepreneurship through the effects of market offerings but also through their methodologies. Nevertheless, the LSM may not be ideal in the following scenarios.

When Mistakes Must Be Limited: First, Eisenmann et al. (2013) state that when start-ups operate in environments where mistakes are intolerable, the LSM may be ill-advised. Circumstances in which a post-launch correction of errors may not be possible fall under this category. Similarly, in cases where mistakes would affect customers' mission-critical activities and trigger a severe societal backlash, including legal consequences, the LSM may not be ideal. For instance, in certain industries such as FinTech and MedTech, data breaches on consumer's privacy can lead to severe consequences for digital start-ups. Thus, it limits the potential for launching a 'half-baked' and minimal digital product to the market.

When Demand Uncertainty Is Low: Second, where there is substantial evidence of unmet demand for a new product, such as a breakthrough treatment for a disease, Eisenmann et al. (2013) maintain that there is less of a need to launch early and seek feedback from customers. In other words, there is high perceived certainty of demand, thereby favoring a causal approach. For instance, a vaccine or treatment for a virus such as Covid-19 arguably has a high perceived demand certainty, thereby suggesting that a linear approach may be more appropriate to new venture enactment. However, as previously noted, uncertainty perceived is subjective and may emanate from an entrepreneur's cognitive biases (McMullen and Shepherd, 2006). Therefore, entrepreneurs must seek to triangulate multiple sources of information that disconfirm their hypotheses before concluding that uncertainty is low or high.

When Demand Uncertainty Is High but Development Cycles Are Long:
In cases where long product development cycles and enormous upfront fixed
costs are needed, it may be impossible to launch early and often. Further, if
demand uncertainty is high and development cycles are long, such as the case
with disruptive new technologies, a fully working product, as opposed to an
MVP may be needed to elicit any meaningful feedback for gauging the level of
demand. Furthermore, Furr and Dyer (2014) argue that a Minimum Awesome
Product (MAP) may often present a better route to innovating with less waste
than an MVP.

More Validation Is Not Better: In a study involving 250 teams in an
American accelerator program, Ladd (2016) found that there was no linear
relationship between validated hypotheses and teams' subsequent success.
He also found that teams that conducted more formalized experiments with
customers performed worse than teams that either conducted one or the other
during the early stages of new venture design. The reason may stem from
erosion of confidence – whereby too much feedback from customers might
cause entrepreneurs and teams to change their idea and eventually become
disheartened or exhausted. Additionally, repeated cycles of MVPs may not
only wear out the entrepreneur but may also increase overheads. Thus, digital
entrepreneurs are advised to maintain a sharp focus on opportunities for rapid
scaling.

False Negatives and Lack of Clear Stopping Rules: Ladd (2016) also
warns against the danger of 'false negatives' – by which good ideas are mistak-
enly rejected because of the absence of clear rules on when to declare victory,
stop experimenting, and begin scaling. He suggests that a 'lean strategy' may
be more useful in setting clear constraints for which markets and methods
are to be considered while testing and fine-tuning the BM. Also, he argues
that if 50 percent of customers in the target segment pay for a prototype, the
BM should be locked in place. However, this argument appears to fly in the
face of digital NVIs built on multisided advertising-based models (Maurya,
2016). Ad-based multisided models may take longer to grow their audience
to a sizeable network that can be monetized effectively. Only when a tipping
point in the user base is reached can it determine how much advertisers will
pay. Furthermore, how much advertisers are willing to pay fluctuates. Thus, an
actual percentage of customers is a complex issue.

Not All Aspects of the BM Need Prioritizing: As earlier noted, Maurya's
(2012) adapted Lean Canvas incrementally prioritizes aspects of the BMC as
the new venture develops. Accordingly, Ladd (2016) found that teams which
focused on target customer segment, value proposition, and channel performed
twice as well as teams that did not give these three components much attention. Therefore, not all aspects of the business model are equally important at
various stages of new venture creation.

Hidden Danger of Assuming Customer Sovereignty: Meanwhile, McMullen (2017) points out the hidden dangers of assuming customer sovereignty in new venture creation. He states that new venture creation revolves around the needs of multiple stakeholders, of which the customer is only one. Thus, while pivoting to meet customers' needs is essential, if it results in the entrepreneur losing passion, there is 'no motive to start the entrepreneurial process, no action in need of a pivot, and no value for stakeholders to claim' (p. 430). Relatedly, Vargo and Lusch (2017) argue that interconnected value co-creation in services ecosystems requires a deeper understanding of the nature and role of technology as well as institutions that frame its multidimensional contexts. Hence, customer sovereignty may not be sufficient in explaining venture performance since multiple interconnected stakeholders interrelate in shaping digital new venture creation and success.

Lean Start-up Is a 'Code for Unplanned': While most criticisms of the lean start-up pick out an aspect of the methodology and moderately criticize it, Masters and Thiel (2014, p. 213) are unequivocal in their stance against its core axioms. They start by arguing that 'leanness' is a mechanism, not a goal. As such, making small incremental changes using MVPs offers little help in finding the global maximum. They recommend that entrepreneurs should focus on careful planning while forgetting MVPs and focus group feedback. They argue that a bad plan is better than no plan, and it is better to risk boldness than triviality.

Overall, most of the criticisms against the LSM suggest that its assumptions may be better suited to a PDE context where digital artifacts can be inexpensively enacted and re-enacted in iterative cycles of experimentation. Likewise, it may simply offer social mechanisms which entrepreneurs in all contexts can pick and choose, then mix and match with other models as needed by the uniqueness of their circumstances. As a result, DT offers another dynamic process model that may complement the LSM.

3.4.2   Design Thinking (DT): Alternative to the Lean Start-up Model

DT, which is a method developed to solve problems for clients (Kelley and Littman, 2001), is a systematic, user-oriented approach to solving real-life problems (Plattner et al., 2009). Being a user-centered design, it focuses on addressing the user's needs and requirements instead of how the problem can be solved technically. It adopts structured and iterative processes in solving user needs. Brown (2008, p. 88) identifies three phases in the IDEO (Innovation Design Engineering Organization) approach to DT: inspiration, brainstorming, and implementation. Inspiration is the purview of the NVI, while brainstorming is the acquisition, development, and testing of hypotheses. At the implementation stage, a definitive prototype is launched.

Table 3.3   Differences between design thinking and lean start-up

Basis for Comparison	Design Thinking	Lean Start-up
Goal	Innovations	Innovations
Scope/Focus	General innovations	Appears digital new venture creation focused
Approach	User-centered	Customer-oriented
Uncertainty	Solve wicked problems identified	Unclear customer problems
Testing	Fail early, succeed sooner	Accelerated feedback loops recommended
Iteration	Iterative	Iterative with pivoting
Ideation	Ideation is part of the process	Ideation is not part of the process; product vision originates from the founder
Qualitative	Ethnographic techniques	Not a focus
Quantitative	Not a focus	Emphasis on actionable, often quantifiable metrics
Business model	Not a focus	Focus
Hypothesis testing	Not a focus	A prime focus
Prototype testing	Yes with connotations of a physical prototype	Yes, but called an MVP, with undertones of a digitized product
Target group	Users (usually end-users, occasionally stakeholders)	Various customer segments – end-users, influencers, economic buyers, etc.

Source: Adapted from Muller and Thoring (2013).

Plattner et al. (2009, p. 113) develop a more comprehensive model of DT which includes six phases. The phases begin with understanding the problem, followed by observations that lead to a so-called *point of view*. Next, ideation, prototyping, and testing follow. The mission of DT, according to Brown and Katz (2011), is to translate observations into insights and insights into products and services that improve lives. It is similar to the LSM in terms of its hypothesis-driven approach but retains distinguishing characteristics. Given that DT has experimentation at its core, the similarities between the LSM are striking. Thus, it may be more worthwhile examining the differences between DT and the LSM. Table 3.3 summarizes the key differences between both methodologies, as discussed by Muller and Thoring (2012).

The differences between the models reveal circumstances under which they may be complementary. To begin, the scope of both approaches is different. While the LSM mainly focuses on new ventures, DT applies to more generic instances of product or service innovation. As such, while the LSM begins with an NVI called a vision, DT projects start with a challenge or 'wicked problems' already identified (Buchanan, 1992). Under these circumstances, the problem is not defined until extensive research has been conducted, from whence ideas are generated. The nature of research at the beginning of the DT project is mostly inductive, qualitative studies that use ethnographic techniques (Kelley and Littman, 2005). Furthermore, insights from qualitative studies are synthesized using several sophisticated methods such as 'Personas,' 'User Journeys,' and 'Causal Maps' (Kolko, 2011) – with the goal of arriving at a so-called 'Point of View.' The LSM, on the other hand, does not work with such synthetic methods.

Another significant difference between the two models can be seen in the distinction between customers, users, and stakeholders. The LSM distinguishes between users, influencers, recommenders, economic buyers, and decision-makers in market segmentation. DT refers merely to users as end-users and stakeholders. Solving the end-users' needs in DT often entails an ideation stage which involves brainstorming and brainwriting. However, since the LSM usually begins with an NVI from the entrepreneur, idea generation is absent in the process (Muller and Thoring, 2012).

Given the distinctions, one could conclude that DT is more generic to most innovation processes and less specific to digital new venture creation. Thus, a combination of both models may be ideal for HDE, where physical prototypes need to be ethnographically tested for more qualitative feedback. In contrast, the LSM appears better suited to the context of purer forms of digital entrepreneurship and offers a more comprehensive basket of social mechanisms that drive new venture realization. It actively embraces experimentation as its core axiom. Consequently, despite its weaknesses, it arguably presents a suitable approach to PDE; but it must be complemented with traditional but iterative new venture creation approaches such as DT, in HDE and traditional forms of entrepreneurship. However, both DT and LSM focus on actor-centric mechanisms, which provide very little insight into the role of non-human agencies embedded in digital technologies.

3.4.3 Sociomateriality Theory and Digital New Venture Enactment

Sociomateriality theory provides a useful theoretical lens for explaining digital new venture creation and performance by considering the role of both human and material agencies (Orlikowski, 2007, 2009; Orlikowski and Scott, 2008; Davidson and Vaast, 2010). Sociomateriality theorists contend that in an age defined by intelligent machine learning algorithms, with their influential actor-independent mechanisms, human-centric explanations of new venture creation provide only partial insights into digital entrepreneurial action (Orlikowski and Scott, 2015).

Thus, the anthropocentrism of entrepreneurship theories such as effectuation and bricolage, lean start-up, and DT give primacy to actor-centric drivers of the entrepreneurial process, with little insight on the role of digital material agencies (Garud et al., 2014, 2018). However, when agency is simply defined as the capacity for action (Latour, 2005), digital artifacts have material agency as they can be assigned functional capacity for action (Faulkner and Runde, 2009; Leonardi, 2011) – a view that is increasingly significant in an age of intelligent systems. That is not to suggest they are the same as human agency, which acts with intentionality and free will. Sayes (2014) explains that to understand how non-human 'beings' act, it is important to first divorce agency from criteria of intentionality, subjectivity, and free will. Accordingly, Latour (2005, p. 72) explains that non-human beings such as digital technologies have agency in that 'they might authorize, allow, afford, encourage, permit, suggest, influence, block, render possible, forbid, and so on.' Against this under-standing, the interrelationships between human and digital material agencies contribute towards a better understanding of the drivers of the digital entrepre-neurial process. Precisely, they change our theorizing of social mechanisms into more sociomaterial mechanism-based explanations, which illuminates the role of digital technologies in entrepreneurship.

Sociomateriality theory is based on a relational philosophy (Barad, 2003, 2007) and the performative argument that humans and objects are first and always a nexus of complex interrelationships that jointly shape each other (Garud et al., 2010; Garud et al., 2018). Therefore, new venture creation is assumed to be performed through the intermingling of human actors and digital material agencies (Pickering, 2010; Cecez-Kecmanovic et al., 2014). As Barad argues, agency emerges as human and material objects *intra-act*. Intra-action is a neologism coined to describe the entangled webs of mutually constitutive agencies between the social and the material. These intra-actions result in 'material-discursive practices' (Orlikowski and Scott, 2015) – whereby the materiality of digital technologies offers affordances which are consciously or unconsciously interpreted and acted out by human agents (Majchrzak and Markus, 2012).

Consequently, Davidson and Vaast (2010, p. 4) conclude that sociomateri-ality in the digital entrepreneurial process 'emerges from the mutual exploita-tion, adjustment and enactment of means-end relationships between human and non-human actors.' Furthermore, sociomaterial routines form the basis of knowledge creation and the reduction in the levels of task-specific uncertainty (McMullen and Shepherd, 2006), with the result being variations in digital new venture ideas, innovation, and outcomes. For instance, the editable and distrib-utable characteristics of digital artifacts offer new sociomaterial mechanisms for inexpensive and collaborative experimentation, flexibility, instant release, and the rapid scaling of digital new ventures (Huang et al., 2017). Likewise, these same characteristics may constrain some actors.

While sociomateriality provides a useful lens for theorizing the role of digital technologies in digital new venture enactment, it has received its share of criticism. Critics of the theory remain uneasy with its philosophical stance that suggests strict symmetry between material and social agents (Mutch, 2013). They advocate a substantialist philosophy that argues for separating material and social agencies (Faulkner and Runde, 2012; Leonardi, 2012). However, Orlikowski and Scott (2015, p. 698) acknowledge the counter-arguments by stating that 're-framing conceptual concerns away from human-centered approaches is a bold move, and we recognize that doing so disrupts long-standing assumptions informing many areas of management.'

Ultimately, the value of sociomateriality lies in its capacity to theorize the complex ways in which mechanisms of digital material agencies embedded in digital technologies, intra-act with human agencies and actor-centric mechanisms, to produce sociomaterial mechanisms that shape digital new venture emergence and outcomes.

3.4.4   Digital New Venture Performance – a Complexity Perspective

Sociomateriality theory is valuable because it avoids reducing causal explanations of entrepreneurial processes to human-centric perspectives only. Thus, it intersects with complexity theory. As Thrift (1999, p. 33) notes, 'the chief impulse behind complexity theory is an anti-reductionist one.' It is anti-reductionist from the perspective that it seeks holistic explanations to new venture creation and performance. Since the entrepreneurial process is one of emergence, it is a process of 'order creation' – a core description of what complexity theory focuses on (Lichtenstein et al., 2007; Schindehutte and Morris, 2009). Digital entrepreneurship operates against a complex and dynamic ecosystem where adapting to change is necessary to drive performance. Adapting new venture enactment to evolving circumstances is itself a process of developing complex adaptive systems.

Therefore, a Complex Adaptive Systems (CAS) theory of complexity sheds light on performance in cases where digital platform creation is the basis of new market offerings. Digital platforms, as noted, create value by facilitating transactions between producers and consumers. CAS theory describes the behavior of such large-scale, highly dynamic systems, which, although driven by the aggregate behavior of individual elements, appear to function in coherent and motivated ways (Anderson, 1999; Tredinnick, 2009). Furthermore, CAS describes the 'meshwork' of interrelated agencies, motivations, and forces that make up the complex system driving digital platform success (DeLanda, 2006).

Benbya and McKelvey (2006) identify the vital characteristics of a CAS. First, they are comprised of heterogeneous agents that interact with each other and their surroundings. These agents may adapt their behavior in an unlimited number of ways. It aligns with the dynamism digital platforms promote, where change can sometimes originate from unanticipated locations and behaviors of actors. Diversity emerges as each agent is different from the other, and the system shapes their actions. The interaction between agents results in the flow of information and knowledge.

Second, CAS exhibit a capacity to anticipate the results of their actions, for which they develop shared schemas (Anderson, 1999; Tredinnick, 2009). Schemas are rules that reflect patterns in experience (Stacey, 1996). These schemas, when combined with each individual agents' schemas, enable a CAS to learn, adapt, and evolve. Since current and future evolution are dependent on history, it makes their evolution equally path-dependent (Tredinnick, 2009). In the digital entrepreneurial context, this flow of information and knowledge within a platform results in rich data and insights, which skilled actors can monitor and respond to in driving performance. Through this lens, organizing is seen as order creation from the perspective that insights result in emergent order, self-organizing, and continuous adaptation.

Being self-organized means that new behavioral patterns emerge as agents interact, with no single agent being able to determine the system's behavior (Stacey, 1996; Anderson, 1999; Benbya and McKelvey, 2006). These systems self-organize when they find themselves between the 'edge of chaos' and the 'edge of order' (Kauffman, 1994). Complexity in the digital entrepreneurial environment is defined by hyper-connectivity and mutual dependencies between actors. As such, digital new venture creation processes are inter-twined in complex webs of socio-technical ecosystems (Leonardi, 2012). These ecosystems operate 'far from equilibrium' and exhibit non-linearity, self-organization, emergence, and co-evolution (McKelvey et al., 2016). Thus, successful digital new venture enactment is determined by the ability of entre-preneurial agents to remain open, flexible, and responsive in creating value for other actors in a complex ecosystem. Thus, a democratic and collaborative form of leadership is critical.

Mechanisms Driving Performance: Accordingly, three mechanisms help explain how adaptive leadership of digital entrepreneurs shapes new venture performance (Reeves et al., 2016). First, digital entrepreneurs need to be realistic about what they can control, what they can shape collaboratively, and what goes beyond the reach of their influence. Also, they need to expect that unpredictable and emergent outcomes will arise from actions at lower levels. Second, agents need to look beyond what they own or control and monitor and address complexity outside the organization's confines. Thus, firm-centric theories that emphasize organizational resources and capabilities as drivers of performance are hard to sustain in this context. Establishing mutually beneficial partnerships with actors in a system helps drive digital new venture performance (Autio et al., 2018). Failure to create value for other stakeholders will result in marginalization and defections. Third, surviving in a CAS is to realize that attempts to control actors at lower echelons of the system are often unproductive and counterintuitive, possibly leading to the collapse of the venture. As such, new ventures must eschew simplistic causal models and avoid trying to manage individual behavior directly. Instead, they must seek to shape the context of that behavior by fostering collaborative, 'leaderful practices' (Raelin, 2011). Consequently, Reeves et al. (2016) suggest mechanisms by which digital entrepreneurial entrepreneurs can conceptualize and enact new venture creation in developing a CAS – summarized in Table 3.4.

Table 3.4   Complex adaptive mechanisms of digital new venture creation

Structural Features	Addressed Threats
1. Heterogeneity – there should be diversity in actors, ideas, innovations, and aspirations	Collapse risk – change from within or outside industry renders venture's business model obsolete
2. Modularity – there should be loose connections between components of the business system and between business systems	Contagion risk – shocks in one part of the business ecosystem spread rapidly to other parts
3. Redundancy – there should be duplication that creates buffering capacity in the business system	Fat-tail risk – rare but involves large shocks to the system such as global financial crisis, viral outbreaks such as Covid-19, terrorism, and political upheavals
Managerial Levers	Addressed Threats
4. Expect surprises, but reduce uncertainty – collect signals, detect patterns of change using digital data analytics, imagine possible outcomes, and take precautionary steps	Discontinuity risk – the business environment evolves abruptly in ways that are hard to predict
5. Create feedback loops and adaptive mechanisms – monitor change, promote variation, experiment, iterate rapidly, innovate	Obsolescence risk – the venture fails to adapt to changing customer needs, competitive innovations, or altered circumstances
6. Foster trust and reciprocity – act in ways that benefit other participants in the overall system and establish mechanisms that ensure reciprocity	Rejection risk – avoid risk of rejection by participants in the business ecosystem

Source: Adapted from Reeves et al. (2016).

The mechanisms for navigating, as well as developing CAS offer practical guidance on behaviors which are needed to drive performance, especially when digital platforms and digital artifacts form the core of NVIs and new market offerings. Some of these behaviors and their social mechanisms are reflected in dynamic models of digital new venture creation such as the Lean Start-up and DT explored above.

3.5   DIGITAL ENTREPRENEURIAL AGENCY AND COGNITIVE MECHANISMS

The nature of complexity and dynamism in the digital entrepreneurial context suggests that traditionally accepted cognitive mechanisms explaining the micro-foundations of entrepreneurial action and performance are inadequate. Likewise, attempts to lionize focal entrepreneurs as drivers of performance may be misplaced. As Nambisan (2017) points out, the locus of digital entrepreneurial agency has become less predefined and more decentralized, thereby disrupting our understanding of leadership in this context. As a reminder, the previous chapter examined cognitive and motivation theories, which purport to explain why some individuals formulate NVIs, why some actors choose to act on them, and why some perform better than others (Baron, 2004). When combined, cognitive models provide explanations for some of the actor-driven mechanisms which enable new venture creation and performance.

3.5.1   Prospect Theory, Perceptual Processes, and Digital New Venture Ideas (NVIs)

To determine why some focal agents formulate and act on NVIs, *prospect theory* and *perceptual processes* have been proposed as cognitive mechanisms which supplement self-efficacy and other established cognitive models in providing micro-foundational explanations of digital new venture creation and performance.

Prospect Theory: Prospect theory deals with the positive framing of risk (Kahneman and Tversky, 1979). It argues that entrepreneurs engage in prospection involving the framing of a situation in terms of losses – whereby loss refers to the economic gains they will forfeit if they do not become entrepreneurs. The 'fear of missing out' then prompts positive framing of risk. Focusing on losses translates into risk-seeking behaviors that prompt entrepreneurial initiatives and entry (Baron, 2004). However, this risk-seeking tendency may, in turn, be plagued by cognitive biases such as optimistic bias (Shepperd et al., 1996), confirmation bias (Nickerson, 1998), planning fallacy, and an illusion of control under uncertainty (Kahneman, Slovic and Tversky, 1982; Kahneman, 2011). These biases result in a tendency to underestimate the risk of starting a new venture. Hence, it suggests that entrepreneurial agents may sometimes be acting on delusional and irrational assumptions. However, the value of this delusion resides in its ability to prompt individuals to start new venture creation based on imperfect knowledge or false assumptions. Only by taking action will they learn if their ideas have value and develop the capabilities needed to drive future performance.

Furthermore, prospect theory maintains that people 'overweight' small probabilities of success but 'underweight' moderate and high probabilities of failure. In the digital entrepreneurial context, it suggests that focal agents may overweight a slim chance of success and underweight moderate to high chances of failure (Baron, 1998; Simon et al., 2000). Such thinking may prompt them to initiate the entrepreneurial process while learning and adapting as they go along. Since digital technologies considerably lower the barriers to starting a digital new venture, prospect theory may provide a plausible explanation. It suggests that some actors believe not starting a digital new venture is missing out.

Perceptual Processes: Perceptual processes, on the other hand, relate to the role of prior knowledge in the formulation of NVIs. It focuses on pattern or object recognition as cognitive mechanisms driving the formulation and reformulation of NVIs into new narratives that guide action. Baron and Ensley (2006) describe pattern recognition as the identification of a complex array of stimuli, which collectively allow perceivers to recognize an object or a complex pattern. It suggests that past experiences help entrepreneurs construct prototypes that represent patterns or categories of objects. Thus, prior experiences help unlock digital technology affordances, resulting in the envisioning of a new combination of market offerings. Accordingly, Gaglio and Katz (2001) suggest that entrepreneurs possess a schema or mental framework which aids their alertness to external stimuli. Cognitive schemas facilitate the search and recognition of changes, as well as market disequilibria. They then match these changes with their mental framework and respond to information that does not match.

However, Grégoire et al. (2010) found that entrepreneurs do not use mental prototypes to recognize and formulate NVIs in technology markets. Instead, they rely on the cognitive alignment of new technologies and markets. With this finding, Grégoire and Shepherd (2012) suggest that digital NVIs result from superficial and structural similarities of digital technology-market combination, while differences in prior knowledge and motivation moderate these relationships.

3.5.2 Counterfactual Thinking and Digital Entrepreneurial Performance

On the question of variance in digital entrepreneurial action and performance, counterfactual thinking has been suggested as an explanatory framework (Nambisan and Baron, 2013). Counterfactual thinking focuses on 'what might have been' (Kahneman and Lovallo, 1994). It presents mechanisms by which entrepreneurs deconstruct the past as a precursor to action in the face of future uncertainty (Baron, 2000). It involves comparing events to 'alternatives that are constructed ad hoc rather than retrieved from past experience' (Kahneman and Miller, 1986, p. 136). It has recently been expanded to include a future dimension that looks at what may yet be (Arora et al., 2013). Ultimately, it suggests that successful digital entrepreneurs are those who constantly imagine new possibilities for change as opposed to accepting the status quo as final. As such, it may also provide answers to the sources of disruptive digital NVIs.

Additionally, entrepreneurs who employ counterfactual thinking may be better at formulating improved task strategies. It may owe much to the fact that thoughts of what might have been yield useful prescriptions for future behavior, heightening success-facilitating intentions and corresponding behaviors (Roese, 1994, p. 815). High-performing entrepreneurs are presumed to be skilled at using counterfactual reasoning to learn from the past. Whereby deconstructing past events to make sense of the future is a cognitive technique that helps develop practical knowledge and ideas (Markman et al., 1993).

3.5.3 Self-Regulatory Processes and Digital Entrepreneurial Performance

Considering that digital entrepreneurs often operate within network-centric innovation ecosystems, where they have less control, self-regulatory processes are seen as essential performance drivers. New ventures that are built around dominant digital platform ecosystems such as the Google App store result in high dependencies between the digital platform leader and a loosely connected network of actors (Nambisan and Sawhney, 2011). While enormous benefits accrue to operating in such environments, they present unique leadership challenges that may affect venture performance, thereby demanding higher-order strategic thinking (Zahra and Nambisan, 2011, 2012). Firms retain less control in these ecosystems, as they must ensure their goals and objectives align with the rules of the digital platform leader. They must also provide sufficient differentiation and independence as they pursue a unique value proposition. Furthermore, the success of the ecosystem may not always result in success for their ventures. Such digital ecosystems raise tensions with an entrepreneur's perceived self-efficacy, thereby calling for a striking of balance between an independent and ecosystem-dependent mindset (Nambisan and Baron, 2013).

Self-regulatory cognitive mechanisms may, therefore, explain how digital entrepreneurs maintain such a balance to drive performance. The multimodal framework of self-regulatory processes includes *self-control*, *grit*, and *metacognition*, which can be interpreted as central to a digital entrepreneurial mindset. These mechanisms explore how individuals monitor, evaluate, direct, and adjust their behavior towards reaching their goals. Indeed, research on cognitive fit suggests that digital entrepreneurs will experience better performance if they choose the self-regulatory model that closely matches the requirements of their ecosystem. In this vein, Hmieleski and Baron (2008) contend that a prevention focus (security and safety approach) is mainly recommended in stable but risky environments, while a promotion focus (achievement and accomplishment approach) is positively linked to performance in dynamic and uncertain environments.

Self-Control: With relation to self-control, it involves resisting strong impulses to engage in actions deemed harmful or out of line with significant goals (Baumeister and Alquist, 2009). Alternatively, it entails resisting impulses to stop performing actions that may be beneficial but not intrinsically enjoyable (Forgas et al., 2011). Research on self-control indicates that individuals vary in their capacity to exercise self-control (Tangney et al., 2004). Additionally, self-control is exhaustible, but at the same time, replenishable (Baumeister and Alquist, 2009; Tice, 2009). Since digital entrepreneurs operate in environments marked by high dependency between actors and ecosystems, they often encounter situations that may deplete their self-control. Therefore, focal agents with high self-control are more likely to act in ways that drive performance, even if that means putting up with scenarios which are not enjoyable. For instance, a digital platform governor such as Apple may demand that all apps upgrade their code to reflect its future goals. Failure to respond would result in an app being removed from the app store. Being forced to upgrade may be costly, frustrating, and stressful for the digital entrepreneur in such platform-based ecosystems. Self-control is therefore needed under such stressful circumstances (Nambisan and Baron, 2021).

Grit (Persistence): While self-control is focused on current actions, grit is concerned with the self-regulation of extended processes. Baron and Henry (2010, p. 49) maintain that 'outstanding performance derives largely from participation in intense, prolonged, and highly focused efforts to improve current performance' in new venture creation. Moreover, being persistent in pursuing long-term goals carries the added benefit of expanding domain-specific knowledge and skills. As such, persistent digital entrepreneurs are likely to generate new knowledge in the process and necessary cognitive resources such as memory, perception, and metacognition, which drive performance. Hence, Duckworth and Quinn (2009) posit that grit is pivotal to understanding digital entrepreneurial performance. Furthermore, Dweck (2015) suggests that it can be consciously developed under the framework of a 'growth mindset.' A growth mindset is rooted in the belief that individuals who believe their talents can be developed through hard work, good strategies, and feedback from others tend to achieve better results than those with a fixed mindset – that is, those who believe their talents are innate.

Consequently, grit is a critical growth mindset explaining digital entrepreneurial performance. For instance, to drive strong network effects, a digital entrepreneur may need to engage in painstaking digital growth marketing activities over the long term via social media and search engine channels. Gaining visibility may be dependent on the algorithmic agencies that power these platforms. Reaching a tipping point between early adopters and an early majority will probably be slow and frustrating. Performance may boil down to actors persisting in search of learning opportunities that help their ventures scale to reach wider audiences. *Dropbox*, for instance, is a well-known case of a digital start-up that initially failed to gain traction. However, through persistent efforts, the actors behind its marketing gained the right combination of growth marketing knowledge that resulted in rapid scaling (Brown and Ellis, 2017).

Metacognition: Finally, *metacognition*, which refers to an individual's awareness and control over their cognitive capabilities (Flavell, 1979), presents another cognitive mechanism which is vital in explaining digital entrepreneurial performance and leadership. Metacognitive abilities include *metacognitive awareness* and *metacognitive resources*. Metacognitive awareness refers to an understanding of what an individual knows about themselves. It suggests that a digital entrepreneur may use this sort of awareness to focus on carrying out actions within their areas of strength while delegating leadership of specific tasks to actors who complement their weaknesses. Meanwhile, metacognitive resources allow entrepreneurs to draw upon the most effective cognitive strategies to bear on a situation (Haynie et al., 2010). As a complexity theoretical perspective suggests, heterogeneity of ideas is needed to drive venture performance. Thus, a single individual hardly possesses all the knowledge and skills required for success.

Since a significant feature of digital technology environments is the high dependency it fosters between actors, successful leadership may boil down to strong metacognition, which assists in determining when collaborating agents are better positioned to lead specific tasks. Strong metacognitive capabilities help focal agents consciously control their cognitions using related mechanisms such as analogical reasoning, think-aloud protocols, and counterfactual reasoning (Nambisan and Baron, 2013). Consequently, metacognitive capabilities also explain how digital entrepreneurs may adopt a cognitively ambidextrous leadership strategy (Fixson and Rao, 2011) in leading dynamic collectives of actors who collaborate in digital new venture creation on their own terms. Using strong metacognition, they are more likely to engage in 'leaderful practices' whereby 'leaderful practice is unrepentant in advocating distinctively democratic values' when approaching specific tasks (Raelin, 2011, p. 203).

In sum, the above-explored cognitive models have helped to provide valuable frameworks for explaining the cognitive mechanisms that drive decision making, action, and performance under digital entrepreneurial uncertainty.

However, since cognition is ultimately enabled by actor knowledge, examining the role of knowledge in digital new venture creation is essential.

3.5.4 Knowledge and Digital Entrepreneurship

Prior knowledge has been identified as a critical ingredient in the birth of NVIs. Thus, examining the role of knowledge in entrepreneurship has a long tradition. Hayek (1945) noted that opportunities arise from the imperfect distribution of information and knowledge in an economy. Individuals with relevant packages of prior knowledge will identify opportunities for new venture creation in different contexts. It is knowledge that contributes towards a reduction in uncertainty, which can stall new venture creation (McMullen and Shepherd, 2006). Knowledge is a source of opportunity, be it knowledge of objective realities, intersubjective knowledge of institutional contexts, or subjective knowledge (Erikson and Korsgaard, 2016). The digital entrepreneurial context tends to be knowledge-intensive, thereby making an understanding of knowledge critical in digital new venture creation. As Davidson and Vaast (2010) argue, digital new venture enactment and performance often hinges on a venture's ability to 'access, create, process, and strategically disseminate knowledge.' Digital products and services embodied in digital artifacts and platform offerings are themselves expressions of knowledge heterogeneity.

Understanding Knowledge: However, it is helpful to take a step back and define what knowledge entails. For guidance, we turn to the Knowledge Management discipline, which defines knowledge as a hierarchy that begins with *data* which when processed, yields *information* (Moteleb and Woodman, 2007); when information is combined with experience and judgment for use in decision-making, it becomes *knowledge* (Kidwell et al., 2000). By breaking down knowledge into its constituent parts, this definition provides a valuable premise for understanding the role of knowledge in the digital entrepreneurial process.

As Polanyi (2009) notes, knowledge can be explicit or tacit. Explicit knowledge can be codified, stored, and possibly transmitted without losses, while tacit knowledge resides in an individual's judgment and experiences, and therefore cannot be easily communicated (Grant, 2007). According to Nonaka and Takeuchi (1995), tacit knowledge can only add value if converted to explicit knowledge. Accordingly, the entrepreneurial process is a process of translating tacit knowledge into explicit knowledge embodied in an emergent hierarchy of artifacts. By initiating NVIs and subsequently acting to convert them into artifacts, entrepreneurs are turning tacit knowledge into explicit knowledge.

Integrating Internal and External Knowledge in Digital Entrepreneurship: Two distinct views tend to dominate a traditional understanding of the role of knowledge in new venture performance. One argument contends that the external environment, such as the state of an industry, is a more potent force deciding a new venture's fate (Porter, 1980), while the other looks internally and sees the resources and capabilities of the venture as being more influential. This internal focus has come to be described as the Resource-Based View (RBV) of the firm (Barney, 1991). RBV holds that it is the resources and capabilities (knowledge included) controlled by a firm that deliver venture performance. It also argues that when a venture's resources are valuable, rare, inimitable, and organized to capture value (VRIO), they deliver a sustained performance (Barney and Clark, 2007). While the RBV has largely considered knowledge a strategic internal asset, Spender (1996) takes it a step further to argue that knowledge is the single most important source of success in today's firms. Consequently, Wiklund and Shepherd (2003) found that knowledge-based resources applicable to the discovery and exploitation of opportunities are positively related to new venture performance.

However, in a digital entrepreneurial context, Lyytinen et al. (2016) argue that digitization reshapes knowledge creation and sharing, which is made possible by the reduced cost of communication and increased speed and scope of digital convergence. Convergence, in turn, increases network knowledge heterogeneity and the need for integration. The result is the redistribution of control and increased demand for knowledge coordination across time and space (Grant, 1996). Given the context, knowledge integration, as opposed to knowledge acquisition, is emphasized because high mobility of knowledge capabilities and resources, which are often vested in individuals, increases value migration, with implications for creating a sustained performance (Amit and Zott, 2001).

Grant (1996) suggests four mechanisms by which digital new ventures can successfully integrate specialized knowledge of co-creators. First, there must be *rules and directives* which establish procedures and guidelines for integrating knowledge. They should be designed such that tacit knowledge is made explicit. Second, a *sequencing* mechanism allows new ventures to integrate specialist knowledge while minimizing communication and continuous coordination. Sequencing organizes new venture creation activities in a time-patterned manner, thereby allowing actors with expert knowledge to independently contribute to new venture creation in assigned time slots. The characteristics of digital artifacts explored above particularly lend themselves to a sequencing mechanism by which tasks can be decomposed, concurrently co-created, and recombined in an agreed time sequence. Third, *routines*, which are simple sequences for coordination, need to be in place. Finally, unlike the other three mechanisms that seek to reduce the cost of communication and learning, group problem solving and decision-making provide the mechanism for navigating a crisis and highly challenging problems. It is a communication-intensive form of integrating new knowledge. Digital entrepreneurs have operationalized some of these mechanisms in agile development models such as *Scrum* and the lean start-up, which offer agile digital new venture co-creation frameworks.

Therefore, while a focal actor's prior knowledge may be relevant in initiating digital NVIs, it is knowledge integration from heterogeneous actors that has the most impact in driving enactment and performance. As such, it is more critical for digital entrepreneurs to develop metacognitive leadership capabilities for integrating external knowledge rather than relying solely on prior and internal knowledge. It implies that digital entrepreneurs need not possess all the necessary knowledge to drive new venture performance. Still, they must learn and constantly weave the capabilities of diverse actors into new venture creation. Thus, absorptive capacity (ACAP) is a required capability.

Knowledge and Absorptive Capacity (ACAP) of Digital Entrepreneurs: Since digital entrepreneurship occurs in a network-centric environment marked by open innovation (Chesbrough, 2006) and rapid technological change, ACAP is deemed a driver of performance. ACAP refers to the ability to identify, assimilate, transform, and apply valuable external knowledge for commercial purposes (Cohen and Levinthal, 1990). Cohen and Levinthal further contend that through its research and development activities, a firm develops collective knowledge about specific areas of markets, science, and technology and how they relate to its value proposition. This knowledge must then be assimilated into the organization's knowledge base to be of value (Pennings and Harianto, 1992).

The firm applies absorbed knowledge in several ways, such as replenishing the existing knowledge base, forecasting technological trends (Cohen and Levinthal, 1994; Lichtenthaler, 2009), reconfiguring existing capabilities (Pavlou and El Sawy, 2006), and developing innovative products and services. Thus, ACAP, directly and indirectly, contributes to venture performance. By cultivating a culture of absorbing and applying knowledge, successful digital entrepreneurial ventures maintain a feedback loop of learning, applying, and upgrading knowledge.

Roberts et al. (2012) note that ACAP is loaded with several underlying assumptions and discuss those under three broad classifications. For one, prior related knowledge is critical to providing a launchpad for acquiring more knowledge. Without sufficient prior exposure, the premise for absorbing more knowledge is absent, thereby implying that ACAP is domain-specific. Accordingly, digital entrepreneurial actors require a degree of relevant prior knowledge. A related assumption is the idea that ACAP depends on the organization's individual members' absorptive capacities. It is not simply the sum of its members, but 'links across a mosaic of individual capabilities' (Cohen and Levinthal, 1990, p. 133). Thus, the transfer of knowledge between individuals and subunits of an organization makes ACAP venture-specific. Finally, since the accumulation of ACAP in one period will permit a more efficient accumulation in the next, ACAP can be thought of as being path-dependent. Given the rate of change in a digital technological context, success may be explained by the development of ACAP and the application of knowledge integration mechanisms.

3.6   DIGITAL NEW VENTURE GROWTH: SURVIVING AND SCALING

As dynamic models of digital new venture creation such as the lean start-up suggest, entrepreneurs may proceed to scale a new venture when product-market fit has been achieved. Therefore, examining the mechanisms by which digital entrepreneurial growth occurs is vital. Given that over 60 years have passed since the inception of Penrose's venture growth theory, it is understandable why the theory has not captured new modes of firm growth. For this reason, McKelvie and Wiklund (2010, p. 274) add a third mode of growth – hybrid. A hybrid mode of growth consists of 'contractual relationships that bind external actors to the firm at the same time as the firm maintains a certain amount of ownership and control over how any assets are used.' It includes franchising, licensing, strategic alliances, and joint ventures. Adding a hybrid mode of growth provides a useful conceptual basis for explaining how digital new ventures grow in a network-centric environment. However, theories on the mechanisms by which hybrid modes of growth occur have been heavily influenced by a traditional network approach to growth.

3.6.1   Growth as a Process in Network-Centric Innovation

As Watson (2007) states, traditional network approaches to growth hinge on the ability of owners to gain access to resources not under their control in a cost-effective manner. It entails three main approaches to analyzing networking and venture growth. A *network magnitude* approach suggests that the greater the size of an entrepreneur's network, the higher the business growth opportunity. Meanwhile, a *network closure* approach (Coleman, 1988) argues that social capital is maximized when entrepreneurs make use of stronger ties (e.g., friends and family), as opposed to weaker ties such as acquaintances (Granovetter, 1973) – reason being, they can easily observe the actions of others, and trust creates strong bonds.

There are five main criticisms of traditional variants of a network approach to growth relevant in a digital entrepreneurial context. First, measuring the linkages between networking and business growth has proven elusive (Storey and Greene, 2010, p. 227). Second, the network magnitude approach emphasizes trust as beneficial rather than market-based mechanisms. Third, the evidence linking business growth to networking is weak (Havnes and Senneseth, 2001). Fourth, network closure was found to be less likely to lead to success than in firms that exploited structural holes – the reason being network position helps identify opportunities. Fifth, a traditional network view is inadequate for explaining growth in a digital entrepreneurial context; because it is based on an assumption of stable inter-organizational partnerships, which is not always the case in dynamic and loosely connected digital ecosystems (Amit and Zott, 2001). Thus, traditional network theories of growth are considered inadequate for explaining the meteoric rise of digital ventures such as Airbnb and Uber (Zervas et al., 2017).

Consequently, a *network position* approach appears a more promising approach to theorizing the growth process of a digital new venture. It argues that growth is more likely to occur when networks are porous and open-ended as it allows for easy transfer of knowledge about opportunities. Thus, successful entrepreneurs position themselves to locate 'structural holes' or influencers between networks. This view appears consistent with the digital entrepreneurial context, where porousness is manifested in the distributed and dynamic nature of entrepreneurial ecosystems in which agents maintain independent and democratic control of resources. As such, successful leadership in a highly complex adaptive network of digital new venture creation has been described as 'weaving' (Raelin, 2016), whereby weaving describes the ability to create webs of interaction across existing and new networks with the goal of mobilizing mutual activities and creating a sense of shared meaning.

3.6.2 Digital New Venture Scaling – a Network Externalities Perspective

Unlike traditional metrics of performance which emphasize profitability, sales, and market share, a network externalities perspective is deemed more relevant to digital new ventures (Katz and Shapiro, 1986; Oliva et al., 2003; Prasad et al., 2010; Maurya, 2016, pp. 29–30). Network externalities is based on Metcalfe's Law (Metcalfe, 1995), which states that a network becomes more valuable as its user base expands. In the case of group forming networks, Reed's Law complements Metcalfe's Law by arguing that the growth of the network can be exponentially larger due to the compounding effect of groups (Reed, 2001). Accordingly, once an inflection point is reached, network effects activate, and exponential growth follows. These laws help explain the meteoric rise of social media networks such as *Facebook* and *WhatsApp* and e-marketplaces such as *Amazon*, where group forming networks have helped to drive many-to-many communications reaching billions of users globally.

However, Hagiu and Rothman (2016) caution that while positive network effects remain critical to value creation for digital new ventures, it can also result in negative network effects if poorly executed. As a result, they caution that growing too fast without figuring out optimal *supply-demand fit* can put stresses on the BM, while leaving the start-up vulnerable to competitors. The supply-demand fit is achieved when buyers are happy to purchase the products or services as providers are happy to supply them. Similarly, growing too early, especially for multisided platform BMs, amplifies problems in the BM, making them harder to fix.

The value of achieving positive network effects in digital entrepreneurship is tangibly explained by Maurya's (2016, p. 9) use of a factory metaphor which states that the user base is like raw materials that a factory converts to finished goods (customers). It involves attracting a large number of users from which conversions can be made to generate revenue. Likewise, Amit and Han (2017) argue that the value of digital businesses resides in positive network effects because it makes it harder for competitors to dislodge. Furthermore, digital ventures may be able to harvest the value of network effects in an infinite number of transactions. It may explain why successful digital new ventures such as *Amazon* and *Uber* initially focus on a *growth to profit* strategy rather than on a *profitable growth* strategy (Davidsson et al., 2009). The idea behind this approach to growth lies in the knowledge that achieving strong network effects through user base growth will open up several possibilities for monetization when economies of scale kick in. Also, given the non-rivalry of digital artifacts, the marginal cost of replication and distributing drops to near-zero after initial development. Thus, BMs are possible that involve giving away the digital product free of charge, while monetizing it through digital advertising.

In line with the Diffusion of Innovation Theory (Rogers, 1995), successful digital new ventures are those that can attract enough users to 'cross the chasm' between early adopters and an early majority (Moore, 1999). As the theory argues, the characteristics of the NVI determine its potential for scalability. Digital new ventures often benefit from the reach of the internet platform, which overcomes the 'tyranny of space' (Lyytinen et al., 2016). Hence, digital new venture growth may also result from being 'born global.'

3.6.3   Rapid Internationalization and Digital New Venture Scaling

Being a digital born global refers to the outcomes of a rapid internationalization process made feasible by the reach of the internet and the distributability of digital artifacts (Evans and Wurster, 1999; Knight and Cavusgil, 2004; Oviatt and McDougall, 2005; Bell and Loane, 2010; Kallinikos et al., 2013). It is also a product of the democratization of digital new venture creation made possible by digital technologies (Aldrich, 2014). Traditional models of internalization suggest a staged process, which is incremental. These models may still be relevant to hybrid and traditional forms of entrepreneurship as they are based on assumptions of the exportation of physical and tactile market offerings.

However, with the enabling power of internet connectivity and the scalable affordances of digital infrastructures, rapid scaling of digital new ventures across geographical borders is central to explaining growth in a digital entrepreneurship context. As Blank (2014) famously pointed out, countries with populations higher than 100 million can afford to look inward, serving local markets. Since most countries have populations less than that, going global is necessary for venture performance and survival. However, whether digital firms choose to go global is defined by multiple factors, including the entrepreneur's willingness to grow, NVI characteristics, and other factors. Consequently, Hazarbassanova (2016) differentiates between passive and active approaches to new venture internationalization. Digital born global ventures are distinguished by the external enablement of the internet and other digital infrastructures, as well as the distributable characteristics of digitized offerings (Gabrielsson and Kirpalani, 2004; Loane et al., 2004).

While digital NVIs are not homogeneous (pure/hybrid modes), Hennart (2014) argues that the NVI and market offering, as well as its capacity for low-cost distribution, is a key characteristic that explains how such ventures achieve strong network effects by internationalization. Therefore, the digitized, non-physical nature of digital artifacts enables high scalability of pure digital ventures (PDE), while in hybrid typologies (HDE), such scalability is constrained (Zhang et al., 2015). Mahnke and Venzin (2003) explain that pure digital new market offerings do not perish or require transportation. They have significant benefits for economies of scale, have no diminishing returns to scale, and their interactivity produces valuable data that enables instant adjustments geared towards satisfying customer needs. Besides, digital new market offerings can be developed by leveraging the capabilities of dynamic collectives and virtual teams dispersed across geographical regions. Owing to the characteristics of digital artifacts discussed previously, multiple actors can network to co-create value across value networks on a piecemeal basis.

As noted, digital infrastructures improve communication between customers and suppliers, help identify new customers and distributors, as well as generate a wealth of data on market trends and global consumer behavior. Moreover, the cloud-based digital infrastructure of dominant players such as AWS and *Google Cloud* allow capital-intensive investments to become available to smaller actors on a 'pay as you go' basis – further discussed in Chapter 4. Resource sharing with large players is partly enabled by technologies such as API which allow systems to share data and resources, resulting in a layered modular architecture of digital new market offerings. The result is a highly networked and hyperconnected global value co-creation environment supported by digital infrastructures.

However, a number of challenges to growth in a digital born global landscape will be explored in Chapter 4. Among them, the low entry barriers imply that market offerings might be easy to imitate in foreign markets. Besides, introducing a new market offering to foreign markets may require educating customers and creating personalizable experiences, which all come with added costs of customer acquisition. There are also cultural differences in growing an international community. Furthermore, differences in internet connection speeds and the quality of ICT infrastructure across countries demand further customization. As will be further examined in Chapter 4, internet regulation and technologies such as the so-called *Great Firewall* of China curtail the reach of the internet and increase costs by compelling businesses to adapt their offerings to meet the requirements of local markets. Thus, digital entrepreneurs are called upon to carefully weigh the cost and benefits of conceiving a truly digitally 'born global' venture.

3.6.4   Growth Mechanisms of Digital New Ventures

While the potential for rapid internationalization can be the result of externally driven, actor-independent mechanisms, digital new ventures can also act to grow their user base through adopting specific social mechanisms. The literature identifies many social mechanisms by which this can be accomplished. Among them, complementarities, novelty, lock-in, and efficiency are mechanisms emanating from continuous digital growth strategies that drive strong network effects and maintain performance (Amit and Zott, 2001). Meanwhile, Huang et al. (2017) identify the generative mechanisms by which digital new venture scaling occurs.

3.6.4.1   Generative mechanisms of digital new venture scaling
As noted, the performance of digital new ventures can be the result of specific actions which digital entrepreneurs take during new venture enactment. The mechanisms by which these actions drive new venture performance have been described as a generative process of rapid user base scaling (Huang et al., 2017). The process is premised on the idea that initial success in growing the user base increases the prospect that more users will follow (Song et al., 2009). Accordingly, three contingent mechanisms are identified. They include *data-driven operation, instant release,* and *swift transformation.* These mechanisms together allow digital new ventures to stay lean, agile, and flexible while growing at speeds not typically observed in more traditional new venture scaling – hence they are described as 'growing on steroids' (Huang et al., 2017).

Data-Driven Operation: Data-driven operation is a mechanism found to be the starting point for growth. It involves the collection of vast amounts of user data, as well as data from other sources to inform growth-oriented initiatives. However, as the lean start-up model prescribes, data-driven operations cannot become an obsession with 'vanity metrics' (Ries, 2011). Activities must combine quantitative data with rich qualitative insights to guide sound decision making (Croll and Yoskovitz, 2013). Digital marketing activities such as user profiling help identify growth opportunities by launching highly targeted marketing campaigns and learning from the data generated. Similarly, decision hedging, which involves analyzing existing and emerging data, was found to aid risk assessment before and during new venture enactment. Fine-grained monitoring of the user bases' data for growth and decline during enactment affords flexible responses to positive or negative signals.

Instant Release: Meanwhile, the instant release mechanism allows digital new ventures to minimize the time between idea and deployment by simultaneously trialing and modifying innovations. Activities under this category include launching, trialing, and reactive modification. It defines the nature of experimentation that drives user base growth.

Swift Transformation: Finally, swift transformation is a mechanism which resembles the lean start-up notion of pivoting. It involves the occasional effort to generate a new wave of scaling by repositioning aspects of the BM in line with significant data-driven insights. Ultimately, these emergent mechanisms extol the virtues of being dynamic, flexible, and responsive instead of sticking with static business plans.

3.6.4.2 Complementarities, lock-in, efficiency, and novelty as growth mechanisms

Other digital growth mechanisms include the use of complementarities. According to Amit and Zott (2001), growing the digital user base through complementarities involves offering a bundle of products and services which together provide more value than the total value of having them marketed separately. Digital new ventures leverage this potential by offering bundles of vertical complementarities such as after-sales services or horizontal complementarities through a one-stop-shop for multiple related but not directly competing products. Horizontal Complementarities in a digital entrepreneurial context can easily be offered through APIs that allow for data sharing. For instance, a digital e-commerce platform such as *Shopify* offers complementarities by using APIs that integrate related services from other actors – for example, plug-ins to integrate payment gateways such as PayPal and Stripe, shipment tracking from DHL, and others.

Meanwhile, lock-in is the extent to which customers are motivated to engage in repeated transactions, such as return visits to a website or digital platform.

Lock-in works by increasing switching costs (Farrell and Klemperer, 2007). Therefore, loyalty programs which reward repeat customers with special offers not only help retain them but also drive advocacy. Other examples of lock-in include familiarity with the use of a product or platform's interface. Familiarity results in efficiency for the customer or user as they need not re-learn a new interface for a similar service. Furthermore, since the utility of digital platform services derives from consumption with other agents (network effects), discussion boards and social media pages facilitate consumer-to-consumer interaction with the potential for influential actors to drive viral dissemination of new market offerings. Meanwhile, novelty drives the growth of the user base when it involves leveraging digital capabilities to bring new offerings to existing markets. Thus, by following customer feedback, a platform such as *Shopify* continues to add novel features that enhance and solidify its growth.

Complementarity, lock-in, novelty, and efficiency jointly offer partial explanations for digital growth strategies that involve creating so-called 'super apps' that merge core services into one. It is made possible by digital infrastructures and the infinitely expansible potential of digital artifacts, which, as noted, remain incomplete by design. Super apps such as Tencent's *WeChat* continuously merge multiple services into one app. One of us who lived in China and watched the service evolve, observes that it was initially a simple messaging app like *WhatsApp*. However, it rapidly evolved to include complementarities such as a payment system for most consumer services, ride-hailing services, food delivery, railway and flight booking, and other public services. Users gain efficiency by using it as a one-stop-shop for performing multiple activities. Likewise, the inclusion of novel services continuously augments its value to users while adapting to their changing needs. Not surprisingly, due to its ubiquity, the app has become more of a public digital infrastructure, as evidenced by its role in fighting the spread of Covid-19 in China through the more recent inclusion of health services.

3.6.5   Digital Growth Marketing Mechanisms

The above growth mechanisms suggest that marketing and sales are more central in digital new venture enactment than digital product development. Indeed, digital marketing activities offer more fine-grained insights on scaling digital new ventures. Digital marketing usually entails using digital technology to get closer to customers, identify, anticipate, and satisfy their needs efficiently and effectively (Chaffey and Smith, 2017, p. 21). Kannan and Li (2017, p. 23) broadly define it as 'an adaptive, technology-enabled process by which firms collaborate with customers and partners to jointly create, communicate, deliver, and sustain value for all stakeholders.' Thus, its departure from traditional marketing practices arises from the realization that in a multi-channel and networked environment, customers are not merely passive receivers of a company's segmentation, targeting, and positioning messages (Kotler et al., 2016, p. 20).

Digital Marketing Mix: Kotler et al. (2016, p. 50) argue that with increased connectivity, digital business environments dictate a shift from vertical to horizontal relationships between a venture and its customers. They propose that the Marketing Mix or 4Ps (Product, Price, Place, and Promotion) in the digital context should be redefined as the 4Cs (i.e., Co-creation, Currency, Communal Activation, and Conversation). The 4Cs represent the digital marketing mix. *Co-creation* is contingent on delivering a superior value proposition by engaging customers in product and service innovation. Meanwhile, *currency* involves using data analytics for dynamic pricing based on market demand and capacity utilization. Likewise, *communal activation* entails the peer-to-peer distribution of services in the sharing economy, where the dormant value of owned products is activated through digital networking (Kannan and Li, 2017). Finally, *conversation* shifts the focus from unidirectional promotion to the engagement of customers through social media networks.

Digital Growth Marketing: More importantly, digital marketing activities that engineer growth into products and services from the very beginning have been described by practitioners as digital *growth marketing* (Huffman, 2018), *growth hacking* (Holiday, 2014; Brown and Ellis, 2017), and gaining *traction* (Weinberg and Mares, 2014). While the word *growth hacker* may conjure up notions of digital criminality, *growth hackers* are digital growth marketers who combine marketing expertise with coding and technical know-how to deliver venture performance. The growth marketer's core activities include improving the performance of digital new ventures through structured testing and optimization of the entire customer journey or marketing funnel. The growth marketing funnel is summarized by the acronym AAARRR which stands for Awareness, Acquisition, Activation, Revenue, Retention, and Referral (McClure, 2007). Growth marketers, unlike traditional marketers, focus on optimizing performance throughout the funnel. They are skilled in the use of tools such as emails, Pay Per Click (PPC) – also Cost Per Click (CPC) – ads, data analytics, platform API integration, and the use of blogs to grow the user base of a new venture at high velocities (Holiday, 2014). Digital growth marketing begins with a good and functional product or content which is developed with growth in mind and refined iteratively from consumer feedback (Brown and Ellis, 2017). Thus, a good product or content that is engineered to self-propagate can drive strong network effects. Tactics such as Search Engine Optimization (SEO), affiliate marketing, targeted PPC campaigns, content research and marketing, social media, and email marketing can be harnessed to grow the user base from early adopters to an early and late majority.

Strategies, Tactics, and Actions: SEO is one of the most critical skills needed in digital growth marketing because user intent is expressed through search terms called keywords. It begins with the basic understanding that search engines exist to help users find specific information to their requests. Additionally, search engines are in a constant battle with web spammers, who seek to rank highly on *Search Engine Results Pages* (SERPS) while offering little or no added value. Thus, the main activities of SEO include keyword research and placement, as well as the development of relevant backlinks that build trust with search engine algorithms, as well as demonstrate authority and relevance.

The strategic placement of keywords and key phrases on web pages can give search engines signals which show their relevance. Without good SEO skills, digital market offerings may never rank highly on SERPS. Since most digital consumers seldom scroll beyond the first page of SERPS (Höchstötter and Lewandowski, 2009), excellent digital products may remain *lost in cyberspace*. Hence, Chaffey and Smith (2017) maintain that it is not the best-designed digital market offerings that succeed but those that are functional and findable. Thus, *findability* is the cornerstone of many SEO and Social Media Optimization (SMO) activities. Digital entrepreneurial agents with good SEO and SMO skills can frugally bootstrap a digital new venture to success by making its products more findable across cyberspace.

However, the challenge for the digital marketer lies in the fact that algorithmic agencies regularly update ranking criteria in ways that are not often transparent – thus, continuous monitoring and experimentation are essential for SEO-driven growth strategies. While SEO is a valuable approach to growing an active user base, regular updates in search engine algorithms can adversely affect new ventures, leading to a loss of strong network effects among those that fall out of favor with algorithmic updates. Furthermore, if SEO is conducted by unskilled actors, the result can be detrimental to venture growth (Aswani et al., 2018). Generally, it would be ill-advised to rely solely on SEO for growth marketing.

Combining SEO with other techniques such as PPC marketing is recommended for growing the user base. PPC marketing enables the accurate targeting of keywords and contextual ad placements on relevant websites and SERPS. It can be a valuable approach to attracting innovators and early adopters. As the name suggests, advertisers pay only when an ad is clicked. Its main disadvantage lies in the fact that if poorly executed, it can become a waste of valuable financial resources. Waste can be the result of poorly targeted ad placements. Since it is based on PPC advertising, it is an expensive but potentially rapid approach to reaching early adopters. While growing the user base is essential, attracting many poorly targeted users results in 'vanity metrics' (Ries, 2011). Hence, a digital growth marketer focuses on actionable metrics such as conversions, cohort analysis, and *bounce rates* (i.e., measurement of visitors exiting a website without interaction). Likewise, they also focus on growth in Page Rank and Domain Authority (Aswani et al., 2018) – that is, the prestige of a website based on its information quality as judged by search engine algorithms. Thus, the combined use of tools such as Google Ads (previously Adwords) with its Keyword Planner tool and Google Analytics is necessary for targeted experimentation that focuses on actionable metrics and conversions (Chaffey and Smith, 2017, p. 384). The Pirate Metrics (AAARRR) by Dave McClure are particularly useful in keeping digital marketers focused on the critical growth metrics in the entrepreneurial marketing funnel (McClure, 2007).

Meanwhile, CPC marketing can be carried out as part of SEO or SMO strategies. While social media networks such as Facebook attract an audience larger than the population of China, success on these platforms often hinges on effective communication strategies as part of inbound marketing (Halligan and Shah, 2009). For this reason, growth marketing through SMO operates on the assumption that digital socialization is about participating in online discussions, sharing ideas and content. Social media marketing is essential because it can support advocacy among users, prompting some to share content. As such, they help the growth marketer to achieve viral growth. *Viral marketing* is a clever SMO activity based on the creation and distribution of shocking or highly informative content that makes for compulsive viewing and sharing (Chaffey and Smith, 2017, p. 428). It may come in the form of content such as a video, an image, or social media message. It involves harnessing the network effects of social media platforms to reach large numbers of people rapidly. Viral marketing requires creative material, shared experience, seeding (identifying sites and social media platforms that act as influencers), promoting content, tracking and monitoring the effects of the message (Holiday, 2014; Brown and Ellis, 2017). Ultimately, digital growth marketing is an inherently sociomaterial practice that involves a dialogic interaction between human and digital material agencies.

3.7 SUMMARY

In sum, digital entrepreneurship is driven by distinctive social, material, and cognitive mechanisms, which provide a combination of inputs that shape digital entrepreneurial processes and outcomes differently. These inputs are the result of digital technology enablers and actor knowledge and means. The outcomes are not always what one would expect in a traditional entrepreneurial process. We develop Figure 3.3 to illustrate how this complex interrelationship between enabling inputs and mechanisms interacts and *intra-acts* sociomaterially to drive digital entrepreneurship.

External Enablers: Given the focus on digital entrepreneurship, digital technology enablers are emphasized here – digital artifacts, digital platforms, and digital infrastructures. That is not to suggest that other enablers in the proximal and distal environment such as regulatory, political, environmental, and socio-economic change do not matter – the emphasis is on digital technology enablers.

Actor-Independent Mechanisms: External enablers are generative and therefore produce actor-independent mechanisms such as resource expansion, resource conservation, combination, and generation. These mechanisms provide potentialities for digital entrepreneurial action.

Actor Knowledge and Means: Digital entrepreneurial actors interact or intra-act with digital technologies and their mechanisms. They input their knowledge and cognitions, as well as provide tangible and intangible means that are equally generative.

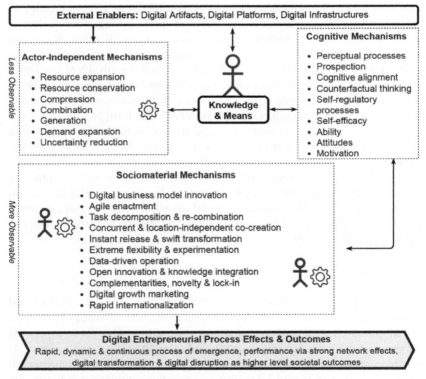

Figure 3.3   Interrelationships driving digital entrepreneurship

Sociomaterial Mechanisms: With the motivation to enact NVIs, a complex web of social and material engagements with digital technologies results in several sociomaterial mechanisms, which are proximal mechanisms driving digital new venture emergence and outcomes. Among them, agile enactment, data-driven operation, and digital growth marketing mechanisms are evident. Sociomaterial mechanisms are the translations of both actor-independent and cognitive mechanisms into more observable and proximal drivers of emergence.

Process Effects and Outcomes: At proximal levels, these interrelationships jointly have various effects on the digital entrepreneurial process. Most critically, the lack of spatiotemporal constraints potentially results in the rapid, continuous, and dynamic emergence of the digital entrepreneurial process compared to traditional entrepreneurial processes. Likewise, strong network effects present a path to venture performance. At the societal level, the effects are digital transformation and digital disruption, which enable hybrid and traditional typologies of entrepreneurship in the digital age. As noted, digital entrepreneurs tend to unlock value by using digital technologies to eliminate traditional entrepreneurial processual inefficiencies. As a result, digital transformation has emerged as a core theme that examines the effects of digital entrepreneurship on the broader economy. The motivation for digital NVIs tends to originate from the need to render more efficient and augmented inert physical artifacts and processes. Therefore, hybrid typologies of digital and traditional entrepreneurship sit in the middle of the continuum between the extremes of PDE and PTE.

3.8   CONCLUSION

By deconstructing the conceptual basis of digital entrepreneurship versus traditional entrepreneurship in the digital age, this chapter presents a solid theoretical foundation for understanding technology-driven activities in the digital and broader economy. Therefore, we set the stage for the next chapter, which explores current changes and trends in the external environment in which digital entrepreneurship occurs.

4. External enablers and barriers to digital entrepreneurship

4.1 INTRODUCTION

This chapter examines the multiple spatial and temporal contexts which frame digital entrepreneurship and entrepreneurship in the digital age. In this respect, it identifies past, present, and future digital technology changes which act as external enablers of digital entrepreneurship and its societal effects. Given that digital infrastructures such as the internet and computing devices are core drivers of the global digital economy, this chapter unbundles the layers of these technologies. In so doing, it identifies the significant changes happening at various layers that present cues for digital entrepreneurial action. Furthermore, it investigates the mechanisms by which the convergence of cloud computing, big data, Artificial Intelligence (AI) and machine learning, as well as IoT, are driving the next wave of digital entrepreneurship. The chapter then examines possible barriers to digital entrepreneurship with potential solutions that offer guidelines for nurturing an enabling and sustaining digital new venture creation against a VUCA (Volatile, Uncertain, Complex, and Ambiguous) ecosystem.

4.2 INTERNET INFRASTRUCTURE AND DIGITAL VALUE CREATION

The internet is the core infrastructure driving digital entrepreneurship and value creation in the digital age. Its basic technology is *packet switching*, which allows a network of computers to communicate. Packet switching allows digitized information to be segmented and routed in discrete data envelopes called packets. Each of these packets is appended transmission control information for routing, sequencing, and error checking, thereby providing a fault-tolerant and efficient mode of telecommunication that can be simultaneously consumed by multiple individuals. It was a radically innovative technology for telecommunication that superseded the less efficient *circuit switching* technology that came before. As with such radical innovations, packet switching spawned an ecosystem for complementary innovations that would only accelerate the emergence of the internet as a global infrastructure for value creation. Accordingly, innovations such as Transmission Control Protocol and the Internet Protocol (TCIP/IP), which were developed in the 1970s, became jointly adopted as standardized modes of controlling the transmission of information across an ever-expanding network of global computers. Its standardization contributed in advancing a culture of openness which has become an integral philosophy of successful internet-driven innovations. Meanwhile, the invention of email by Ray Tomlison and the World Wide Web (W3) by Tim Berners-Lee created some of the first 'killer apps' running on the internet.

Several independent organizations provide the governance structure of this critical infrastructure. For instance, the Internet Corporation for Assigned Names and Numbers (ICANN) is a non-profit organization that governs the allocation of unique identifiers such as IP addresses, domain name ownership, and top-level domain name extensions. Likewise, the Internet Engineering Task Force (IETF) is an open global community of network operators and researchers overseeing the technological development of the internet. Meanwhile, the World Wide Web Consortium (W3C) is the organization that sets open programming standards for the web, such as HTML5 (HyperText Markup Language 5), and CSS3 (Cascading Style Sheets v3). Nevertheless, while open standards are promoted, a battle for dominance rages between open and proprietary standards, with implications for the future of the internet as a platform for innovation (Zittrain, 2008).

4.2.1   The Internet and Digital Economy Enablement

Value creation in the digital economy would not exist without the internet. For perspective, the World Bank estimates that the GDP of the global economy reached $87 trillion in 2019 (World Bank, 2021). Nested within the global economy is the digital economy, whose GDP is harder to estimate due to the lack of an agreed definition. Hence, estimates vary from between a low of 4 percent to a high of nearly 23 percent of global GDP (UNCTAD, 2019). Accenture, whose estimates are considered most accurate, defines the digital economy broadly as a share of total economic output derived from several digital technology inputs (Knickrehm et al., 2016). This definition includes inputs such as digital skills, digital technologies, and digital artifacts used in the production of digital-related goods and services. The digital economy's growth rate is much greater than the traditional economy – and may have been further accelerated by the Covid-19 pandemic (OECD, 2020). Curiously, it is an uneven economy that is highly concentrated in two main regions of the world – North America, led by the United States, and Asia, led by China. As of 2018, some 90 percent of the market capitalization value of the world's top

70 digital platform-based firms was split between the United States and China at 68 and 22 percent respectively (UNCTAD, 2019).

Essentially, value creation in the digital economy is inextricably linked to access and the quality of digital infrastructures such as the internet. Hence, it is essential to examine the multi-layered architecture of the internet and the changes occuring within each layer which act as external enablers of digital entrepreneurship and value creation in the digital age. This architecture is depicted as an hourglass model, which can be deconstructed into four main layers (Laudon and Traver, 2019, p. 119) as represented in Figure 4.1 and examined in more detail subsequently.

4.2.2   Network Layer and External Enablers

The base is the network layer that carries internet traffic in a first- and last-mile relay. First-mile internet connection is mainly carried by ever faster fiber optic cables which are replacing co-axial cables. These cables primarily run along coastlines and underground on land. Satellite networks equally provide internet access. However, unlike fiber optic cables, satellite networks generally have higher latency. Fiber optic cables use light to transmit data, making them faster than co-axial cables or satellite connections.

At the last mile, regional hubs, Local Area Networks (LAN), and DSL (Digital Subscriber Line) provided by Internet Service Providers (ISPs) relay internet connection into homes and offices. In countries of the Organisation for Economic Co-operation and Development (OECD), the last-mile internet connection infrastructure is currently being upgraded to bring gigabit per second (Gbps) data transmission to homes and mobile devices. Some countries such as South Korea and Singapore have already begun rolling out 10 Gbps internet connection infrastructure to households and businesses in urban areas, which means low latency, high throughput, increased reliability, and security of data transmission (OECD, 2020).

In emerging economies, increased adoption of fast mobile broadband (4G and 5G) has helped countries such as China and India to leapfrog over the digital divide (Welsum, 2016). Consequently, these changes enable digital entrepreneurship by driving growth in demand for digital services. Similarly, in an age where the sale of smartphones, tablets, and ultrathin laptops has eclipsed desktops, unique mobile phone subscriptions grew to 5.2 billion globally in 2020, with 3.8 billion connections to the mobile internet (GSMA, 2020). As a result, instead of being geographically tethered, value co-creation in the digital age is increasingly becoming mobile and location-independent. Furthermore, with the rollout of next-generation 5G technology, with its low latency and high throughput, more people and devices are expected to come online in the next decade. In 2021, DataReportal reported that some 60 percent

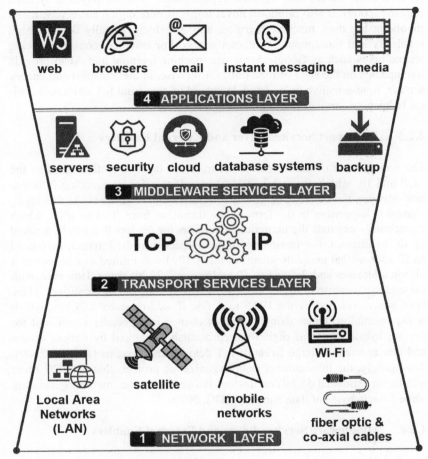

Source: Adapted from Laudon and Traver (2019).

Figure 4.1   Layered modular architecture of the internet

of the world's population had internet access – which means there is latent demand for digital services from 40 percent of the world's population which is yet to come online (Kemp, 2021).

The improved infrastructure supports the surge in M2M (Machine-to-Machine) communication and the demand for data-intensive and high bandwidth services such as 4K High-Definition (HD) video streaming and real-time AI systems. Consequently, it is critical to the external enablement of hybrid forms of digital entrepreneurship where the Internet of Things

(IoT) creates mutual and complex dependencies of cyber-physical systems (Ashton, 2009). It also promotes novel forms of pure digital entrepreneurship involving big data, machine learning, and AI which typically demand high reliability and throughput of internet access. For instance, consumer-facing technologies such as Google Maps use machine learning and AI to provide live updates on the state of road traffic. Likewise, in the transport and energy sectors, time-sensitive upload and download of data from IoT devices is critical to keeping services running reliably and safely.

4.2.3   Transport Services Layer and External Enablers

The second layer of the internet is the transport layer. It is dominated by the TCP and IP, which are standardized technologies for transmitting information between the network of global computers on the internet. At this layer, change is happening in the form of the transition from IPv4 to IPv6, which significantly expands the numerical identifiers for devices that can be hooked up to the internet. For computers to be connected to the internet, they need an IP address that uniquely identifies them. IPv4 was limited to a little over 4 billion addresses and defined an IP address as a 32-bit value. However, with the massive increase in IoT devices, IPv4 was running out of identifiers. Thus, IPv6 was developed by the IETF to define IP addresses by 128 bits, which is exponentially greater than IPv4. This change is especially significant for driving hybrid forms of digital entrepreneurship, marked by remote access and management of large fleets of IoT devices and systems (Ashton, 2009). Accordingly, the International Data Organization projects that by 2025, there will be an estimated 55 billion devices hooked up to the internet, generating some 73 zettabytes of data annually (IDC, 2020).

4.2.4   Middleware Services Layer and External Enablers

Meanwhile, the third layer consists of middleware services such as storage, security, and file systems. At this layer, major changes are happening in the move from on-premise to cloud-based infrastructure. Ubiquitous cloud computing has resulted in efficiencies regarding how data is stored, processed, and accessed across the internet by various actors. Central to cloud computing is virtualization, which is a technology that separates hardware from software by pooling resources into a central location for self-service. Pioneered by Amazon in the early 2000s, it is not surprising that Amazon Web Services (AWS) maintains leadership in the provision of rentable public, hybrid, and private cloud infrastructure. Cloud services providers such as AWS, Google Cloud, and Microsoft Azure equally provide complementary offerings such as Content Delivery Networks (CDNs) and load balancers across data centers. They are equally equipped with uninterruptible power supply, and robust physical and cyber data security infrastructure. CDNs cache digital content across multiple distributed servers and redirect users to servers within geographical proximity. Latency is reduced as users in a region are directed to geographically closer servers to access digital content. Reduced latency greatly improves the speed of access, as well as the user experience (Nygren et al., 2010).

Driven by models such as IaaS (Infrastructure as a Service) and PaaS (Platform as a Service), cloud technology providers significantly lower barriers to entry by driving down the cost of owning and managing digital infrastructure for all classes of entrepreneurial actors. Accordingly, scarce resources are not wasted in substantial upfront costs associated with building and owning such systems. The result is the democratization of digital entrepreneurship by which multiple participating actors can create new ventures with minimal resources. By some estimates, certain services that required over $2 million to start with a prototype in the 1990s could be started for as little as $50,000 by 2016 due to the proliferation of scalable cloud computing (Baller et al., 2016, p. 42). Given its significance, we expect cloud computing to have a major role in driving the next wave of digital entrepreneurship.

4.2.5 Applications Layer and External Enablers

Finally, the fourth and topmost layer of the internet is the applications layer. It includes consumer-facing technologies such as web browsers, email clients, instant messaging, and media players. At this layer, changes from Web 1.0 through to the current Web 3.0 continue to have significant implications for the external enablement of value creation in the digital age. Under Web 2.0, digital platforms became core centers for value creation in the digital age. With the current Web 3.0, a semantic web is born where AI systems and their machine learning algorithms increasingly use big data to create, unlock, and optimize economic value. AI systems employ machine learning algorithms to crunch big data in real-time, and therefore they often require cutting-edge computer processing and storage infrastructure. Thus, when coupled with the availability of rentable, affordable, and scalable cloud infrastructure, barriers to pure digital entrepreneurship based on resource constraints are significantly lowered. Not surprisingly, disruptive innovations such as blockchain and machine learning, and AI are currently occurring at this layer. Blockchain is a supposedly tamper-proof distributed digital ledger driving emerging innovations in cryptocurrencies such as Bitcoin and Ethereum.

The current state of change occurring at various layers of the internet's architecture indicates that change is the only constant in this environment. Hence, one can expect more of such in the future. Since change in the environment represents an external enabler of entrepreneurship, changes occurring

across the four layers of the internet's infrastructure converge to provide a catalyst for current and future forms of digital entrepreneurship.

4.3   COMPUTING INFRASTRUCTURE AND EXTERNAL ENABLEMENT

While the internet represents a central infrastructure driving the digital
economy, it is ultimately consumed across a network of computing devices
that combine to form the global digital infrastructure. At an abstract level,
computers are sophisticated adding machines that contain processors, memory,
and storage. They receive inputs and conduct calculations using algorithms to
convert into outputs. Computers power the information age by processing
data and expressing it in binary codes which use only two digits – one and
zero. Algorithms, tightly coupled in a computer's memory, measure, compare,
and manipulate binary digits, allowing a computer to perform tasks such as
organizing processes, regulating the operation of machines, analyzing data,
and simulating the behavior of dynamic systems.

4.3.1   Microprocessors, Data Storage, and External Enablement

The processing power of computers determines the speed at which they
conduct calculations and offer capabilities for multitasking. In the 1960s,
a radical innovation resulted in the arrival of the integrated circuit, which was
a device containing hundreds of transistors, diodes, and resistors on a tiny
silicon chip. The *Intel 4004* became the first single-chip microprocessor
released in the early 1970s. Its arrival galvanized the trend in chip miniaturization contrasted by ever-increasing processing power in keeping with Moore's
Law. Currently, ever more powerful microprocessors such as those built on the
Intel multi-core architecture power some of the most capable general-purpose
computing used in digital value creation.

Likewise, ARM (Advanced RISC Machines), whose unique microchip
designs result in low power consumption and heat generation, has been
vital to the adoption of light, portable, battery-powered computers such as
smartphones, laptops, tablet computers, and embedded smart systems. Thus,
advances in such microprocessing capabilities culminated in the release of
the iPhone in 2007, which ushered in the smartphone revolution. Since then,
ever more powerful hand-held computing devices continue to be placed at
the fingertips of consumers. Digital entrepreneurs are then empowered to
develop applications that take full advantage of the advanced microprocessing
capabilities of hand-held computing devices. As a result, in 2021, smartphones
and tablet computers eclipsed desktops as the primary web client, according
to DataReportal (Kemp, 2021). Pervasive computing and mobile internet con-

sumption in the hands of users change consumer behavior and therefore enable digital entrepreneurship by increasing the demand for digital services.

Meanwhile, improvements in data storage technologies converge with powerful microprocessors in improving the overall infrastructural basis for digital entrepreneurship. For instance, fast Solid State Drives (SSD) have been developed to complement legacy Hard Disk Drives (HDDs), whose magnetic data storage and retrieval speeds are comparatively slower than SSD. Thus, SSDs are increasingly replacing HDDs since they combine a higher data transfer rate with greater storage density, improved reliability, and low latency on a more compact device. Improved storage combined with powerful miniaturized chips increases the speed at which computers can process, store, and retrieve vast amounts of data at affordable rates. This partly enables the proliferation of scalable cloud computing solutions that support digital entrepreneurship by democratizing technology access.

4.3.2 Chip Miniaturization, Smart Sensorization, and External Enablement

Concurrently, another class of miniaturized microprocessors has been accelerating the trend towards smart connected devices. Smart connected devices ultimately result in the sensorization of value chains. Examples of smart sensorized microprocessors include the digital signal processor (DSP) which is used in several digital telephones and modems. Unlike powerful microprocessors used in general-purpose computing, smart sensors do not have to perform elaborate computations at great speeds. Unlike regular base sensors, intelligent sensors combine embedded microprocessors, storage, diagnostics, and network technologies to digitize, store, and transmit analog signals. Using wireless technologies such as Wi-Fi, Bluetooth, Near Field Communication (NFC), and Radio Frequency Identification (RFID), they can transmit data through secure gateways to LAN, databases, and cloud computing systems for analysis.

With inexpensive nanochips, billions of smart sensors have been designed to perform specialized information processing tasks. Tasks performed by smart sensors include the sensing, measuring, compressing, and filtering of a continuous stream of real-world analog signals such as heat, pressure, motion, and light. Since they often simulate the five sensory capabilities of human beings with greater accuracy, they drive the disruption of value chains via the creation and deployment of autonomous systems, which eliminate the role of human agents. Hence, they are usually enablers of hybrid forms of digital entrepreneurship involving the embedding of DSPs into IoT devices and cyber-physical systems. The continuous stream of data from human and M2M interactions provides the raw materials for AI development, which is yet another revolution mainly occurring within the spheres of purer forms of digital entrepreneurship (PDE).

Accordingly, the convergence of smart sensors with embedded network technologies and storage drives the so-called Fourth Industrial Revolution (Schwab, 2017) or Second Machine Age, marked by the 'digitization of just about everything' (Brynjolfsson and McAfee, 2014). By blurring the lines between digital, physical, and biological spheres, digital entrepreneurship is enabled through the combination and generation of new digital and physical artifacts such as smartwatches, smart speakers, and smart cars, which provide value-creating services for individuals and organizations.

4.4   DOMINANT DIGITAL PLATFORMS AND EXTERNAL ENABLEMENT

Upon the enabling infrastructure of both the internet and advanced computing capabilities, digital platforms have emerged as critical value creation ecosystems of the digital economy. While digital platforms form the core of new venture ideas in digital entrepreneurship, dominant platforms also double as digital infrastructures. As noted, they have a more significant value creation footprint because they are based on enabling value-creating interactions between producers and consumers (Parker et al., 2016, p. 5). Not surprisingly, digital platform-based organizations such as Google and Apple rank among the most valuable global companies. Their value is largely derived from interactions on their platforms, which result in copious amounts of data that can be analyzed to create value through innovative business models. By facilitating the exchange of goods, services, and social currency, dominant digital platforms expand value creation opportunities to all participants. Through business models such as SaaS and PaaS – discussed subsequently – they have become infrastructural to all forms of entrepreneurship in the digital age.

4.4.1   Dominant Digital Platforms as External Enablers

Dominant digital platforms are external enablers of entrepreneurship as they change the economics of doing business across borders by reducing the cost of cross-border interactions and transactions. Likewise, their strong network effects create marketplaces and user communities with global reach, which offer entrepreneurs a vast base of potential customers with efficient and effective ways of targeting them (McAfee and Brynjolfsson, 2017). Hence, digital entrepreneurs with limited resources have become micro-multinationals and digital born globals using platforms such as eBay, Amazon, Facebook, Alibaba, and Google. Accordingly, in 2016, McKinsey reported that some 86 percent of digital technology-based start-ups were born global (Manyika et al., 2016).

Additionally, these platforms often employ and provide access to consumer-facing AI technologies that connect producers and consumers with speed and precision. For instance, the Google Ad platform (formerly Google Adwords) enables entrepreneurs of all sizes to research markets using complementary in-built tools such as Google Keyword Planner, precisely estimate Total Addressable Markets (TAM), and target users with pinpoint accuracy. The functionality of Google's Ad platform is also further enhanced by complementary APIs (Application Programming Interfaces), allowing it to integrate with several digital services such as Google Analytics, Agency Analytics, and Shopify. Through data analytics, critical insights are generated to optimize the effective reach of global customers, and reduce uncertainty in the digital entrepreneurial process.

4.4.2 Enabling Role of Dominant Platforms across Industries

Value creation in virtually every industry today is shaped by one or more dominant digital platforms. In the FinTech industry, for instance, platforms such as Robinhood and eToro are democratizing access to trading in stock markets. Others, such as PayPal and Stripe, have revolutionized the ease with which digital payments are securely captured by merchants. Likewise, start-ups such as Revolut and N26 are disrupting the traditional banking system by democratizing access to everyday banking services. Meanwhile, platforms such as Bitcoin and Ethereum more recently adopted blockchain technology to develop cryptocurrency offerings that enable new forms of financial transactions. In the least developed economies, the adoption of mobile money has significantly reduced inefficiencies associated with money transfer and the lack of access to essential banking services. Platforms such as M-Pesa in Kenya and MTN have developed digital wallets which facilitate money transfer via smartphones across Africa. Likewise, platforms such as WorldRemit have proven disruptive to incumbents such as Western Union and MoneyGram by providing cost-effective international money transfer solutions.

In EdTech, digitization has driven rapid growth into a mega-industry estimated to reach $404 billion globally by the end of 2025, at the current growth rate (HolonIQ, 2020). MOOCs (Massive Open Online Courses) such as Coursera, Udemy, and Skillshare are digital platforms that facilitate access to critical skills needed for value creation in the digital age. Not only are they ideal distribution platforms for EdTech entrepreneurs, but they also allow participants to select and develop skills on an on-demand basis. Similarly, other more specialized digital platforms have been created by educators with deep knowledge of their industry. Consequently, novel forms of EdTech entrepreneurship such as *digital teacherpreneurship* are becoming common, with platforms such as Khan Academy and TeachersPayTeachers representing outcomes of this form of digital entrepreneurship (Buckley and Nzembayie, 2016; Shelton and Archambault, 2018).

Meanwhile, global talent and work-based platforms, such as Upwork, LinkedIn, GitHub, and Fiverr, enable digital entrepreneurship by lowering the cost of searching and integrating critical skills needed in digital value creation. Entrepreneurs can co-create value with a heterogeneous cast of loosely connected knowledge assets on an on-demand basis. On-demand co-creation significantly reduces costs associated with hiring full-time employees. Relatedly, other platforms such as ThemeForest and Canva provide access to ready-made and customizable web and content designs from highly skilled actors that speed up and greatly reduce the cost of developing and deploying digital services.

Finally, in the e-commerce space, Amazon, Alibaba's Tmall, and eBay, with their strong network effects, stand out as platforms for the sale and distribution of both digital and non-digital goods. Given the influence of such platforms, worldwide e-commerce sales reached an estimated $26.7 trillion in 2020 amid a global pandemic (UNCTAD, 2021).

4.5   TECHNOLOGY CONVERGENCE AND NEXT-WAVE DIGITAL ENTREPRENEURSHIP

The evolution of digital technologies as examined above has culminated in a tipping point in which the convergence of cloud computing, big data, IoT, machine learning, and AI cumulatively drive the next wave of digital entrepreneurship and its societal consequences of digital transformation and digital disruption (Siebel, 2019). These technologies mainly enable digital entrepreneurship by offering the twin benefits of resource expansion and resource conservation, which both empower and enable small digital innovators. As a result, digital technology convergence presents almost infinite possibilities for new venture ideas based on the combination and generation of digital artifacts and platforms geared towards solving age-old societal problems.

As Stanford and MIT scholars, Erik Brynjolfsson and Andrew McAfee, point out, we are on the cusp of a Second Machine Age (Brynjolfsson and McAfee, 2014). Unlike the First Machine Age (Industrial Revolution) which was marked by the complementary integration of human labor with machines, the Second Machine Age results in the automation of several cognitive tasks, thereby eliminating human intervention in several roles. Some of these roles, such as legal services, accounting and bookkeeping, medical practice, and proofreading, were previously thought to be too complex for machines, thereby privileging human actors. Digital technology convergence is therefore driving a classic Schumpeterian creative destruction, with creative combinations of digital and cyber-physical offerings upending several legacy systems of value creation and competition, while positively maximizing economic productivity (Porter and Heppelmann, 2014, 2015). Accordingly, the World Economic Forum estimates that the next wave of digital entrepreneurship will result in the digital transformation of economies with productivity gains that 'deliver around $100 trillion in value to business and society over the next decade' (World Economic Forum, 2016b). However, to understand how these technologies interrelate to drive the next wave of digital entrepreneurship, and the resultant digital transformation and digital disruption, it is essential to first dissect them independently.

4.5.1 Cloud Computing

Cloud computing is arguably the glue that binds the other converging technologies together. As noted earlier, it sits on the middleware services layer of the internet's layered modular architecture. Cloud computing is the on-demand availability of a shared pool of configurable computer hardware and software resources. It is comprised of computer networks, servers, data storage, and applications, among others, that can be quickly provisioned via the internet with minimal management from the user. Cloud computing follows the paradoxical computing trend whereby the exponentially powerful growth in capabilities is contrasted by rapidly falling per-unit costs (Marston et al., 2011).

Virtualization and Containerization: Technically, cloud computing is made possible by two main technologies – virtualization and containerization. Virtualization is the use of software to simulate hardware functionality, while a container is a lightweight, self-contained, and executable operating system running the virtualized environment. Containerization is powerful because it liberates software code and all its dependencies, enabling it to run uniformly and consistently on any infrastructure. Virtualization and containerization jointly result in cost-effective and reliable use of computer resources. To understand how these technologies achieve this, it is essential to contrast a virtual and traditional architecture (Figure 4.2 below).

A traditional architecture sizes and provisions hardware to handle anticipated peak demand. Hence, idle computing in times of low demand renders a traditional data architecture wasteful. Contrarily, virtualization allows infrastructure resources to be shared across several applications on an on-demand basis, thereby resulting in a significant increase in hardware utilization. The optimal use of computing resources contributes to the dramatic decrease of cloud computing costs for all users.

Public, Private, and Hybrid Clouds: Cloud infrastructure can be public, private, or hybrid. The public cloud is owned by a third party and can be rented and used on an on-demand basis. The private cloud, as the name suggests, is

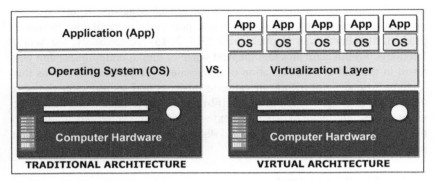

Figure 4.2   Traditional versus virtual architecture

owned by an organization for its exclusive use. The hybrid cloud offers greater flexibility by combining the best of public and private cloud for specific needs. For instance, an organization such as a bank may store its customers' sensitive bank account data on a private cloud and simultaneously leverage resources of a public cloud for less sensitive information such as marketing communication.

Pioneered by AWS in 2002, other major players such as Google Cloud and Microsoft Azure have emerged with differentiated offerings. According to reports from Gartner (2021), end-user spending on the public cloud grew from over $270 billion in 2020 to $397 billion in 2021, with AWS as the leading provider. Given the advances in cloud computing infrastructure, several organizations have moved all of their operations to the public cloud. Hence, traditional data centers are being disrupted as Cisco estimates that cloud data centers are already processing some 94 percent of workloads. For instance, organizations with data-intensive and bandwidth-hungry services, such as Netflix, Dropbox, and Uber, have already shut down and moved all or a significant portion of their technology operations onto AWS.

Cloud Service Models: The success of cloud computing is not driven solely by the technology but, more importantly, by innovations in the business models behind them. Cloud service providers have pioneered three main service models that create value for various groups of actors – Infrastructure as a Service (IaaS), Platform as a Service (PaaS), and Software as a Service (SaaS). These models are summarized in Figure 4.3.

With IaaS, a cloud provider such as AWS EC2 (Elastic Compute Cloud) rents out scalable networking, storage, servers, and virtualization resources. The user typically accesses these services through a self-service dashboard which gives them control over the entire infrastructure. PaaS provides access to infrastructure as well as the tools for building custom applications. The cloud provider maintains the infrastructure and software tools, allowing the user to focus on application development. Finally, SaaS is among the most common consumer-facing cloud service models. With SaaS, the service provider delivers and manages software and applications via internet tools such as web browsers and seldom requires downloading them. With near-zero maintenance costs, guaranteed uptime availability, advanced cyber and physical security, low latency, and disaster recovery, among others, digital entrepreneurs can focus limited resources and time on bringing digital innovations to market in rapid iterations.

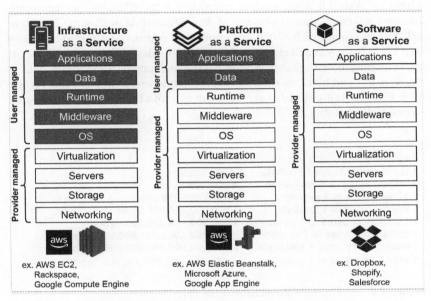

Figure 4.3   Cloud service models explained

Ultimately, the consequence of various rentable cloud service models is the lowering of entry barriers for meeting the needs of all classes of actors – skilled and unskilled. For instance, the digital entrepreneurs behind the Dropbox SaaS platform eventually migrated much of their on-premise infrastructure to take advantage of Amazon's AWS S3 (Simple Storage Service) IaaS offering (AWS, 2020). It is helpful to think of it as a B2B transaction between two classes of cloud service providers. Dropbox offers its software-based cloud services to end-users on either a B2C or B2B basis. The example illustrates the attractiveness of cloud service models in lowering participation costs for all classes of actors. With scalable and unlimited computing power at their disposal, digital entrepreneurs with extreme resource constraints can rapidly bring digital artifact and digital platform innovations to market.

4.5.2   Big Data

Cloud computing services are essentially designed to store and process data that today comes in large troves. Big data is data too large and complex to be processed using traditional centralized computer processing architectures – generally described as 'scale-up architectures.' As previously noted, the advent of Web 2.0 introduced an interactive web, whereby user-generated content resulted in copious amounts of data. Meanwhile, with some 20 billion IoT devices connected by 2020, enormous data streams continue to be generated via M2M communication. To fully grasp big data, it is essential to begin by examining how digital data is measured and stored. Simply put, data is stored in bits and bytes, as shown in Figure 4.4, where eight bits make up one byte. Bits of data are stored as zeroes and ones with a bit being the most atomic representation of data.

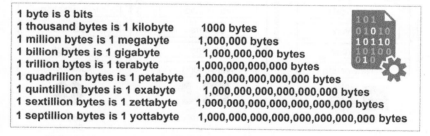

1 byte is 8 bits		
1 thousand bytes is 1 kilobyte	1000 bytes	
1 million bytes is 1 megabyte	1,000,000 bytes	
1 billion bytes is 1 gigabyte	1,000,000,000 bytes	
1 trillion bytes is 1 terabyte	1,000,000,000,000 bytes	
1 quadrillion bytes is 1 petabyte	1,000,000,000,000,000 bytes	
1 quintillion bytes is 1 exabyte	1,000,000,000,000,000,000 bytes	
1 sextillion bytes is 1 zettabyte	1,000,000,000,000,000,000,000 bytes	
1 septillion bytes is 1 yottabyte	1,000,000,000,000,000,000,000,000 bytes	

Figure 4.4   Digital data measurement units

Having examined Figure 4.4, now consider the estimates that the total amount of data generated, captured, copied, and consumed by users in 2018 was 33 zettabytes, which grew exponentially to 59 zettabytes in 2020 and is on course to reach 175 zettabytes by 2025. Human civilization is increasingly digital-centric – hence the exponential estimates are plausible. For instance, in 2020, some 500 million tweets, 294 billion emails, and 65 billion WhatsApp messages, and 72,000 hours of video content were generated each day (Vopson, 2021).

Unlike 'small data,' big data requires 'scale-out architectures' that use thousands of processors to crunch data in real-time. Accordingly, without the advances in cloud-based infrastructure discussed above, big data processing is hard to achieve. Relatedly, software technologies have been designed to leverage scale-out architectures for processing big datasets in parallel. For instance, the MapReduce programming model developed by Google in 2004 and Hadoop – Yahoo's implementation of MapReduce – are open-source technologies widely available for managing big data (Siebel, 2019, p. 38).

However, there are characteristics of big data that entrepreneurs need to consider in unlocking value. These characteristics are captured by the 5V framework of big data – Volume, Variety, Velocity, Veracity, and Value (Anuradha, 2015).

Volume: The size of the data must be big enough to determine the potential value and insights that can be extracted from it. Hence, big data is typically described as data larger than terabytes and petabytes.

Variety: Traditional data processing tools such as spreadsheets and Relational Database Management Systems (RDBMS) typically capture and store data in a structured manner. However, big data combines structured, semi-structured, and unstructured data. Since digital platforms such as social media networks facilitate user-generated data, such data comes in a wide variety. Hence, big data tends to draw from text, images, audio, and videos, and then completes missing data through *data fusion* – that is, the process of integrating disparate sources and varieties of data for the production of more consistent, accurate, and valuable information.

Velocity: Meanwhile, velocity refers to the speed at which data is generated and processed to meet user demands and challenges. Services driven by big data often need to capture, process, and generate insights in real-time, thereby making velocity an essential characteristic of big data.

Veracity: Furthermore, the quality of big data is critical to generating accurate and reliable insights that do not misrepresent reality. Hence, veracity is an essential feature of big data which moves beyond volume to emphasize reliability. In an age where life-changing decisions are made using big data, veracity is equally critical.

Value: Finally, big data is only valuable when analyzed to yield information and insights. Without insights that aid decision-making and action, big data is of little to no value. Hence, big data is hardly discussed without analytics which generates descriptive, diagnostic, predictive, and prescriptive insights.

Ultimately, big data presents metaphors for digital entrepreneurial action as the possibilities for solving societal problems become endless. Since economic value creation often entails providing affordable solutions to consumer needs and wants (i.e., problems), digital entrepreneurs are increasingly unlocking the potential of big data to solve age-old problems across industries and societies. Hence, digital entrepreneurship typically occurs along a data value chain. The data value chain begins with generation, collection, storage, analysis, and the transformation of data into insights; then proceeds to monetization in the form of selling advertising, operating e-commerce, transforming traditional goods into rentable services, and the renting out of cloud infrastructure (UNCTAD, 2019).

4.5.3   Artificial Intelligence, Machine Learning, and Deep Learning

The challenge of analyzing big data to create value is the province of AI and machine learning. AI is the arm of computer science and engineering that develops intelligent machines and computer software that mimic the cognitive abilities for learning and problem solving, typically associated with humans. Machine learning is a subset of AI, which constitutes algorithms designed to learn experientially and from examples. Algorithms are a set of instructions that computers can follow to execute an action. For instance, search engine algorithms from Google follow a set of instructions to rank results from search engine queries by order of relevance.

Machine learning algorithms typically build a model based on a sample or training dataset to make predictions and make decisions in an approach described as supervised learning. With supervised learning, one or more inputs are given in a labeled sample dataset, and the algorithm determines an output for inputs that were not part of the sample dataset. Supervised machine learning could be active, which means an algorithm learns iteratively. It could also be classification learning, which means it assigns objects into categories, and it could be regression-based, which means it estimates the relationship between variables. With a high level of accuracy in making predictions, an algorithm is said to have learned. Supervised learning is ideally suited to tasks where data scientists can predict the features that can be extracted from an algorithm and less so for unpredictable outcomes. For instance, activities of narrow AI such as training an algorithm to distinguish between a car and a motorbike is more straightforward than predicting if an individual is on the verge of committing a crime. Deciphering criminal behavior is a complex activity that requires general and complex intelligence.

Accordingly, a high-performing subset of machine learning known as deep learning emerged around 2010 to tackle more unpredictable scenarios. Deep learning uses sophisticated mathematical models and hardware in a 'neural network' for learning from big data. A neural network mimics the network of neurons in the human brain, and is therefore moving AI closer to the realms of general human intelligence. It forms a layered hierarchy of algorithms that analyze input components, thereby allowing it to arrive at more abstract outputs. Deep learning is even more powerful in unsupervised learning algorithms, whereby such algorithms take a set of data with only inputs and build a complete representation. Hence, unsupervised learning algorithms are helpful in analyzing big data because they can discover hidden patterns without human intervention, detect anomalies, cluster items, associate frequently occurring events, and decompose datasets into multiple components.

For instance, using a large dataset, a deep learning algorithm may predict that a particular individual is a potential credit risk and therefore recommend rejecting a loan offer. In e-commerce retailing, unsupervised learning algorithms drive mass personalization as online advertising can be tailored to each individual by analyzing data from their online behavior against a huge dataset. Most remarkably, Google's DeepMind made headlines in 2016 when its AlphaGo algorithm beat a human professional champion, Lee Sedol, in the Asian strategy game of Go. An infinite number of moves are possible in the game of Go, and thus it requires highly intuitive human intelligence, previously thought to be beyond the reach of machines. Yet, AlphaGo was just the beginning as its subsequent versions exhibit exponentially more powerful deep learning capabilities.

The computational resources needed to analyze big data through deep learning are immense. Therefore, computer hardware improvements such as powerful new GPUs (Graphics Processing Units) from Nvidia enable digital entrepreneurs to train algorithms in neural networks exponentially faster and less expensively than was possible before. A GPU is a specialized processor originally designed to accelerate the rendering of graphics. High-performance GPUs on Google Cloud (Google Compute Engine), AWS EC2, and Microsoft Azure provide robust and scalable hardware resources for machine learning and data-intensive deep learning. Consequently, such convergence of technologies enables and drives digital entrepreneurship because the ability to develop and apply sophisticated AI and machine learning algorithms to solve everyday problems is now democratically available to under-resourced digital entrepreneurs.

4.5.4   The Internet of Things (IoT)

Finally, the IoT is yet another converging technology which is particularly critical to driving the next wave of digital entrepreneurship. As noted, advances in information and communications technology have converged to enable intelligent, connected products and services that constitute complex, modular, and layered cyber-physical systems. These products are commonly described as 'smart' for their cyber-physical composition. As noted, emerging wearable technology products such as Fitbit and Garmin, and consumer-facing products such as Google Home and Amazon's Echo are examples of such smart products.

Edge: A typical IoT product has three broad layers. The first layer is the edge, which is a general reference to a number of network-enabled technologies such as smart sensors, actuators, appliances, and IoT gateways. Edge technologies are capable of sensing, collecting, storing, and transmitting data over a computer network. Smart sensors, for example, are critical edge devices capable of detecting, measuring, and indicating any specific analog signal such as light, heat, motion, sound, and moisture. Such edge devices can be designed to convert and store analog signals as electrical signals and then, using layered network technologies, transmit them over the internet. Some are equipped with bidirectional communication and control capabilities, which means they can be monitored and controlled remotely towards resolving problems. For instance, when paired with machine learning algorithms, IoT devices can be used to predict equipment failure and prescribe an accurate maintenance date.

IoT Platform and the Organization: The IoT platform is the bridge between the edge and the organization at the next layer. IoT platforms are designed to ingest, federate (i.e., aggregate), and normalize large volumes of varied data from edge devices in real-time (see Figure 4.5 below). Applications may be developed for IoT platforms to monitor, control, and optimize products and processes. Hence, IoT applications have become central to digital transformation initiatives across traditional value chains. For example, the smart grid is changing the power grid which had remained largely unchained since its invention. The smart grid is fitted with several IoT edge devices which remotely communicate in real-time. As a result, electricity consumption is monitored across regions remotely while simultaneously generating big data. It has resulted in more efficient use of electricity and accurate billing of consumption through smart metering.

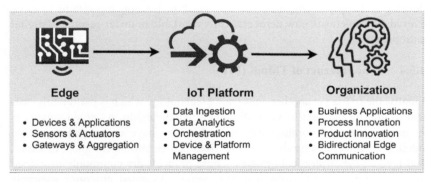

Figure 4.5   *IoT layers and value creation*

4.6   DIGITAL ENTREPRENEURSHIP: BARRIERS AND POTENTIAL SOLUTIONS

While changes in the broader digital technology environment generate external enablers, several barriers place restrictions on current and future forms of digital entrepreneurship. However, these barriers may also be interpreted as external enablers of digital entrepreneurship as they represent problems searching for innovative solutions. Consequently, they are discussed and followed by potential short-term, mid-term, and long-term solutions which entrepreneurs and policymakers have considered, are considering, or have already applied in different regions of the world.

4.6.1   Digital Divides and Skills Gap

Most notably, internet infrastructure remains unequal, unaffordable, and unreliable in many countries and regions of the world, resulting in digital divides along the lines of gender, geography, age, skills, and income dimensions (World Bank, 2016, p. 5). Hence, some 40 percent of the world's population currently remains offline, potentially exacerbating existing inequalities across societies. The Covid-19 pandemic laid bare some of these inequalities as societies with poor internet infrastructure failed to reap the benefits of remote work, health care, and education (United Nations, 2021). Before the pandemic, internet penetration in the developed world stood at 87 percent, 47 percent for developing countries, and 19 percent for least developed countries, with access among women being a significant problem (ITU, 2019). Simply put, without appropriate infrastructural investment, digital entrepreneurs will find it difficult to take advantage of opportunities in cyberspace.

To compound the problem, digital divides along the lines of skills appear to be even more pernicious. Digital skills required to unlock the full economic potential of advanced digital technologies are in short supply. Hence, a digital skills gap exists, with several businesses having difficulty finding critical digital technology talents. Worse still, competition for existing talents renders them expensive to acquire, thereby favoring big incumbents with extensive financial resources. For perspective, a report by the European Commission (2020) indicated that 58 percent of Europeans had basic digital skills, while 33 percent had more advanced skills. However, skills were unevenly distributed along sociodemographic lines, with over 80 percent of digital natives between the ages of 16 to 24, individuals with high formal education, and students possessing basic digital skills. However, only 35 percent of citizens aged 55 to74 and 30 percent of retirees had basic digital skills.

With the digital transformation of society, basic to intermediate digital skills only assist in performing non-tech work. Moreover, while the digital skills divide remains a much bigger problem in the least developed countries (80 percent currently lack basic skills), in advanced economies, some 40 percent of the population still lack basic digital skills (ITU, 2020). The result is a digital skills divide, which threatens to exacerbate existing problems of inequality across all levels of society. Therefore, even when the internet infrastructure gap is closed, a skills gap prevents individuals and societies from taking advantage of opportunities for value creation in cyberspace. It is indeed an urgent issue as the next wave of digital entrepreneurship will require intermediate to advanced digital skills.

However, while advanced digital skills are critical, technical proficiency on its own is insufficient. Therefore, an overemphasis on STEM (Science, Technology, Engineering, and Mathematics) education at the expense of equally important non-tech competencies may be misplaced. The ability to identify and unlock the hidden potential of digital technology, use platforms to recruit global talents, conceptualize, lead, and realize digital technology projects, and develop novel business models are among the complementary digital entrepreneurial capabilities needed beyond advanced technical proficiency. Accordingly, the World Economic Forum suggests that digital entrepreneurs require a blend of technical skills such as programming and app development, with non-technical skills such as critical thinking, creativity, problem solving, and negotiations (Milano, 2019). In an increasingly complex world marked by the proliferation of next-generation digital technologies in every societal activity, having a range of skillsets is vital to unlocking, creating, and capturing value.

Potential Solutions: To address digital divides and skills gaps, several policy options exist. Regarding an infrastructure gap, the obvious solution is to invest in the development of advanced, next-generation digital technology infrastructures. More importantly, infrastructure development must be informed by affordability. Therefore, national policies must prioritize the rollout of affordable high-speed broadband and next-generation mobile networks to both urban and rural populations. As noted, AI, IoT, and machine learning are technologies that require rapid internet access and high data throughput for real-time data crunching and predictive analytics, which are hard to achieve with network latency.

To close the skills divide, integrating digital literacy into all education systems from an elementary level is recommended as a long-term strategy. As basic digital literacy skills are necessary to perform non-tech work, individuals and societies without them will become increasingly marginalized. Hence, a World Economic Forum (2016a, p. 3) report on the future of education identifies ICT literacy as a foundational skill along with traditional skills such as numeracy, science literacy, and financial literacy. Meanwhile, the report also identifies critical thinking, creativity, communication, and collaboration as competencies needed to approach an increasingly complex world. Finally, persistence, adaptability, leadership, and initiative are among the critical character qualities identified. It is essential to point out that most of the competencies and qualities identified are digital entrepreneurial growth mindsets – discussed in Chapter 3. Therefore, digital entrepreneurship education could be a feature of virtually every higher education program at cross-disciplinary levels.

In the near term, favorable immigration policies geared towards attracting and retaining highly skilled immigrants are a potential solution to the digital skills gap. Likewise, the development of digital literacy skills cannot be left solely to the traditional education system. Governments must support initiatives to democratize access to those skills for individuals who currently lack them. Incentivizing business models that fill skills gaps among the adult population is necessary. Encouraging upskilling via MOOCs such as Coursera and Udemy can be part of policy initiatives whose mechanisms include recognizing qualifications beyond college degrees and certificates.

4.6.2 Digital Credit Access

Besides digital divides, access to credit presents yet another significant barrier to digital entrepreneurship. While access to credit remains a problem for most entrepreneurs, digital entrepreneurs face a more uphill battle. Most traditional financial institutions follow credit rules that heavily favor the creation of physical and tactile goods, and the use of physical artifacts as collateral security. However, digital entrepreneurship is often based on the creation of intangible information-based digital artifacts and digital platform services deemed ill-suited as collateral. Accordingly, digital entrepreneurs struggle to access debt finance through bank loans. Debt finance policies are therefore out of step with value creation in small innovative digital firms with a higher risk-return profile, which depend on venture-specific capabilities and intangibles (OECD, 2019a).

In the European Union (EU) for instance, poor digital credit access is further compounded by the stigmatization of failure and a banking culture that generally has an aversion to risk – a phenomenon made worse by the 2008 financial crisis. It partly explains Europe's relatively inferior performance in the digital platform economy and next-wave digital technology development compared to the United States and China. McKinsey reports that as of 2018, Europe's spending on software and digital technology services was only 8 percent of the global total versus 77 percent for the United States. Likewise, equity finance remains underdeveloped, with over 90 percent of the EU's venture capital funding concentrated in eight member states. It has led to a European paradox whereby poor performance in the digital economy is ironically not due to the lack of advanced digital skills or infrastructure (Bughin et al., 2019).

Potential Solutions: Solutions to the digital credit gap have been seized by entrepreneurs and policymakers in some regions as an opportunity. Venture capitalists and entrepreneurs in countries like the United States have stepped in to fill the void. Accelerators such as *Y Combinator* and *Dreamit Ventures* have been instrumental in providing digital entrepreneurs with solutions to digital credit access. Moreover, digital entrepreneurial failure is not stigmatized but worn as a badge of honor. Successful digital ventures such as Stripe, Dropbox, Airbnb, and Reddit are among some 2,000 ventures that Y Combinator is credited with launching. With an enabling ecosystem for digital entrepreneurship, it is no wonder the United States continues to lead and attract digital talents from across the globe. For instance, the founders of Stripe were initially denied credit for their first digital venture (later named *Auctomatic*) back home in Ireland. However, after moving to the United States and going through the Y Combinator program, they developed and sold it for $5 million. Through the same program, they continued the sequel of success by founding Stripe as a US competitor to PayPal, which is currently among the top 70 global digital platform companies by market capitalization (Irish Times, 2014; UNCTAD, 2019).

As fast-growth new ventures often come from digital technology industries, a good line of credit is required to nurture their emergence. However, that does not imply a lack of prudence in funding digital entrepreneurial initiatives. Since digital entrepreneurs can often experiment with new venture ideas at low cost, perhaps a preferable approach to convincing creditors and investors is to begin by bootstrapping. Financial bootstrapping signals a commitment by entrepreneurs to their new venture ideas. Likewise, bootstrapping has been associated with innovativeness and resilience in start-ups. Therefore, digital entrepreneurs increase their chances of getting credit when early steps have already been taken to demonstrate the viability of digital new venture ideas, resulting in actionable and tangible metrics. Such an approach also has the benefit of reducing information asymmetries which give some creditors concern. Thus, early traction can be used as a mechanism for assessing viability. If traction shows viability at a quantitative and qualitative level, financial service providers can mitigate risks through an incrementalist approach that expands funding as additional traction is achieved.

To further mitigate risks, the digital new venture idea should be examined by the degree to which it is dependent or independent from dominant digital platforms. For instance, an app-only digital new venture idea that is heavily reliant on its relationship with Google or Apple app stores is vulnerable to policy changes and actions taken by these platform leaders. Therefore, financial providers can evaluate risk by the degree to which a digital new venture exhibits the potential for independence from dominant platform channels. That is not to suggest that high-risk propositions that are reliant on dominant platforms should not get access to credit. The key is to be aware of the risks and mitigate accordingly. One way of mitigating the risks could be by providing credit incrementally as the venture develops profitably. When data reveals promise through traction, access to credit can be scaled to allow the venture to harvest as much value from the business while expanding its portfolio beyond the dominant platform.

Nevertheless, some new digital ventures may need a massive injection of cash to get off the ground. Under such circumstances, entrepreneurs should take early steps to reduce demand uncertainty via small-scale experimentation. In cases where digital entrepreneurs are willing to share equity, a few guidelines are recommended. First, equity finance providers should avoid short-termism. A short timeline for expected returns may be unrealistic for certain ventures, as reaching a tipping point in search of strong network effects can take time. Furthermore, a *growth to profit* model is necessary when an idea is highly disruptive. Since the internet promotes winner-take-all market dynamics, a slow pace of growth for some ventures could increase the risk of being overrun by a fast-moving and well-resourced competing new entrant. Market disruptors such as Amazon, Uber, and Airbnb illustrate how a growth to profit, as opposed to a profitable growth model, is the logical step when new venture ideas are disruptive. Thus, a bold but risky credit move that takes a long-term view may be the only solution under some circumstances. Value capture in the form of profitability may only occur when critical mass and market dominance are achieved. Investors can then expect the venture's operational costs to achieve parity with incoming revenue initially, and subsequently surpass it to deliver profitability.

4.6.3 Regulatory Uncertainty and International Policy Fragmentation

In a similar vein, regulatory uncertainty and international policy fragmentation raise additional barriers to digital entrepreneurship. Governments and regulators typically strive to create a healthy ecosystem for innovation and entrepreneurship. They design laws to protect the public from deliberate and unintended consequences. For instance, in the United States and EU, anti-trust regulations exist to protect small digital entrepreneurs from the anti-competitive practices of big incumbents. However, regulatory frameworks traditionally lack the agility to adapt to technological change. Given the exponentially greater pace of change in the digital technology landscape, slow-moving regulatory frameworks are often out of step with change. Likewise, with the global nature of digital innovation, coordination and consensus on regulation are even more difficult to achieve, leading to fragmentation. When regulation does catch up, it sometimes ironically results in unintended consequences that are hard to predict, with potentially damaging ramifications for small digital new ventures.

Regulatory Fragmentation and Unintended Consequences: Regulatory uncertainty and fragmentation increase complexity, with the knock-on effect being a rise in the cost of compliance for small digital ventures, which instead favors well-resourced big firms. Digital technology convergence often blurs the lines between consumers, producers, and 'prosumers' in digital marketplaces, raising questions regarding regulatory scope. Furthermore, cross-border transactions tend to cut across jurisdictional boundaries, which creates regulatory ambiguities. For instance, enforcing infringements on intellectual property rights have often proven challenging beyond national borders. Additionally, attributing blame in digital commerce is even more problematic when AI is applied (OECD, 2019b). Regulatory and policy guidelines are fragmented across the globe, thereby erecting cost-related barriers to digital entrepreneurship. For instance, the California Consumer Privacy Act (CCPA), the EU's General Data Protection Regulation (GDPR), and ePrivacy Directive are well-meaning regional privacy laws illustrating the issue of regulatory fragmentation.

GDPR, a stricter privacy protection law, has been found to unintentionally harm competition by favoring big technology organizations such as Facebook and Google. As Johnson et al. (2020) found, following the new GDPR, data sharing online reduced, but market concentration increased among web technology vendors by 17 percent in favor of big incumbents. Websites were found to drop smaller vendors in favor of big technology companies who are perceived to be better equipped to cope with increased regulatory complexity and ambiguity. Other studies complement these findings by revealing that GDPR introduces new uncertainties and due diligence costs, resulting in decreased investment in EU venture deals, with a much higher drop among foreign investors (Jia et al., 2020).

Digital Taxation and Fragmentation: Regarding digital taxation, there are also challenges in developing regulation that is fit for the digital age. Since digital entrepreneurship is often based on multisided business models and the sale of intangibles, new ventures can often 'scale without mass' across geographical boundaries (Brynjolfsson et al., 2008). As such, where value is created, appropriated, and captured can become challenging to compute from a taxation perspective. Moreover, the growth of the on-demand or gig economy has led to the rise in non-standard work, which often does not fit nicely within legacy taxation frameworks. Likewise, emerging technologies such as blockchain and the resulting trade in cryptocurrencies present new challenges for digital taxation. Meanwhile, digital business taxation discussions have proven contentious among OECD countries. One proposal is to have digital businesses taxed by the jurisdiction where the most value is created and captured, while another suggests imposing a global minimum tax rate.

Consensus has been hard to reach, leading to digital taxation policy fragmentation. Some countries have proceeded with unilateral digital taxation legislation as an interim measure, primarily aimed at big digital technology companies. There are concerns that unilateral taxation only helps to exacerbate regulatory fragmentation. Potential issues such as indirect taxation, double taxation, and trade disputes arise, resulting in new uncertainties that inhibit digital entrepreneurial action. Without agreement between countries, a digital taxation landscape is emerging that may prove complicated to navigate, with added compliance costs for small digital ventures.

Algorithmic Harm, Cryptocurrency, and Cybercrime: Meanwhile, regulators are equally grappling with the potential for harm and criminality which emerging technologies present. Big data, machine learning, and AI pose significant risks to individual liberties. Information asymmetries in AI-aided decision-making, privacy violations, and bias threaten to overshadow the benefits of the technology. Opaque decision-making, gender bias, racism, violation of individual privacy, and nefarious use of data have been identified, which illustrate the potential for algorithmic harm. Hence, there appears to be a genuine need to regulate AI and machine learning in everyday decision-making (European Commission, 2019).

For instance, facial recognition AI developed by *Clearview AI*, a company that provides digital surveillance technologies to law enforcement, sparked a global backlash. In particular, regulators are examining potential privacy violations regarding the scraping of some three billion images from across social media pages on the web for use in its algorithms. Relatedly, a number of facial recognition AI technologies have displayed high levels of error in determining the gender of dark-skinned people. Some of these risks from AI may be the product of a flawed design or use of data without correcting for possible biases. Regardless, a trust deficit has developed as citizens become informed and thus wary of algorithmic harm (Tufekci, 2015).

In another domain, governments around the world are still grappling with the emergence of relatively newer technologies such as blockchains and the cryptocurrencies based on them. A study by the Law Library of Congress (2018) finds that governments worldwide oscillate between restricting cryptocurrencies and embracing them. Still, some are making efforts to create government-regulated cryptocurrencies (so-called *GovCoins*) via traditional institutions such as central banks. The challenges are daunting as cryptocurrencies are increasingly favored by cybercriminals for money laundering, drug trafficking, and internet fraud. While blockchain holds promise as a revolutionary financial technology, its downsides, some of which are yet to become apparent, invite new regulatory and policy scrutiny. With laws remaining inconsistent, ambiguous, and uncertain, digital entrepreneurial initiatives based on blockchain may be impeded by reduced investment.

Digital Protectionism, Trade Disputes, and Geopolitical Rivalry: At the same time, digital protectionism, trade disputes, and geopolitical rivalry present new regulatory and policy challenges. The protectionist policies of some governments restrict access to specific markets, further fragmenting the landscape of the digital economy (Lund and Manyika, 2017). National borders still matter as countries control the free flow of data by erecting legal and technical barriers. For instance at present, China's internet infrastructure design is akin to a gigantic national intranet, which uses the so-called 'Great Firewall' technology to restrict access to most major foreign social media platforms such as Facebook, Twitter, and YouTube, search engines such as Google, email services such as Gmail, and even cloud storage systems such as Dropbox – the list is long. Accordingly, access to about one-fifth of the world's internet population remains off-limits to many foreign digital entrepreneurs. Thus, for some 800 million internet users in China at present, data flows largely remain within national borders. Essentially, the country could disconnect from the global internet if it chooses to. Even more sinister is the concern that such internet censorship technologies are being exported from China to other centrally controlled regimes as it develops their internet infrastructure, giving dictators a national internet kill switch. While technologies such as Virtual Private Networks (VPNs) and proxy servers can be used to circumvent such firewalls, they are also the object of increasing technical and legal restrictions.

Nevertheless, by shielding its digital entrepreneurs and internet market from foreign competition and outside influences, China has gained certain advantages over western nations. For one, its digital entrepreneurs have been successful at developing replicas of foreign digital technologies for its enormous local market. With capabilities locally honed, China has emerged as a powerhouse for next-generation digital technology development. Hence, the country is currently at the forefront of investments in next-generation technology developments such as AI, machine learning, and 5G. With fewer obstacles to collecting vast data pools from its citizens due to relatively relaxed privacy protection laws compared to say the EU, China has emerged as a leader in AI and machine learning – recall that AI feeds off big data. Accordingly, China's digital entrepreneurs are at the very cutting edge of advancements in speech recognition, computer vision, human behavior modeling, AI-driven MedTech, and related fields.

Having conquered the local market, they naturally look to scale globally, but often do so under their home country's regulatory and policy guidelines. However, western governments led by the United States have begun to demand reciprocity while contesting overseas Chinese expansion into their home markets. As such, digital entrepreneurs from China and their ventures increasingly find themselves in the crosshairs of geopolitical, cultural, and international trade disputes. For instance, several countries recently erected regulatory and policy barriers regarding the adoption of Huawei's next-generation 5G technology, citing national security concerns and a lack of trust. Likewise, digital platforms from China, such as TikTok and WeChat (Weixin), have recently become pawns in a geopolitical game of chess, culminating in a 2020 ban in countries like India.

Potential Solutions: While regulation and national policies are essential in maintaining a healthy digital entrepreneurial ecosystem, regulators and policymakers need to do so with thoughtful considerations of the potential for unintended, harmful consequences. They must remember that the very foundation of internet technology is premised on a principle of openness. However, protectionism and regulatory fragmentation are predominantly social problems threatening the promise of the internet as an open platform for innovation. Therefore, it is in everyone's best interest to maintain openness and dialogue.

The voices of every group must be heard in formulating and revising global laws and policies, given that much is at stake. A loud minority with privileged access to digital technology knowledge cannot be left to legislate on behalf of groups that may not even be present at policy and regulatory tables. Moreover, given the digital skills divide, it is arguably not equitable to legislate on behalf of people who may not yet be knowledgeable about digital technologies. Hence, 'education before legislation' must become a guiding philosophy. Besides, since the digital economy is not geographically contained, common ground based on shared interests must be sought in cooperating and coordinating regulatory and policy efforts across borders. Likewise, regulators and policymakers must guard against the dangers of a one-size-fits-all approach.

Meanwhile, when disputes eventually arise, a representative forum for mediation needs to be in place. Such a forum could be within existing global cooperation frameworks such as the World Trade Organization (WTO) or other independent world bodies. Efforts in this direction are already underway in the EU and OECD. However, these bodies must be more inclusive. History and geography cannot be allowed to determine destiny in a digitally enabled world.

4.6.4   Cybersecurity Threats

While regulatory and policy barriers present a daunting challenge, cybersecurity threats further complicate the global digital innovation landscape. As value creation increasingly centers around digital technologies, so does illegal activity. As a result, activities such as ransomware attacks, DDoS (Distributed Denial of Service) attacks, malware, credit card fraud, identity theft, and phishing scams are currently among the most frequent forms of cyberattacks. As data has become a key driver of economic value, an underground economy for stolen data has emerged in the so-called dark web. Cyber criminality can erect barriers to digital entrepreneurship by increasing the cost of participation and disincentivizing engagement. It can result in damages such as the destruction of mission-critical data, financial theft, lost productivity, intellectual property theft, destruction of critical infrastructure and post-attack disruption, and reputational harm, among others.

Next-Generation Technologies and Cybersecurity: With particular reference to next-generation digital technologies such as IoT and big data, several threats have become apparent lately. Indeed, IoT devices have greatly amplified the threat of cyberattacks. As the World Economic Forum (2021) reports in its Global Risk Report, attacks on IoT devices increased more than 300 percent in the first half of 2019, as they make perfect targets for abuse and sabotage. A smart grid, for instance, can be taken offline in a ransomware attack, with destructive consequences for entire cities and countries.

In a ransomware attack, hackers infect computers with malware and restrict access to files while threatening to destroy data permanently or dump it on the dark web if a ransom is not paid. The severity of ransomware threats was perfectly illustrated when the Irish Health Services (HSE) was attacked in May 2021 amid a global health pandemic. While data was being restored, patients could not make appointments with doctors. The causal trail for possible deaths associated with such an attack is even harder to establish. Meanwhile, Colonial Pipeline, which is currently the largest pipeline infrastructure in the United States for refined oil, suffered a ransomware attack in the same month. The attack led to a temporary fuel shortage on the East Coast of the United States. Consequently, industry experts warn that ransomware is currently the fastest-growing cybersecurity threat as it promises high returns for criminals, contrasted with a very low risk of getting caught. Its importance made it a central subject for discussion at the 2021 G7 summit.

In more state-sponsored attacks, hackers infect IoT devices with spyware and use them for eavesdropping and espionage. Even when IoT devices are not targeted for ransomware, DDoS attacks are also possible. A DDoS attack occurs when an attacker knocks a site offline by flooding it with more traffic than it can handle. The attacker accomplishes this by infecting multiple computers with malware which are then used to create a botnet. The botnet, with its 'zombie computers,' can then be directed towards a target server or website, thereby overwhelming it. DDoS attacks can be crippling because they may disrupt a critical digital service needed by an entire country. For instance, in 2021, Fiducia and GAD IT, a German company that provides technology for the country's cooperative banks, suffered a DDoS attack that temporarily disrupted banking services across the country. Such attacks have been massively scaled by IoT devices. For instance, in February 2020, Amazon reported that its AWS Shield foiled one of the largest DDoS attacks ever carried out at a record-breaking 2.3 Tbps (Terabits per second) – that is, about 20 million requests per second (Cimpanu, 2020).

Additionally, IoT devices generate copious amounts of valuable data, which make prime targets for data theft. They collect and distribute data that is potentially sensitive for individuals, corporations, and nation states. Therefore, big data is at risk of being stolen and sold on the dark web, or used by a nation to gain trade and military advantages. An illegal marketplace for brokering data exists estimated to be in the billions of dollars. While law enforcement authorities have successfully shut down dark web marketplaces such as Silk Road and DarkMarket, they often re-emerge in other forms. Stolen data can be traded and used to facilitate other attacks, such as phishing attacks that seek to extort money from individuals and organizations. A phishing attack occurs when an attacker uses social engineering to manipulate victims into opening an email or instant message while masquerading as a trusted entity. As people are usually the weakest link in cybersecurity, phishing attacks can be precursors to a vicious cycle of varied attacks.

Digital Technology Weaponization: In a similar vein, the internet has been weaponized and used as a tool in cyber warfare involving state-sponsored actors and organized crime. Governments are honing cyber offensive and defensive capabilities. For instance, Stuxnet is a well-known malicious worm that was launched against Iran's nuclear program. The scale of the attack suggested that a well-resourced governmental entity was behind it. Worse still, state-sponsored attacks are now being directed at private organizations and individuals in other countries. For entrepreneurs developing sensitive and extremely valuable technologies, state-sponsored attacks on private businesses presents a new threat level. When a government launches an attack against a private organization in another country, it is never a fair fight. The sheer amount of resources it deploys overwhelms most private businesses. The purpose is often to steal secrets, cripple critical infrastructure, or weaponize information to meet strategic political, military, and economic goals.

Speaking of information weaponization, it is primarily facilitated by social media platforms. The tools of information weaponization are usually sophisticated machine learning and AI systems, automated software bots, and natural language generation for the creation and dissemination of disinformation at scale. Private social media platforms such as Facebook and Twitter have become new battlegrounds in disinformation warfare. First, an attacker conducts reconnaissance of a target and then proceeds to create realistic content with AI-assisted tools. They may also sponsor ads that precisely target and manipulate a specific group. Attackers may plant false content into social media groups with the help of bots, and subsequently drive engagement. As false content overcomes factual information and spurs belief, an attack is complete. As observed during the 2016 US presidential election, such attacks can interfere with the democratic process of a nation. With AI's ability to craft convincing 'fake news' articles and 'deep fakes,' threat levels have been significantly elevated.

Moreover, machine learning algorithms may inadvertently integrate misleading and weaponized information into big datasets that amplify disinformation. The ease with which social media disinformation can spread at scale means that individuals and organizations risk having well-constructed brand images tarnished overnight, among other threats. Worse still, social media platform owners are under increasing regulatory pressure to mitigate such attacks. Ultimately, digital entrepreneurs in all industries can safely assume that any digital innovation deployed in cyberspace can be subject to all kinds of threats.

Potential Solutions: However, several solutions already exist while others are being explored. First, to fully appreciate cyberattacks, it is essential to entertain the somewhat abominable thought that cybercriminals are innovators and entrepreneurs. Innovation and entrepreneurship are not always forces for good. As Baumol (1996) reminds us, there are three types of entrepreneurs in society – productive, unproductive, and destructive. Productive entrepreneurship is the object of this book and entrepreneurship education in general. It centers around value creation for the greater good of society. Unproductive entrepreneurship extracts value from society without contributing much to its creation. Destructive entrepreneurship is the 'evil twin' of productive entrepreneurship as it destroys society for personal gain. Thus, cybercriminals can be described as destructive digital entrepreneurs who leverage digital innovation tools to destroy society while extracting value for themselves. In the digital space, the outcome is a flourishing economy on the dark web where malware, exploit kits, and cyberattack-for-hire abound. Since today's cybercriminals display high levels of sophistication, intelligence, and self-organization, productive digital entrepreneurs are gifted with value-creating opportunities by resolving the challenges presented by their 'evil digital twins.' Thus, digital new venture ideas can be born out of anticipating and foiling the actions of destructive digital entrepreneurs. The opportunity is massive as cybersecurity ranked among the top five globals risks of 2020, according to a World Economic Forum report (2021).

With particular reference to IoT devices, cybersecurity should be a key consideration in all product designs at a technical level. On a positive note, McKinsey (2020) reports that proactive cybersecurity is now a primary consideration in developing IoT devices from the very inception and throughout the value chain. Meanwhile, computer scientists point to the potentialities of combining blockchain technology with IoT devices to secure cyber-physical systems (Khan and Salah, 2018). Hence, cybersecurity is no longer an afterthought but is increasingly becoming a feature of most cyber-physical system engineering.

Relatedly, there are positive headwinds as the G7 submit of 2021 placed cybersecurity among the top global risks in search of solutions. Deeper global coordination on cybersecurity is a possible outcome of current debates among the world's most powerful nations. As cybersecurity threats cut across geographical boundaries, joint efforts between law enforcement agencies can help dismantle illegal marketplaces on the dark web. Undercover cyber law enforcement officers on darknets may help take down and deter cybercrime by making darknet markets unsafe for criminal activity. For instance, Europol reported that an operation involving several countries successfully took down DarkMarket, a large underground market on the dark web with over 500,000 users, 2,400 sellers, with transactions estimated at over €140 million mainly carried out with bitcoins (Europol, 2021).

However, law enforcement is but one layer of cybersecurity. Basic education is needed at national levels. As such, digital literacy skills aimed at individuals and organizations must incorporate techniques for foiling internet attacks based on social engineering. Individuals and businesses must be trained in good cybersecurity housekeeping, such as the regular updating of software systems. For instance, most websites that get hacked are often found to be running outdated PHP versions. PHP, which stands for Hypertext Preprocessor, is a dynamic web programming language that runs on Apache web servers. It is regularly updated and triggers other updates from millions of open-source web development services like WordPress, Joomla, Magento, and WooCommerce, which depend on the technology.

Regarding social engineering attacks, some organizations have come up with innovative solutions for training and raising the levels of alertness among employees. Techniques used include randomly performing phishing attempts at their own employees (including management) to assess their levels of sophistication in dealing with similar cyber threats. Employees who fall prey to such attempts in company drills are reminded or cautioned, thereby keeping mission-critical teams on high alert at all times.

Finally, concerning cyber threats masterminded by governments, it is safe to assume that a cyberwar is currently an ongoing reality, albeit covertly. Given its potential to cause tremendous harm to citizens through acts of sabotage, cyber defense must be considered a strategic military priority for countries. Hence, several nations are currently honing cyber offensive and defensive capabilities following attacks by suspected state actors. Unlike kinetic warfare, cyber warfare leaves room for plausible deniability. In cases where entrepreneurs develop and manage sensitive technologies, additional resources from a cyber defensive military unit may be needed to fend off attacks from a well-resourced state-sponsored actor.

4.6.5   Digital Technology Fragmentation

Cybersecurity combines with digital technology fragmentation to erect further technical barriers to digital entrepreneurship (World Economic Forum, 2021). Fragmentation, as noted above, is problem enough at regulatory, policy, infrastructural, and skill levels. However, technology fragmentation occurs at more proximal levels of digital new venture creation. Hence, its effect is more directly felt by digital entrepreneurs. Technology fragmentation is a general reference to the multiplicity of platforms or technology standards that are designed to serve a similar purpose. Fragmentation locks users into self-contained and closed ecosystems, with the primary objective being the maximization of company value while offering a curated user experience.

Technology polarization of the digital economy can be good for innovation when kept to a minimum, as it reduces monopoly and promotes competition. However, it can increase the cost of developing and maintaining digital experiences. For instance, Apple's iOS and Google's Android are two dominant app ecosystems with different development frameworks that require exclusive sets of skills. Developing for both platforms doubles the workload and cost of acquiring talent. Furthermore, sudden requests for app version upgrades occasionally call for a complete overhaul and redeployment in keeping with new technologies and governance standards imposed by the platform leader. Failure to respond risks an immediate existential threat to app-based businesses dependent on these ecosystems. Additionally, backward compatibility (i.e., interoperability with an older legacy system) is at times not supported, resulting in time-consuming tests of app versions across new and older devices, coupled with the potential loss of user base from failed upgrade attempts. As consumers use many devices to consume digital content, digital entrepreneurs have to deal with the technical challenges of developing and maintaining omnichannel experiences.

However, digital technology fragmentation is not a new challenge. For example, competition for dominance in web browser technology has resulted in 'browser wars' between providers since the 1990s. While organizations such as the W3C have always stepped in to support open standards such as HTML5 and CSS3, browser competition persists with regular updates aiming to outdo the competition. As such, the web developer's job is made more complicated as several lines of code have to be written and regularly updated to ensure cross-browser compatibility and usability of digital content. For instance, the decision by web browsers to discontinue the support of Adobe Flash in 2020 has rendered a sizeable chunk of interactive web content unusable. Digital entrepreneurs have been forced to invest in redeveloping legacy Adobe Flash-based content in the new technology standards such as HTML5, CSS3, and JavaScript. Others who could not afford the cost of adapting have either seen their user base diminish significantly or been put out of business altogether.

Currently, a similar trend is emerging as companies race to position their offerings as dominant designs in next-generation digital technologies. For instance, in the machine learning and AI space, format fragmentation increases the time and resources needed to build, train, and release neural networks. Developers are confronted with a daunting array of tools such as PyTorch, Theano, TensorFlow, and Caffe, each developed based on different technical frameworks. Additionally, developers get locked into a particular framework as migration or transfer between standards is often not supported. Similarly, IoT and cloud technology fragmentation lead to deployment issues as devices and systems are not designed to plug into each other. In the cloud computing space, the market is consolidating around a few key providers such as Amazon, Microsoft, and Google, with their proprietary cloud technology designs.

Potential Solutions: There is the need to agree on self-regulatory technology standards in many areas that ensure the interoperability of next-generation digital technologies. There is precedence to such an agreement, as exemplified by the success of PCI-DSS (Payment Card Industry Data Security Standard) in maintaining a healthy ecosystem for online payment processing. PCI compliance is now a self-regulatory framework designed and agreed upon by leading credit card companies to facilitate the secure processing of payments online and to combat fraud. Standardization is the very reason the internet has largely remained an open platform for innovation. Standards provide specifications and technical information on technologies, services, and processes. Creating standards typically involves a wide range of individual, organizational, and governmental actors seeking consensus. While not exactly a legal framework, standards have been referenced in legal proceedings for guidance.

Advances in next-generation digital technologies call for standards that ensure interoperability between AI tools, cloud storage systems, and IoT devices. Standardization can ensure platform independence by enabling data portability, allowing apps and devices to be moved freely between vendors. In this regard, a model-driven architecture (MDA) is a recommended solution for AI designs. MDA refers to a software design that uses models as a set of guidelines for structuring design specifications. It offers an abstraction layer that simplifies programming and speeds up the development of AI and IoT applications. MDA allows developers to focus on relevant issues and avoid worrying about extra details or data types. Likewise, to avoid cloud vendor lock-in, platform independence can be achieved through a multi-cloud deployment approach. Digital entrepreneurs can minimize risks by limiting their dependence on one vendor or technology provider. Hence, they must first determine if a cloud development environment allows them to write applications for modules in multiple programming languages. Likewise, such an environment should allow application portability and the cross-platform deployment of AI and IoT applications (Siebel, 2019, p. 184).

4.7   SUMMARY AND CONCLUSION

By exploring changes and challenges in the digital technology environment, this chapter has shed light on the external enablers and barriers to current and future forms of digital entrepreneurship. Accordingly, it has explored emerging trends in the digital infrastructure landscape that provide the supporting framework for digital entrepreneurship and digital transformation. It began by exploring and highlighting significant changes in the critical infrastructure of the internet, dominant digital platform infrastructure, and computer processing and storage infrastructures, which are foundational technologies for present and future forms of digital entrepreneurship. Subsequently, it examined the convergence of four key technologies (AI, big data, cloud computing, and IoT), which are poised to shape future forms of digital new venture creation while completely transforming and disrupting legacy value creation systems in the process. Finally, barriers are identified along with potential solutions that are already being considered towards overcoming them. Therefore, building on the current and previous chapters, the next chapter provides practical guidelines for digital new venture creation in a digitally-enabled world.

5.   Pragmatic model of digital new venture creation

5.1   INTRODUCTION

While the previous chapters have provided a solid theoretical and contextual basis for appreciating digital entrepreneurship, digital transformation, and digital disruption, the actual practice of digital new venture creation is yet to be addressed. Accordingly, this chapter offers a pragmatic model for digital new venture creation. As such, aspiring digital entrepreneurs, educators, policymakers, and managers are equipped with a blueprint for structuring the proactive search and realization of digital opportunities. This model is based on the outcome of a longitudinal action design research study (Coghlan, 2019) conducted in a digital entrepreneurship context, underpinned by existing theory and current industry practices (Nzembayie, 2019). Thus, it is inclusive enough to be applied in the multiple contexts in which digital entrepreneurship and entrepreneurship in the digital age emerge. Since the model offers guidelines that are applicable to all forms of entrepreneurship in the digital age, it has potential for adaption and application in a much broader entrepreneurship context.

5.2   PROCESS MODEL DEVELOPMENT: FROM THEORY TO PRACTICE

Following on from the theoretical foundations explored in the previous chapters and the empirical findings from our research, we develop a pragmatic model for digital new venture creation. We undertook an action design research study that involved the real-time creation of a digital new venture in the EdTech sector. By grounding our research in a structured process, we were able to translate our tacit knowledge into explicit knowledge on the best and next practices of digital new venture creation. Our approach has been validated in multiple scholarly publications and academic conferences (Nzembayie, 2019; Nzembayie et al., 2019; Nzembayie and Buckley, 2020).

The study enacted a pure digital new venture idea in an EdTech context over four years while documenting every interaction as part of the research. The core action design research project sought to leverage enabling digital technology change to develop digital education games for the primary education sector. Since going live in 2018, the new venture has attracted some 700,000 early adopters in nearly a million web visits called *sessions*. Thus, iterations of Minimum Perfect Products or MPPs (discussed subsequently) were used to validate the new venture idea and market offering progressively. Meanwhile, the study also reveals how changing external conditions such as the Covid-19 pandemic can accelerate the success of a new venture by exponentially increasing demand for its offerings. Hence, from April to June 2020, a surge in demand, combined with digital growth marketing skills, led to a rapid user base growth.

The result is an evidence-based and theory-supported pragmatic model for digital new venture creation depicted in Figure 5.1. The model constitutes two distinct but interrelated phases. Phase 1 is the *Ideate* and *Evaluate* (IE) phase, while Phase 2 is the *Enact* and *React* (ER) phase. We subsequently expand on the two phases, providing fine-grained tactics and actions required to increase the odds of developing successful digital new ventures. As noted in Chapter 2, success is broadly defined as venture survival and growth.

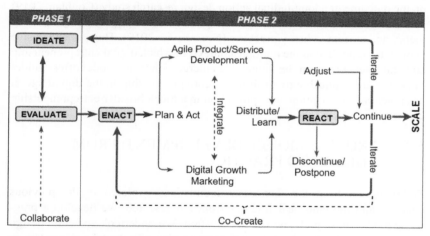

Figure 5.1   Pragmatic model of digital new venture creation

Digital entrepreneurship theory, as reviewed in Chapters 2 and 3, explains that entrepreneurship is a complex, multidimensional process of emergence. We distilled this generic understanding of an entrepreneurial process into Figure 2.1 in Chapter 2. The lower echelons of the early stages of new venture emergence are critical. At nascent phases of early-stage entrepreneurship, entrepreneurs formulate new venture ideas against external enablers and evaluate them to gain opportunity confidence. Confidence prior to new venture creation is a product of perceived uncertainty and the willingness to bear uncertainty. Demand uncertainty reduction is particularly critical at nascent phases. Therefore, sizing markets and estimating demand are usually activities of most proactive searches that aim to reduce the chances of creating a product or service without market demand. Likewise, confidence can be the result of the means entrepreneurs and self-selecting actors bring to new venture creation.

Ultimately, value creation is the goal of all forms of productive entrepreneurship. As noted, productive entrepreneurship creates value by solving problems for society. Problems are the needs and wants of consumers. Hence, new venture ideas and market offerings can be assessed in terms of how well they solve a problem for a targeted segment. Chapter 3 examined the implications for new venture creation when digital artifacts and digital platforms form the core of new venture ideas and market offerings. As noted, the composition of new venture ideas is a major source of variance regarding how different typologies of entrepreneurship in the digital age emerge. Upon the successful subjective, intersubjective, and objective assessments of new venture ideas against external enablers, entrepreneurs and stakeholders are better positioned to commit time, resources, and effort towards realizing them, leading to various outcomes.

At proximal and micro levels, immediate outcomes are products and service offerings launched into an industry and new organizations in many cases. At the macro and distal levels, outcomes are transformative or disruptive when they alter market and economic systems. In Chapter 4, we examined how digital technologies and the outcomes of digital entrepreneurship are affecting economic systems by way of digital disruption and digital transformation. Rooted in these theoretical and contextual understandings, we develop our model and substantiate it with examples from our own empirical study and practical experiences as serial digital entrepreneurs.

5.3   PHASE 1 – IDEATE AND EVALUATE

Phase 1 is a pre-enactment phase focused on the birth of the digital new venture idea and primarily aimed at lowering the levels of demand uncertainty while self-assessing and strategizing to overcome resource scarcity. A number of steps are discernible at this stage, as depicted in Figure 5.2.

Step 1 – Ideate and New Venture Idea: Ideation is the conceptual and dialogic process of generating a rudimentary new venture idea. Rudimentary suggests that ideas need not be perfect at this step. Likewise, as many ideas as possible could be generated. Such ideas could be the result of a proactive, reactive, or fortuitous search. However, the emphasis is on a proactive search that develops a structured environmental scanning process geared towards

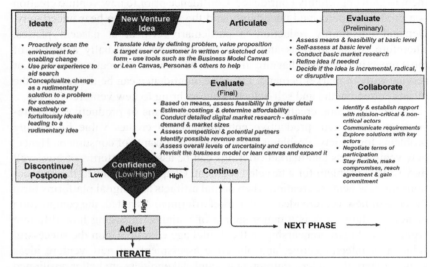

Figure 5.2   Phase 1 expanded – ideate and evaluate

identifying enabling digital technology-related change. It is not to suggest that
new venture ideas do not emanate from fortuitous or reactive search. However,
given that this model is ultimately geared towards promoting digital entrepreneurial practices in a structured manner, a proactive approach is emphasized.

In proactive search, digital technology-related change is a broader reference
to the cause-effect relationships that form around digital technologies at a societal level. For instance, innovations in next-generation technologies such as
cloud computing, discussed in Chapter 4, have driven demand in cloud-based
hosting and the disruption of on-premise hosting services. The demand for
cloud-based services, in this instance, is an example of a consumer behavioral
change that is digital technology-driven. Thus, in a proactive search, identifying a technology trend should seek to anticipate what changes it is causing and
the non-digital technology changes occurring because of it.

Proactive search is not a random act and is often aided by prior knowledge
and direct experiences with real-world problems. Real-world problems are
problems in our immediate physical environments. Hence, aspiring digital
entrepreneurs could begin by exploring problems in their immediate environments with the potential for a digital technology-aided solution. They must
remember that resolving inefficiencies in society remains a primary (but not
the sole) impetus behind the formulation of digital new venture ideas. Most
external enabling mechanisms relate to issues of inefficiency. Inefficiency
is simply defined as the failure to make the best use of time and resources.

A careful analysis of digital ventures such as Uber, Airbnb, PayPal, Stripe, Dropbox, Google Search, AWS, and many more, reveals that resolving some form of societal inefficiency was a chief impetus behind their new venture ideas. Google, for instance, set out to make the search for information in cyberspace more time-efficient. Uber set out to make the process of ride-hailing more time-efficient for consumers while at the same time enabling car owners to optimize the use of their cars (resource optimization). At an abstract level, such inefficiencies are linked to the spatial and time-bounded nature of our physical world, as suggested in Chapters 2 and 3 – see Figure 3.1 for instance. Accordingly, brainstorming based on problem-solution pairing from encountered problems of inefficiencies can inform the departure point for steering the search for digital new venture ideas and value creation opportunities.

Traditional business frameworks such as STEEPLE (Social, Technological, Economic, Environmental, Political, Legal, and Ethical) and VUCA (Volatile, Uncertain, Complex, and Ambiguous) offer useful proactive environmental scanning tools. In using them, we recommend that entrepreneurs ask twin questions from their perspective and the consumer's perspective. In the first question, STEEPLE raises the *what* while VUCA (Bennett and Lemoine, 2014) answers the *how* in the second question. Based on asking these questions, a third and final *what* question focuses on what a technology-related change is enabling from the perspective of the entrepreneur and the consumer. Hence, we develop Table 5.1 as a conceptual tool for structuring such digital new venture ideation exercises.

The table can be used by educators and practitioners as a structured template for the proactive generation and preliminary evaluation of digital new venture ideas. Identifying what is happening, how it is happening, and what it is enabling helps clarify the nature of change and what opportunities for value creation are embedded in it. Using the VUCA framework, change could be described as volatile or gradual, uncertain or predictable, complex or simple, ambiguous or obvious. For instance, a technological change may increase demand for a product or service in an obvious manner. It may then result in a new venture idea that provides an obvious solution, thereby creating the potential for intense market competition. Obvious product/service offerings may be less defensible due to intense competition. Consequently, the pressure for a high degree of innovativeness of new venture ideas and market offerings increases significantly. Contrarily, change that is ambiguous and complex may result in ideas that are not so obvious, thereby creating conditions for a defensible first-mover advantage. These possibilities should be interrogated as part of ideation.

Proactively identifying and interpreting change in this manner entails keeping an eye on authoritative and credible industry, governmental, and technology information sources. We recommend Chapter 4 as a good departure point for

Table 5.1   Conceptual tool for structuring environmental scanning and ideation

WHAT change is happening?	HOW is it happening?
Socio-cultural	Volatile or gradual
Technological	Uncertain or predictable
Economic	Complex or simple
Environmental/Ecological	Ambiguous or obvious
Political	
Legal	
Ethical	

WHAT is the change enabling for the entrepreneur and the consumer?	
Demand expansion:	*Entrepreneur:* Does it increase demand for a particular product or service?
	Consumer: What new solutions to old problems does change offer me?
Resource conservation:	*Entrepreneur:* Does it save resources for bringing a product or service to market?
	Consumer: Does it conserve resources I need in performing a particular activity?
Resource expansion:	*Entrepreneur:* Does it increase the amount of resources needed to create a new product or service offering?
	Consumer: Does it increase the number of resources I need for solving a problem?
Combination:	*Entrepreneur:* Does it allow two artifacts to come together to provide new functionality or augment a legacy system?
	Consumer: Does it allow me to merge services into one artifact?
Generation:	*Entrepreneur:* Does it allow for the creation of new artifacts?
	Consumer: Does a new artifact solve an existing problem for me?
Uncertainty reduction:	*Entrepreneur:* Does it reduce various forms of uncertainty in the entrepreneurial process?
	Consumer: Does it remove an uncertainty I usually had to deal with?

WHAT is the change enabling for the entrepreneur and the consumer?	
Compression:	*Entrepreneur:* Does it increase the speed at which a new market offering can be created, distributed, or iterated?
	Consumer: Does it save me the time needed to perform an activity in my daily life?

sensing digital technology-related change. A subscription to updates from credible sources, as evident in Chapter 4, can aid external alertness. Through regular email updates and a constant visit to credible technology-related sources, digital entrepreneurial practitioners will seldom miss critical changes that stimulate ideation. Given the rapid rate of change in the digital technology landscape, regular updates are needed to keep abreast with current affairs beyond what is currently reviewed in Chapter 4.

Step 2 – Articulate: The next step is the articulation of ideas. Articulating ideas is a dialogic process of making them explicit in a communicable form. There are two benefits to this exercise. First, it is a reflective process that enables entrepreneurs to refine rudimentary ideas, making them clearer to themselves. Indeed, scholars studying practice have long identified that when ideas are tacit, they are hard to formulate into strategies that others can understand and develop (Schön, 1984, p. 243). Second, well-articulated ideas are easier to communicate towards gaining stakeholder buy-in. Stakeholder buy-in potentially increases the resources needed for realizing the new venture idea.

Visualizing the idea through descriptive writing and basic sketching is essential for a dialogic interaction with an idea. Tools such as the Business Model Canvas (Osterwalder and Pigneur, 2010) and Lean Canvas (Maurya, 2012) have been developed to assist in articulating new venture ideas. The focus of these canvases at this step should be on clarifying the problem an entrepreneur is trying to solve and expressing it as a succinct value proposition or solution. They also focus on identifying the potential target users or customers of a solution. Hence, personas of market segments should be sketched out as part of the articulation exercise (Miaskiewicz and Kozar, 2011). Finally, articulation should typically result in the development and refinement of a brief jargon-free statement of what an idea resolves and for whom. Learning to write a successful elevator pitch is a useful technique for articulating new venture ideas. An elevator pitch is a 30-second statement of what a new venture idea is about (David, 2014).

Step 3 – Evaluate Preliminarily: Following articulation, the next step is to conduct a preliminary evaluation. The goal is to rapidly assess market demand, competition, potential partners, and available means. Since external causes of venture failure include a lack of market demand, demand evaluation is critical in determining if an idea is a sound basis for new venture creation (CB

Insights, 2021). Digital tools such as Google Keyword Planner (incorporated into ads.google.com), Similarweb, Google Trends, and Ubersuggest from Neilpatel.com can help assess demand in a bottom-up approach. According to a DataReportal report, an estimated 98 percent of internet users searched for information via a conventional search engine in 2021, with Google commanding 92 percent of the search engine market share (Kemp, 2021). The same data also shows that 98.9 percent of internet users visited a social media channel in 2021. Accordingly, tools and data from search engines and social media platforms offer a valuable resource for digital growth marketing research. They can be especially useful when new venture ideas are based on a Business-to-Consumer (B2C) model. For instance, customer demand can be extrapolated from data on monthly searches conducted by consumers, filtered by location and other parameters. Thus, by describing the value proposition of a new venture idea from the consumer's perspective, skilled actors can arrive at several search terms that consumers may be using to express their needs. Using these search terms to query search engine platforms and databases is a valuable technique for acquiring data that aids bottom-up evaluation of market demand. Digital growth marketers use such techniques as an early step in growth marketing involving data-driven decision-making geared towards reducing demand uncertainty (Huffman, 2018).

For instance, in one of our entrepreneurial education activities, a group of students came up with an idea for a new digital venture that meets the demand for healthy eating among digital natives. Their proposed solution was to develop an app that provides self-service recipes for making healthy meals aimed at Generation Z – that is, those born around the mid to late 1990s. Among the search terms chosen to assess demand, the term 'healthy lunch,' which was entered into Google Trends, immediately revealed that it spiked and dipped at regular intervals annually, over a five-year period. They then triangulated that information with data extracted from Google Keyword Planner and Ubersuggest, which showed related search terms and the level of difficulty involved in ranking highly on Google *Search Engine Results Pages* (SERPs). Next, they identified key marketplace actors and used Similarweb to approximate their monthly search volumes. By combining multiple data sources, they arrived at a plausible demand assessment, resulting in an estimate of the Total Addressable Market (TAM). In the end, the nascent entrepreneurs felt confident in their idea but were under no illusion regarding how much work it would take to realize it successfully. Educators and practitioners can use such exercises in evaluating new venture ideas towards gaining opportunity confidence.

However, it is essential to point out that not all new venture ideas lend themselves to such techniques for demand evaluation. In cases of radical and disruptive innovations, for instance, demand may be harder to assess. Therefore, a design-based approach which combines digital research tools with a more experimental, ethnographic, and autoethnographic approach may be more helpful in evaluating market demand (Brown and Katz, 2011). In addition, potential consumers may be unaware of a digital technology solution to an old problem. For instance, Drew Houston, the founder of Dropbox, reported being frustrated with forgetting his USB memory stick, leaving him with a laptop and no files to work with. It led him to imagine a cloud-based solution that made files available anywhere on any device with internet access. The result was Dropbox, whose benefits consumers did not immediately perceive, as evidenced by its initial market failures. However, through digital growth marketing, customers were eventually educated into seeing how it solved a problem they had all along. As a result, Dropbox is today an essential tool for collaboration involving geographically decentralized teams. At present, it has a market capitalization of approximately \$12 billion.

Beyond reducing demand uncertainty, digital entrepreneurs must look internally to assess their confidence levels regarding capabilities for realizing the new venture idea. Self-assessment of their abilities, material means, networks, and motivation will help determine if confidence is high or low for pursuing an idea. Self-assessment is a metacognitive exercise with the added benefit of indicating where extra resources and capabilities may be needed and what sort of actors potentially make valuable co-creators. It may also identify gaps in an entrepreneur's abilities, thereby pointing them towards further self-development and training. As noted in Chapter 3, strong metacognition has been identified as a cognitive mechanism driving digital entrepreneurial performance.

Step 4 – Collaborate: Based on a preliminary assessment in the previous step, entrepreneurs identify and survey potential mission-critical and non-critical collaborators. This step is premised on the assumption that co-creation is a feature of virtually all entrepreneurial processes. However, it is not compulsory to collaborate at this stage for reasons discussed subsequently. Since entrepreneurship is hardly a solo activity, initially identifying key supporting actors helps build confidence in the possible realization of new venture ideas. Entrepreneurs should evaluate collaborating actors based on their ability to provide new means and capabilities critical to realizing the new venture idea. In addition, they should distinguish between mission-critical actors and non-critical actors. Mission-critical actors are those whose skills, knowledge, or resources are indispensable in advancing the idea. They could be external assessors such as investors, finance providers, skilled partners, and team members. Non-critical collaborators could be actors on digital talent platforms who sell their skills on an on-demand basis.

For instance, in our study, LinkedIn proved useful in identifying critical partners for product development based on a B2B (Business-to-Business) negotiation. As our action design research project involved creating digital games for education, we quickly determined that game programming skills which we did not possess were critical to realizing our new digital market offering. By negotiating contractual agreements with an experienced team of programmers in the Netherlands, we gained mission-critical commitment that increased our confidence in realizing the new venture idea. Other platforms such as Fiverr helped hire specific non-critical, on-demand talents such as logo designers and voice artists. Previously articulated ideas are communicated to mission-critical actors using techniques such as an elevator pitch, presentation, or discussion to gain commitment and understanding of requirements. We learned that the more visual the form of communication, the more powerful it is at gaining clarity and critical stakeholder comprehension. It is therefore valuable for entrepreneurs to hone communication capabilities. Likewise, they should be very flexible and open to ideas from potential partners at this stage.

For mission-critical actors such as investors, they may also follow the previous steps to evaluate the new venture idea and the entrepreneur behind it. Ideas could also be further modified or changed at this step. In the end, commitment could be given if key actors assess the idea to be a sound basis for action and if a high level of confidence in the entrepreneur's capabilities is perceived. Hence, questions regarding the focal entrepreneur's background and prior knowledge are necessary for assessment. For entrepreneurs, their personal stories are under the spotlight, and they can control how that story is communicated and interpreted. Depending on the idea and venture-specific characteristics, important decisions such as equity-based commitment will have to be made by the focal entrepreneur. Difficult conversations must be had at this step as disagreements between partners often features as a key reason for venture failure (Khelil, 2016). Only actors who provide real value and commitment should be classed as mission-critical and worthy of equity ownership. A decision to share ownership of a new venture is probably one of the most difficult decisions an entrepreneur will have to make at such an early stage. Such a decision will also depend on entrepreneurial motivations and how much control an entrepreneur intends to have on the venture.

Meanwhile, it is essential to point out that given the uniqueness of every new venture idea and the capabilities of entrepreneurs, mission-critical collaborators may not be needed at an early stage or throughout new venture creation. Some new venture ideas can be bootstrapped by an entrepreneur, only with non-critical collaborators who may not be interested in an equity stake. Likewise, some collaborators will emerge at various stages in the entrepreneurial journey. Others may require a proven concept before committing. As digital technologies promote the democratization of entrepreneurship, several independent actors often enter the digital entrepreneurial process on their own terms at different stages. New venture creation can occur with a dynamic cast of loose collectives. Therefore, collaboration based on giving equity stake may be bypassed initially. Ultimately, contextual factors such as idea-specific, entrepreneur-specific, and venture-specific characteristics will determine how collaboration unfolds towards opportunity confidence and throughout the journey.

Step 5 – Evaluate 'Finally': Having identified and sought the commitment of potential collaborators, all activities across previous steps are now assessed to arrive at a final evaluation. A final evaluation is the last step before concluding if an idea is an opportunity with a high confidence level in pursuing it. With the possibility of obtaining new means from potential collaborators, a feasibility assessment helps determine if the idea can be realized successfully. Relatedly, details on costings may be estimated to assess affordability or formulate a strategy for new venture creation and market entry. For instance, limited financial resources will influence how entrepreneurs deploy resources to enter a market. As poor access to credit has been identified as a barrier to digital entrepreneurship in Chapter 4, perhaps entrepreneurs may decide to realize a new venture idea by bootstrapping it (Khelil, 2016).

In our action design research study, we were bootstrapping our digital new venture along with contracted, mission-critical, but independent collaborators who shared the story of their digital entrepreneurial journeys with us. One entrepreneur noted that he did not opt for venture finance because his venture was not deemed 'interesting' to investors. However, he sought and gained the commitment of a mission-critical partner who was a skilled game developer that he previously worked with at another organization. Together, they shared the same vision for their new venture idea and overcame financial limitations by opting for bootstrapping. Bootstrapping worked by holding full-time and part-time jobs at various times while they slowly developed their venture, which was the game development organization we were collaborating with. When the venture was mature enough to earn them a basic wage, they quit their jobs to focus on it full-time. Currently, they run a thriving digital game creation venture in the Netherlands. By evaluating the idea against their resources and capabilities, the entrepreneurs felt confident enough to pursue their new venture idea within available means.

To further reduce demand uncertainty, the initial evaluation conducted at Step 3 of this phase will have to be solidified with a more detailed demand assessment geared towards estimating actual market sizes. At this step, industry frameworks such as TAM, SAM (Serviceable Available Market), and SOM (Serviceable Obtainable Market) provide useful demand assessment tools (Chi, 2021). Table 5.2 defines these tools and offers an example of how they can be applied.

Along with market demand evaluation, entrepreneurs should also examine other factors, such as competition and key marketplace actors. Analyzing existing competition can give confidence in the viability of an idea. The

Table 5.2   *Calculating TAM, SAM, and SOM in demand assessment*

Tool	TAM (Total Addressable Market)	SAM (Serviceable Available Market)	SOM (Serviceable Obtainable Market)
Definition	TAM assesses the viability of an idea based on the maximum amount of revenue it can capture from a market. Not even the most successful businesses capture 100 percent of the TAM. However, it helps to determine if a problem is big enough to justify starting a new venture in the first place	SAM narrows down to the portion of the TAM a venture is targeting. Narrowing down could be based on geography, demographics, and other characteristics. SAM encourages entrepreneurs to define market segments more objectively. It typically results in about a fraction of the TAM	SOM further narrows the SAM to a more realistic cross-section of the market that will generate revenue in the immediate to long term. Even when a market segment is identified, competition often means that a much smaller segment will be addressed initially or eventually
Question	What is the total size of the market?	What portion of the total market can you realistically capture?	What portion of the serviceable available market can you reach?
Example	In 2020, a US entrepreneur looking to enter the global video games market arrived at a conservative estimate from industry reports that his TAM was roughly $150 billion	The video gaming entrepreneur decided to focus on the North American video games market, estimated at $60 billion, thereby constituting his SAM	The entrepreneur decided that he was only going after the North American mobile games market, which the reports estimated at $15 billion, thereby providing his SOM. As the example suggests, a final SOM of $15 billion is a far cry from a global TAM of $150 billion

presence of successful market players may suggest that an idea is viable, meaning an innovative new market offering could result in success. Contrarily, a very strongly positioned marketplace actor may be difficult to challenge, especially considering that the internet promotes winner-take-all market dynamics. However, the absence of competition should lead entrepreneurs to question the idea to determine why none exists. Non-existent competitors may indicate that the idea is not worth pursuing. It may also indicate that a market has been defined too narrowly and indirect competitors have not been considered. Alternatively, it may positively suggest that an idea is radically or disruptively innovative. In other cases, an entire industry could be at an early stage of evolution, implying that non-existent direct competition is normal.

Relatedly, non-existent competition may indicate that an idea is ahead of its time. In which case, a risk of failure exists from entering the market too early (CB Insights, 2019). Meanwhile, several competitors in a mature industry may suggest market saturation. A saturated market may increase pressures for a high degree of product/service innovation. Thus, if a new venture idea is based on bringing an imitative offering to a saturated market, it may limit the potential for success. In this case, only a disruptive new market offering could increase confidence in the likelihood of success.

Finally, possible revenue streams should be identified. Since entrepreneurial failure has also been associated with developing a product/service offering that customers are unwilling to pay for, the dangers of commoditization should be assessed (CB Insights, 2019). Commoditization arises when consumers view goods with economic value as mere commodities. Under such circumstances, a valuable offering may not be able to attract enough paying customers to create a sustainable or profitable venture. Commoditization may result from cut-throat industry competition, disruptive technological breakthroughs, the entry of a dominant and well-resourced market competitor, among others (Shih, 2018). A technology breakthrough could significantly reduce the cost and barriers to developing a product or service, leading to abundance and a significant drop in prices. For instance, in the early days, when mobile app development was still a novelty, the cost of hiring developers was relatively high. However, as app development knowledge proliferated, along with new technologies such as app-creation platforms for non-programmers, several free apps were created and became available in the app stores. As a result, business models based on selling premium apps were greatly affected as consumers began to see certain app-based services as mere commodities to be obtained freely. To make matters worse, dominant digital platforms routinely and unethically price-compete with smaller platform-dependent entrepreneurs, further depleting the chances of generating profit.

Step 6 – Decide on Levels of Confidence: Based on a final evaluation, digital entrepreneurs should determine if the level of confidence in pursuing the idea is high or low. Recall that opportunity confidence is an actor's evaluation of a new venture idea and the degree to which it is deemed a viable basis for new venture creation. High levels of confidence indicate that demand uncertainty, trust in the entrepreneur's means and capabilities, and resources from collaborators render possible new venture creation and success. Contrarily, a low level of confidence may stem from high demand uncertainty revealed by market research, doubts in a focal entrepreneur's capabilities to realize the idea, lack of resources, and poor timing, among others. For instance, a more in-depth evaluation of the market may have revealed that a key market player would require a more disruptive new venture idea to challenge. As the digital environment promotes winner-take-all market dynamics, some market segments with dominant players make little room for imitative or incremental product/service offerings. Thus, it requires adjustments in the new venture idea, the approach to innovation, or discontinuation.

Consequently, three broad categories of outcomes are possible in Phase 1. First, with a high level of confidence, entrepreneurs should naturally continue to Phase 2. Confidence suggests that an idea is a viable business opportunity worth pursuing. Contrarily, if the level of confidence is low, it may be advisable to discontinue or postpone the pursuit of the idea. By quitting quickly, entrepreneurs can return to the first step of ideation. Meanwhile, a low level of confidence may also result in a decision to adjust an idea, continue with it, or adjust it by revisiting and revising key steps in Phase 1. Finally, given that ideation and evaluation can be relatively inexpensive, multiple ideas can be initiated and evaluated concurrently before making a more significant commitment in Phase 2.

5.4   PHASE 2 – ENACT AND REACT

With a high degree of opportunity confidence in Phase 1, entrepreneurs begin Phase 2 – the ER phase. To enact an opportunity means to take action towards realizing it. To react is to stay flexible and responsive to knowledge arising from the process of new venture creation. Enacting new venture creation is initiated by planning project-specific activities under two main categories: agile product/service development and digital growth marketing. The two broad categories are tightly integrated and, therefore, not mutually exclusive. Phase 2 is premised on the logic that digital new venture creation is defined by the constant initiation, forking, merging, and termination of diverse activities grouped under the two broad categories (Nambisan, 2017).

Phase 2 builds on some of the strengths of a hypothesis-driven approach to new venture creation, reviewed in Chapter 3, and which were validated in our own longitudinal study and experiences as digital entrepreneurial practitioners. Figure 5.3 subsequently captures the steps in this phase.

Step 1 – Plan and Act: Planning is an activity that decomposes digital new venture creation into projects that are prioritized to optimize the chances of early success. Hence, it aligns with agile development principles which encourage planning incrementally and often throughout new venture creation (Ghezzi and Cavallo, 2020). Planning defines the objectives of each iteration of product/service development and digital growth marketing, in addition to integrating both groups of activities tightly. Digital growth marketing objectives may be defined around Dave McClure's AAARRR (Awareness, Acquisition, Activation, Revenue, Retention, and Referral) framework reviewed in Chapter 3 (McClure, 2007). Prioritization under the two main categories of marketing and product/service development remains a vital planning activity since entre-

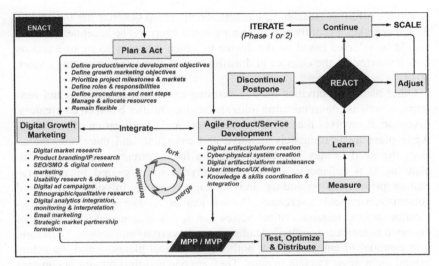

Figure 5.3   Phase 2 expanded – enact and react

preneurs seldom have unlimited resources. Therefore, finding the most efficient and optimal path to success by running experiments via digital customer acquisition channels is critical (Weinberg and Mares, 2015). Since running out of resources is a major contributor to venture failure, prioritization cannot be overstated (Khelil, 2016; CB Insights, 2019). Advantageously, digital products and service offerings are never complete and therefore continue to evolve long after the initial launch. It is a product of the modifiable characteristics of digital artifacts, among others, as examined in Chapter 3. It is especially true of pure digital new venture creation, where products and services based on digital artifacts can be reprogrammed and modified seamlessly 'on the fly.'

As noted in Chapter 3, success in a digital entrepreneurship context is often defined by achieving strong network effects through user base growth (Huang et al., 2017). Therefore, finding an optimal path to developing an early user or customer base should be a key consideration at this step. Likewise, planning incremental releases of products/service offerings builds on the assumption that if entrepreneurs run out of limited resources, the venture can continue, even if that means being a scaled-down version of the original idea and market offering (Ries, 2011). Furthermore, digital entrepreneurs may find that a scaled-down first iteration of a minimal digital product or service satisfies a market segment competently. Hence, prioritization could also focus on conquering a beachhead market before adding functionality that caters to a wider market segment. A beachhead market is a smaller market segment with specific characteristics ideal for distributing and learning about a new product or service offering. Beachhead markets can also help generate the initial cash flow that makes a venture self-sustaining in the interim. The beachhead market should be selected based on the degree to which it is easy to capture and on how it maximizes the chances of drawing lessons that result in scaling (Aulet, 2013).

Other planning activities include defining immediate procedures and next steps, as well as communicating roles and responsibilities between co-creators. Likewise, it involves the careful management and prioritization of resources. Agile planning is ultimately iterative and emergent, and therefore emphasizes the need to stay flexible. While the focal entrepreneur facilitates it, planning is a collaborative and cooperative activity geared towards promoting project understanding and agreement among mission-critical and non-mission-critical co-creators. As we learned in our study, miscommunication among mission-critical actors can result in a misunderstanding of expected outcomes, eventually leading to cost overruns and delays. Therefore, it is essential to emphasize that both digital project planning and the actors behind them never operate in silos. They are one and thus remain in constant communication and coordination throughout new venture creation. It is not unusual for digital growth marketing and agile product/service development to be undertaken by the same individuals. Cases of extreme resource scarcity and bricolage require focal actors to oscillate between digital marketing and product development roles. Under such circumstances, entrepreneurs must possess, continuously develop, and combine varied skillsets for realizing new venture ideas. As a result, they can expect to find themselves working longer and harder than other collaborators initially.

Eventually, planning outcomes should be documented and stored in a centralized location to keep mission-critical co-creators 'on the same page.' Documentation does not imply producing a highly detailed text that no one reads. Ideally, it should be highly visual and succinct. In this regard, agile project planning and communication tools and techniques such as product roadmaps, release planning, product, and sprint backlogs can be leveraged to structure, capture, and communicate planning outcomes (Layton et al., 2020). Meanwhile, cloud-based digital project management tools and systems such as Asana and Slack can be leveraged to keep co-creators in constant communication. Constant communication assists in catching problems early. Given the importance of this step, it is normal to expend a bit more time in planning before execution. However, this cannot be interpreted as a carte blanche for paralysis by analysis, whereby the overthinking of imperfect circumstances results in a continuous looping of the planning step without progressing to taking actual action. Planning should therefore focus on what is sufficient to jump-start concrete action. It is essential to remember that flexibility is a critical element of planning, which means actions can proceed under imperfect circumstances with the possibility for accommodating and adjusting to new knowledge and resource inputs along the journey.

Step 2 – Acting Concurrently: Accordingly, planning is rapidly followed by concrete action. Concrete action is the concurrent process of enacting two sets of tightly interwoven and planned activities towards releasing a concrete market offering. The two sets of interwoven activities are digital growth marketing and agile product/service development (Layton et al., 2020). Recall that digital growth marketers are skilled actors who engineer growth into a product or service from inception (Huffman, 2018). Whether a new market offering is a digital artifact/platform or cyber-physical system, digital growth marketing can always begin before product or service development.

Digital Growth Marketing: Without digital growth marketing, digital new ventures may fail even when they have a well-designed offering meeting an actual customer need. Indeed, getting lost in crowded cyberspace is a real threat for new digital ventures. Therefore, to gain visibility, digital growth marketers design activities geared towards engaging consumers in a manner that creates a viral loop which results in exponential self-propagation of a new market offering (Penenberg, 2009).

Activities such as setting up a web presence in the form of a website or social media channel are usually quick and easy first steps in digital growth marketing. Websites could be developed on the same domain name and server upon which a finished digital product or service will be promoted, distributed, marketed, or consumed. Since digital growth marketing involves marketing to human and algorithmic agents, it departs from a purely customer-centric notion associated with traditional marketing. Thus, sending a signal to search engine algorithms through SEO (Search Engine Optimization) techniques is an essential long-term growth marketing strategy to give digital market offerings future visibility (Chaffey and Smith, 2017, pp. 368–83). From our experience, what does not seem to have changed over many years of search engine algorithmic updates is the fundamental rule that major search engines such as Google rank websites based on trust. Longevity, regularity of content updates, and relevant inbound links are all mechanisms for signaling trust from the perspective of a search engine such as Google.

For instance, digital growth marketers understand that multiple data points, such as the age of a website domain name and relevance of inbound links, are used by algorithms to determine how highly a web page ranks on Google's SERPs. Content marketing is a central strategy that integrates this understanding into building trust with search engines such as Google and human consumers. Content can be used to engage and delight an early user base via social media channels, who are encouraged to share them, thereby building relevant inbound links that signal authority and trust to search engines. In addition, content such as video, audio, full articles, and short posts can be used in pre-launch promotional activities geared towards generating buzz around a future product or service (Huffman, 2018, pp. 102–4).

Thus, growth marketing may entail promoting products and services which are still being developed using content. Promotion need not be direct but could include the subtle use of informative content to build trust among end-users and algorithms. Typically, rich audio and visual content are used to give information about an upcoming product or service. At the same time, the audience is encouraged to sign up for news on updates or engage in product testing. Feedback from such pre-launch activities is then captured and analyzed to inform the continuous and iterative process of agile product/service development. A plethora of creative digital growth marketing techniques exist. However, an exhaustive examination is beyond the scope of this book. Likewise, chosen techniques are often venture-specific and should therefore be adapted to the nature of each new venture idea. Nevertheless, given its importance, digital growth marketing capabilities should be a critical component in developing digital entrepreneurial capabilities. A couple of practitioner publications reviewed in this book provide excellent case studies of digital growth marketing (Weinberg and Mares, 2015; Brown and Ellis, 2017).

In our action design research study, digital growth marketing began by deciding on a brand name, followed by research and registration of a chosen and branded domain name. Subsequently, researching potential intellectual property issues with brand names while launching a primary WordPress site was also part of this initial step. Then content marketing efforts began by identifying and planning articles for blog posts based on research that assessed keyword demand using tools such as Google Keyword Planner and Ubersuggest. Soon after, the writing of 20 initial articles was outsourced to ghost-writers on Upwork. These articles were content posted on the website, which was only a blog at an early stage.

At the same time, social media channels were also being registered, while integrations with Google Analytics and Google Search Console were set up with the website. A sitemap was developed and submitted via Google Search Console, enabling search engines to crawl and index 20 web pages containing the 20 articles. These first steps in digital growth marketing were being undertaken while agile development was being initiated. Since we were creating a games-based education site as part of our action research study, branding of games and user interface designs were tightly interwoven with growth marketing. For instance, growth marketing efforts included designing a brand identity that was subsequently embedded into games as part of a long-term strategy of user-driven brand name penetration. This effort was successful as the brand name later became a top search term used to find the site over time, while *direct* website visits became a dominant channel for customer acquisition – that is, 41 percent of website traffic as of 2021. As the example indicates, digital growth marketing and agile development are not discrete activities but are tightly interwoven into a symbiosis from inception.

Agile Product/Service Development: Meanwhile, the concurrent sub-process of agile development aims to create and distribute product/service functionality in usable increments. It involves coordinating various knowledge assets and skills towards delivering an MPP. If an MPP is not feasible, entrepreneurs could settle for a Minimum Viable Product (MVP) as suggested by the lean start-up model reviewed in Chapter 3 (Ries, 2011; Eisenmann et al., 2013). However, MVPs do not tend to emphasize quality, thereby increasing the risk of producing and shipping inferior iterations of products or services. Moreover, as noted in Chapter 3, the weaknesses of an MVP risk increasing overheads, among others. Hence, we recommend entrepreneurs aspire for an MPP, which is a flawlessly designed and well-functioning essential product that fulfills the core needs of an initial target group.

Aiming for the delivery of iterations of MPPs has three main advantages. First, entrepreneurs are managing scarce resources in bringing ideas to market. Therefore, getting it right the first time is critical to finding an efficient path to success and generating a virtuous circle of waste reduction and resource optimization. Second, if entrepreneurs were to run out of resources, an MPP could become the basis of a successful but scaled-down new venture. Third, an MPP greatly enhances digital growth marketing activities, which are often based on a good product or service. A perfect product or service has the benefit of ensuring that growth marketers' feedback from early adopters is accurate, and ideas are not rejected due to false positives and false negatives.

Step 3 – Test and Optimize: To fine-tune a product into an MPP, it should be tested extensively at an internal level and then optimized by eliminating faults before distribution. Testing and optimization must be done from the end-user and customer's perspectives. Growth marketers can be instrumental in ensuring usability by identifying a small group of potential early adopters for very small-scale qualitative and ethnographic testing. Distributing or shipping poorly designed products risks generating negative word-of-mouth.

For instance, in our action design research study, our MPP was two well-coded education game templates used to create multiple learning activities for the target market. First, we developed and tested games extensively for coding errors and cross-browser compatibility. Furthermore, we created a revision game exercise from the school assignment of a five-year-old pupil who was a member of the target group of consumers. Almost instantly, we learned that the time programmed for answering specific questions in our game was limited for a young learner with poor motor skills. The result was a frustrating experience for the learner. Consequently, we optimized the games by fixing bugs in the code and increasing the time needed to answer time-limited learning questions.

Step 4 – Distribute, Measure, and Learn: Having tested and optimized the MPP at an internal level, distribution to a larger audience of target consumers occurs. Distribution is where digital growth marketing skills are most needed. First, a soft launch, whereby a limited pilot digital promotional campaign is aimed at a target customer segment and rigorously monitored for feedback may be carried out. The soft launch is the first iteration of the *measure* and *learn* feedback loop (Ries, 2011). Measurement occurs as results are analyzed to generate insights that are used to refine the MPP for a dedicated distribution at scale. It could also be used to drive experimentation that determines what the optimal configuration for a successful promotional campaign might be. Poorly set up digital advertising campaigns can result in wasteful spending. For instance, in our experience, we came across marketers launching a Google Ad campaign geared towards driving traffic to a website that was poorly optimized for speed. The result was poor user engagement with the website, as evidenced by a high bounce rate due to the slow loading of web pages.

Digital platforms such as Google and Facebook Ads are tools that enable flexibility in terms of how digital ad campaigns are run to test and optimize products and services. These platforms are powerful because they allow entrepreneurs to target users using specific parameters such as demographics, gender, geography, search terms, type of device, and time of the day. Data analytics tools should already be in place to enable measuring and learning from promotional campaigns (Croll and Yoskovitz, 2013). Key performance indicators (KPIs) identified at the planning step should guide digital promotional campaigns. For instance, analytics data from A/B testing can aid decision-making that optimizes conversion rates. Likewise, analytics can reveal insights on user behavior and engagement across digital marketing channels. Following optimization from a soft launch, a hard launch campaign is carried out. The campaign is geared towards generating substantial insights upon which to base critical decisions at the reaction step.

Step 5 – React: At this step, digital entrepreneurs react to the lessons drawn from distributing and promoting the MPP in a hard launch campaign, as well as external enabling conditions. With a dedicated campaign in place, growth marketing activities generate critical insights, leading to three classes of decisions. First, entrepreneurs are likely to continuously *adjust* products/services and marketing tactics based on emerging feedback. Adjustments could be minor or major. A minor adjustment could include a quick update to a process, product, or service based on emerging insights. Following minor adjustments, entrepreneurs could then *continue* to scale.

In our study, positive feedback, coupled with external changing fortunes brought about by the Covid-19 pandemic were maximized to accelerate growth. For instance, a single act of digital growth marketing experimentation ensured that the positive turn of market events was seized and acted on to drive growth in referral traffic. Referral traffic is traffic from other sites to yours. It is a valuable metric because it can also signal trust to search engine algorithms, creating a virtuous circle of viral growth. In this instance, we experimented and adjusted by swapping around the order of social bookmarking icons on the social media sharing widget (AddThis) embedded on the website. Through this act, we discovered that our users preferred sharing our games on Google Classroom. Simply moving Google Classroom above Facebook, Twitter, WhatsApp, and other social bookmarking icons saw exponential growth in its referral traffic from about 1,000 sessions (site visits) a month to over 9,000 at peak months during the pandemic. To date, referrals from Google Classroom alone have accounted for roughly 100,000 of the nearly one million visits to the website, with a higher average session duration, compared to other channels. This example perfectly illustrates the critical role digital growth marketing plays in making adjustments that lead to venture success. Besides such minor but critical adjustments, a significant adjustment could mean continuing with another iteration of the enactment phase or iterating the fundamentals of the new venture idea altogether. Iterations on the fundamentals of new venture ideas indicate returning to Phase 1.

Second, entrepreneurs could also react by continuing based on positive or negative feedback. Positive feedback may mean that campaigns based on the MPP have confirmed key businesses hypotheses, and the venture should scale to maximize the opportunity (Maurya, 2016). However, entrepreneurs must avoid the dangers of confirmation bias when feedback appears positive. They should look for disconfirming evidence before deciding that an experiment based on launching an MPP is successful. A decision to scale is a big one, and it means that demand uncertainty has mainly been reduced or eliminated. Likewise, such a decision should revisit all aspects of the business model to ensure that the venture can grow sustainably in the future. Entrepreneurs could approach more investors with an evidence-based business plan at this stage, geared towards seeking additional venture finance depending on venture-specific characteristics. However, whether positive or negative, feedback could result in a decision to continue with another iteration of Phase 1 or Phase 2. Entrepreneurs may have learned significant lessons from the first iteration of an MPP, which reveals the consumer's needs more accurately. They may need to repeat Phase 2 by generating another iteration of an MPP based on new insights.

Contrarily, a significant lesson could reveal that the initial idea does not form the basis of a viable new venture. Entrepreneurs may choose to return to Phase 1 and begin the entire process all over. Alternatively, a decision to react may mean discontinuing or postponing new venture creation entirely. For example, customers may deliver a resounding rejection of the idea and market offering, leading to a termination decision. Alternatively, an MPP offering could be well received by consumers, but learning reveals that the venture may not capture enough revenue to remain sustainable or profitable. Hence, entrepreneurs may choose to exit by disbanding. Finally, regarding postponement, there could be several reasons for this. For instance, entrepreneurs may learn that the market is not ready for a product or service. Likewise, other enablers may not be in place, meaning an idea is ahead of its time. Entrepreneurs may then postpone new venture creation until the time is right.

5.5   CONCLUSION

Our research-informed model and the concrete steps embedded in it increase the odds of creating a successful digital new venture. Thus, it offers a useful pragmatic tool for novice digital entrepreneurs, entrepreneurship educators, business incubators, and policymakers invested in nurturing the growth of young digital ventures. However, it is essential to reiterate that as with every model or guideline aimed at an unpredictable phenomenon such as entrepreneurship, adopters are advised to adapt it in context. Its modularity is its ultimate strength. Modularity implies that some steps in the process may not be needed under certain circumstances. Some of these circumstances relate to the levels of perceived uncertainty discussed in Chapter 2. Ultimately, our model should be viewed as an artifact that organizes and triggers creativity. As such, its material agency should enable, rather than constrain, the fluidity of thought and action based on unique and ever-changing circumstances. Through such creative and thoughtful application, readers are equipped with guidance for steering and nurturing digital new venture creation.

6. Synopsis: digital new venture creation and disruption

6.1   INTRODUCTION

The previous chapter provided a digital entrepreneurial process model based on our empirical research and extensive experience in digital new venture creation. The model also forms the basis of our teaching of entrepreneurship in university and corporate circles. Throughout this book, we have argued and demonstrated that the digital entrepreneurial process differs in a substantive way from traditional entrepreneurial processes, and therefore represents a paradigmatic shift or significant disruption to entrepreneurial theory and practice. Utilizing this model in practice and entrepreneurship training – with a growth mindset – can raise the 'batting average' of most digital entrepreneurs, particularly those who require guidance at the commencement or various stages throughout new venture enactment. Used in the intended manner, this text provides pragmatic and evidence-based guidance for nurturing digital entrepreneurial practice among a variety of actors – nascent, novice, serial, or portfolio digital entrepreneurs. At a minimum, this text will help nascent or novice entrepreneurs to increase their venturing confidence to a point where they can rigorously evaluate and then implement their venture ideas in a more disciplined way than they would have before consulting the advice in the text. The remainder of this chapter subsequently synopsizes key themes discussed in the book and brings the current volume to a conclusion.

6.2   CONCEPTUALIZING AND CONTEXTUALIZING DIGITAL ENTREPRENEURSHIP

The book commenced by introducing digital entrepreneurship as a disruptive approach to new venture creation in the digital era. It also advances a conceptual framework for defining and differentiating digital entrepreneurship and its two main typologies – pure and hybrid. Thus, it contributes to reducing conceptual fuzziness regarding what constitutes digital entrepreneurship versus entrepreneurship in the digital age more broadly. This framework is represented visually by Figure 1.1, which we reintroduce here.

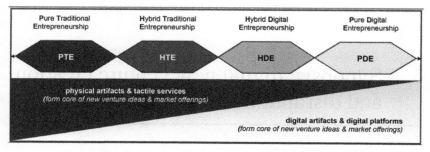

Figure 1.1   Typologies of entrepreneurship in the digital age

We exploit the concepts of digitization and physicality to differentiate entrepreneurship by the extent to which each is core or peripheral to new venture ideas and market offerings. This logic is anchored in the argument that what entrepreneurs act on is an important source of variance determining how various processes emerge. Digitized market offerings are outcomes of ideas embodied in digital artifacts and digital platforms. When applied across the economy, in a process called digitalization, outcomes of digital entrepreneurship have a transformative and disruptive impact on society at large. This process of creating and applying digital artifacts and digital platforms to the economy has undermined traditional theories of value creation, particularly those rooted in assumptions of spatial and temporal boundedness. Innovation and value chain models that assume processual discreteness and linearity are harder to sustain. This book explains how this paradigm-shifting form of entrepreneurship emerges with a clear focus on the digital entrepreneurial process.

6.3   THEORETICAL DOMAIN OF ENTREPRENEURSHIP

It is difficult to grasp a novel phenomenon without situating it in its historical context. Hence, having conceptualized digital entrepreneurship along an entrepreneurship continuum, the book then traces the evolution of contemporary entrepreneurship thought in Chapter 2 while highlighting developments that have led to current debates in the entrepreneurship discipline. As such, it illustrates that entrepreneurship thought has co-evolved with economic thought through the decades. Consequently, the distinctive domain of entrepreneurship scholarship has come to revolve around the IO nexus, with the pursuit of opportunity as its processual focus. However, the opportunity construct and the question of discovery versus creation have proven elusive, leading to conceptual and theoretical quandaries.

Consequently, the remainder of the chapter focuses on more recent developments which have contributed to moving the discipline beyond the opportunity impasse. The opportunity construct has been decoupled into the sub-constructs of new venture ideas, external enablers, and opportunity confidence. Hence, an entrepreneurial process model can be developed that includes external enablers, which are the sources of actor-independent mechanisms that play an input role in driving new venture emergence. Likewise, it contains new venture ideas initiated and refined by entrepreneurial agents (focal and collaborative agents) who provide the micro-level input mechanisms that drive new venture creation at proximal levels towards various outcomes. By combining the latest thinking in the domain, we developed a unifying and comprehensive entrepreneurial process model that functions as an analytical framework. It is captured in Figure 2.1 and subsequently reintroduced here. This framework provides us with the starting point for differentiating between the digital entrepreneurial process and the more traditional processes in successive chapters.

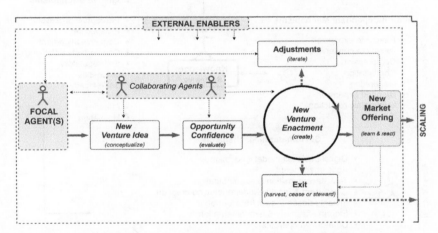

Figure 2.1   Comprehensive conceptual model of the entrepreneurial process

6.4   DIGITAL ENTREPRENEURSHIP AND PARADIGMATIC SHIFT

By integrating relevant interdisciplinary concepts, constructs, and theories, in Chapter 3, we dissect the extent to which digitization upends several traditional assumptions of innovation and entrepreneurship. By exploiting the concepts of physicality and digitization, the chapter provides a conceptual basis for differentiating while at the same time establishing the relationship between digital entrepreneurship and other forms of entrepreneurship in the digital age. Hence, it examines the three interrelated technologies and their actor-independent mechanisms that play varying roles in digitizing and digitalizing entrepreneurship. It explains that digital artifacts and digital platforms form the core of new venture ideas and new market offerings in digital entrepreneurship at its purest, while digital infrastructures are external enablers of all forms of entrepreneurship in the digital age. When actor-independent mechanisms of digital technologies externally interact with agent knowledge, means, and cognitive mechanisms, it results in sociomaterial mechanisms. Sociomaterial mechanisms become proximal and more observable drivers of digital new venture creation, resulting in distinct outcomes. Figure 3.3, which illustrates these interrelationships, is subsequently reintroduced here.

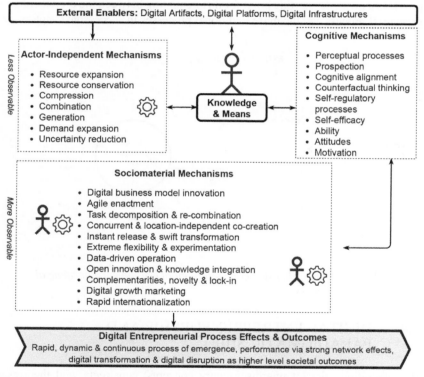

Figure 3.3   Interrelationships driving digital entrepreneurship

We also noted that this is both significant and paradigm-shifting as data-driven products and services become the basis of economic value creation. Economic value creation mainly operates in the context of what is termed 'economics of bits' – marked by the creation of non-rival digitized market offerings which do not get depleted when consumed and can be maintained at nearly zero marginal cost. At a micro level, the result is the potential for the rapid, continuous, and dynamic emergence of the digital entrepreneurial process compared to more traditional entrepreneurial processes defined by physicality. Meanwhile, success becomes mainly defined by achieving positive network effects, manifest in a large and engaged user base. Accordingly, the value of discrete and linear models of innovation and new venture creation get upended. At the same time, traditional success measures such as profitability, growth in employees, and sales are not immediately relevant. It thus explains the *growth to profit* model that successful digital ventures such as Amazon and Uber have been known to adopt during their emergence.

6.5   NAVIGATING THE DIGITAL ENVIRONMENT: ENABLERS AND BARRIERS

Chapter 4 unpacks the digital technology enablers and barriers undergirding the digital entrepreneurship ecosystem and entrepreneurship in the digital age. Given the Volatile, Uncertain, Complex, and Ambiguous (VUCA) environment against which entrepreneurship in the digital age emerges, such technological unbundling is essential to understand the forces driving digital entrepreneurship and its effects – that is, digital transformation and digital disruption. Hence, the chapter begins by examining the core internet infrastructure and its layered modular architecture. Then, by reviewing the four layers of the internet architecture, the chapter highlights the changes happening within each layer that cumulatively act as external enablers of digital entrepreneurship and value creation in the digital age.

Subsequently, the computing infrastructure is analyzed by emphasizing enabling changes in microprocessing capabilities, storage, and miniaturization. Additionally, the convergence of disparate but related technology domains is assessed in terms of the roles played in driving the next wave of digital entrepreneurship, defined by creating pure digital and complex cyber-physical systems as market offerings. Accordingly, cloud computing, AI (Artificial Intelligence) and machine learning, big data, and the Internet of Things (IoT) are emphasized as four core technological domains shaping the future of digital value creation. However, several socio-technical challenges present barriers to digital value creation that digital entrepreneurs and policymakers must address to maximize the potential of these enabling technologies. These challenges are examined alongside potential practical, technical, and policy solutions. Consequently, the reader emerges from the chapter equipped with a lucid appreciation of the proximal and distal opportunities and challenges driving value creation in the digital age.

6.6   PRAGMATIC DIGITAL ENTREPRENEURIAL PROCESS MODEL

Without practical guidelines, this book would be incomplete. Hence, Chapter 5 addresses such a need by offering an evidence-based pragmatic model of the digital entrepreneurial process in Figure 5.1, reintroduced here subsequently. A process model of practical utility provides a vital tool for ensuring that aspiring digital entrepreneurs, policymakers, educators, and students are equipped with a valuable framework for steering digital new venture creation and practice-based education. The model provides step-by-step guidelines for nurturing digital new venture creation structured in two phases. Phase 1 is the *Ideate* and *Evaluate* phase, which offers fine-grained tactics, tools, and techniques for proactively developing digital new venture ideas and assessing them to determine if they form a sound basis for entrepreneurial action.

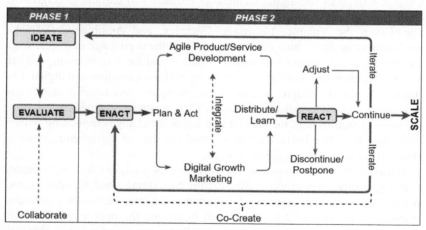

Figure 5.1   *Pragmatic model of digital new venture creation*

Phase 2 is the *Enact* and *React* phase, which furnishes users with invaluable toolsets, skillsets, mindsets, and techniques for navigating the tightly interwoven sub-processes of digital product/service innovation and digital growth marketing. By following the recommendations embedded in the model, practitioners will increase the odds of arriving at a scalable digital new venture. Moreover, the model's solid grounding in theory, research, and practice should give users confidence in adapting and applying it creatively as determined by the uniqueness of every context.

6.7   CONCLUSION

In sum, the 21st century has ushered in unprecedented changes in how value is created by and within society. This transformational change has been driven by the unpredicted and unprecedented changes brought on by the digitization and digitalization of 'just about everything.' Technologies such as the internet, computing infrastructure, AI, machine learning, cloud computing, big data, and the IoT, and the synergistic interrelationships between them, usher in many exciting opportunities for nascent, novice, serial, and portfolio entrepreneurs. What has been missing to date is a clear roadmap to help the entrepreneur and educator navigate their way through the VUCA environment that they collectively face in this digitally enabled world. Entrepreneurs in traditional businesses will find this book useful in helping them transform their businesses, allowing them to compete and win in this exciting new world. However, digital entrepreneurs or nascent, novice, or experienced entrepreneurs considering entering the pure or hybrid digital domains will derive the most benefit from this text. We have provided a research-validated and 'road tested' process model which can work for digital entrepreneurs of all types – if the text is consulted with a growth mindset. We expect this model to evolve as the external environment becomes even more VUCA, and hyperconnected. However, we have demonstrated here that the underlying mechanisms driving digital entrepreneurship identified in our research, and incorporated into our process model, will endure, helping to guide digital entrepreneurs towards successful new venture emergence.

The advent of enabling digital technologies has changed the entrepreneurial landscape forever, as shown in this book. Now more than ever, these technologies are helping to democratize entrepreneurship in the digital age – for those who are lucky enough to have access to them. Ultimately, we aim to foster 'successful digital business venturing' geared towards sustainable individual and societal value creation in the digital age. Finally, we hope that the benefits of the knowledge and enterprises digital entrepreneurs create may proliferate to individuals and societies currently unlucky not to have access to these 'game-changing' digital technologies.

Glossary of terms

- *Actor-independent mechanisms*: Causal pathways or processes originating from external enablers and material agencies which interact to influence the entrepreneurial process in less observable ways.
- *Affordance:* A relational construct which describes the hidden potential of technology that eventually get materialized by a discerning actor. The opposite is a technology *constraint*.
- *Artificial Intelligence (AI):* Intelligence displayed by machines which tends to mimic aspects of human intelligence such as language processing, image recognition, learning and pattern recognition.
- *Big data:* Varied data that arrives in increasing volumes and needs to be computed with great velocity for value creation, typically using machine learning algorithms.
- *Bounce rate:* A percentage-based performance metric for determining how well users are interacting with a website or digital platform.
- *Bricolage:* An actor-centric theory of the entrepreneurial process which offers mechanism-based explanations as drivers of new venture creation under extreme resource scarcity. Mechanisms such as resourcefulness, making do, and the repurposing of existing resources are considered central in explaining new venture creation under resource constraints.
- *Business Model (BM):* The logic describing the processes by which an organization creates and captures value from customers.
- *Business Model Innovation (BMI):* Changes made to enhance the processes by which an organization creates and captures value from customers.
- *Cloud computing:* The availability of computer resources such as storage and processing power on an on-demand basis with only minimal management from the user.
- *Cognitive mechanisms:* Causal pathways or processes influencing new venture creation, which originate from an actor's thought processes and motivations. Examples of cognitive mechanisms include self-regulation, self-efficacy, and counterfactual reasoning.
- *Constraint:* The opposite of the technology *affordance* construct that suggests way in which technologies may impose restrictions on human action.

- *Content Delivery Network (CDN):* A distributed network of servers designed to load website content fast. It works by directing users to geographically closer servers, thereby reducing latency in data transmission.
- *Core:* If an element is indispensable to the existence of an entity or phenomenon, it is core. The opposite is peripheral. For instance, digital artifacts and digital platforms are core elements in all typologies of digital entrepreneurship.
- *Cost Per Click (CPC):* In digital advertising, it is the charge that an advertiser pays a publisher when their ads are clicked – also Pay Per Click (PPC).
- *Design Thinking:* A user-centered approach to conceptualizing and building products and services.
- *Digital artifacts:* A collective construct used to describe digitized components or 'quasi-objects' that technically exist as bits of data and form all or part of a product or service offering. Examples include mobile apps, digital content, software in general, digital games, and websites. Unlike physical artifacts, digital artifacts are uniquely defined by their capacity for distribution over cyber space.
- *Digital born global:* A digital new venture that internationalizes rapidly from its very inception, enabled above all by the reach of the internet and digitization
- *Digital disruption:* A general reference to the upending of traditional value creation processes, theories and practices by digitization and digitalization.
- *Digital entrepreneurship:* Entrepreneurship in which digital artifacts and digital platforms form the core of new venture ideas and market offerings.
- *Digital growth marketing:* A form of entrepreneurial marketing in which growth is engineered into products and services from the ground up.
- *Digital infrastructure:* A collective construct for digital technologies that support the value creation activities of a vast and diverse cast of actors. Examples include the internet, open standards, broadband, microprocessors, 5G networks, dominant digital platforms, and cloud computing.
- *Digital platform:* A software-based system whose architecture is designed to host complementary offerings in cyberspace, thereby facilitating the bringing together of producers and consumers.
- *Digital transformation:* A general construct that captures the multiple changes resulting from the digitization and digitalization of traditional value creation processes.
- *Digitalization:* A construct that describes the socio-technical process of applying digitizing techniques to traditional value creation processes. It is pivotal to explaining digital transformation and digital disruption.
- *Digitization:* The technical process of encoding analog information as bits of data or ones and zeroes. It is pivotal to differentiating digital entrepreneurship.

- *Effectuation*: An actor-centric theory of the entrepreneurial process which offers a number of mechanisms as explanations of new venture creation. Actor-derived mechanisms such as co-creation, affordable loss, and experimentation are deemed critical to explaining new venture emergence.
- *Entrepreneurial process:* The process by which individuals initiate and evaluate new venture ideas and subsequently act to transform them into new market offerings and new organizations.
- *External enabler (EE):* External stimuli capable of prompting the initiation of new venture ideas, influencing the process of realizing them, and shaping new venture outcomes. They are the result of changes in external circumstances such as technology, economy, legal, and political conditions.
- *Hybrid Digital Entrepreneurship (HDE):* A typology of entrepreneurship in which digital artifacts and digital platforms combine with physical artifacts and tactile services to jointly form the core of new venture ideas and new market offerings.
- *Hybrid Traditional Entrepreneurship (HTE):* A typology of entrepreneurship in which physical artifacts and tactile services form the core of new venture ideas and market offerings; however, market offerings are significantly enhanced by the application of digital artifacts and digital platforms which remain peripheral to the core offering.
- *Infrastructure as a Service (IaaS):* Cloud-based business model that provides access to scalable networking, storage, servers, and virtualization resources on an on-demand basis.
- *Internet of Things (IoT):* An industry-originated description of cyber-physical systems and market offerings.
- *Lean startup:* A model of new venture creation which advocates agile experimentation as a central mechanism for managing the uncertainty of the entrepreneurial process.
- *Machine learning:* A branch of Artificial Intelligence (AI) that involves teaching machines to learn from data.
- *Mechanisms:* Causal pathways or processes by which a cause produces an effect; alternatively described as intermediate causes.
- *Minimum Perfect Product (MPP):* An essential but flawlessly designed product that meets the consumer's needs and forms the basis for eliciting accurate feedback.
- *Minimum Viable Product (MVP):* An essential product that is designed to meet the consumer's needs and elicit feedback.
- *Network effects:* The idea that the value of a product or service increases with more users adopting it; alternatively referred to as demand-side economies of scale.
- *New venture idea (NVI):* A rudimentary conceptualization of a product or service combination geared towards creating value for consumers.

- *Opportunity confidence (OC):* The degree to which a new venture idea has been evaluated and deemed a sound basis for new venture creation. OC could be low, high, or both.
- *Peripheral:* If an element is peripheral to an entity or a phenomenon, it means that entity or phenomenon can still exist in a meaningful way without it. For instance, digital artifacts such as Apple Car Play and Android Auto are peripheral to a modern car's functionality.
- *Physicality:* Defined by physical and, therefore, tactile qualities.
- *Platform as a Service (PaaS):* A cloud-based business model that provides access to infrastructure as well as the tools for building custom applications on an on-demand and subscription basis.
- *Pure Digital Entrepreneurship (PDE):* A typology of entrepreneurship in which digital artifacts and digital platforms solely form the core of new venture ideas and new market offerings.
- *Pure Traditional Entrepreneurship (PTE):* A typology of entrepreneurship in which physical artifacts and tactile services form the core of new venture ideas and market offerings, with limited to no application of digital artifacts and digital platforms.
- *Search Engine Optimization (SEO):* A digital marketing activity geared towards ensuring that digital contents are visible on the top of organic Search Engine Results Pages (SERPS).
- *Service-Dominant Logic:* A theoretical assumption which contends that value co-creation is best conceptualized as the exchange of services involving the use of skills and knowledge by an actor for the benefit of another, as opposed to the production and exchange of tangible and intangible goods.
- *Social mechanisms:* Actor-dependent causal processes that underlie actions such as new venture creation. They are generally considered more observable than other types of mechanisms. Examples of social mechanisms include co-creation and agile experimentation.
- *Social Media Optimization (SMO):* The practice of distributing and ensuring that content is visible via social media channels.
- *Sociomaterial mechanisms:* Causal processes that underlie actions such as new venture creation, but which are predominantly the result of mutually constitutive interrelationships between human and material agencies. These mechanisms cannot be explained comprehensively by solely focusing on the role of human actors. Examples include data-driven operations and digital growth marketing activities.
- *Sociomateriality:* A theoretical assumption which contends that social activity is best understood in terms of mutually constitutive interrelationships between human and material agencies.
- *Software as a Service (SaaS):* A cloud-based business model that rents out centrally hosted software for use on an on-demand and subscription basis.

- *Typology:* A unique form of theory in which a complex web of cause-effect relationships are integrated into a coherent, typified, and easy-to-remember profile.
- *Value creation:* The economic process of meeting the needs and wants of society through product and service development and related business activities such as marketing, distribution, and human resource management.
- *Viral marketing:* An approach to digital marketing that makes for compulsive viewing and rapid dissemination of content from person to person.

Bibliography

Ajzen, I. (1991). The theory of planned behavior. *Organizational Behavior and Human Decision Processes, 50*(2), 179–211.

Ajzen, I. (2005). *Attitudes, personality, and behavior*. London: McGraw-Hill Education.

Aldrich, H. (1999). *Organizations evolving*. Thousand Oaks, CA: Sage.

Aldrich, H.E. (2014). The democratization of entrepreneurship? Hackers, makerspaces, and crowdfunding. In *Annual Meeting of the Academy of Management* (Vol. 10, pp. 1–7).

Aldrich, H.E., & Kim, P.H. (2007). Small worlds, infinite possibilities? How social networks affect entrepreneurial team formation and search. *Strategic Entrepreneurship Journal, 1*(1–2), 147–65.

Alvarez, S.A., & Barney, J.B. (2007). Discovery and creation: Alternative theories of entrepreneurial action. *Strategic Entrepreneurship Journal, 1*(1–2), 11–26.

Alvarez, S.A., & Barney, J.B. (2013). Epistemology, opportunities, and entrepreneurship: Comments on Venkataraman et al. (2012) and Shane (2012). *Academy of Management Review, 38*(1), 154–57.

Amit, R., & Han, X. (2017). Value creation through novel resource configurations in a digitally enabled world. *Strategic Entrepreneurship Journal, 11*(3), 228–42.

Amit, R., & Zott, C. (2001). Value creation in e-business. *Strategic Management Journal, 22*(6–7), 493–520.

Anderson, P. (1999). Perspective: Complexity theory and organization science. *Organization Science, 10*(3), 216–32.

Andreessen, M. (2011). Why software is eating the world. *Wall Street Journal, 20*(2011), C2.

Anuradha, J. (2015). A brief introduction on Big Data 5Vs characteristics and Hadoop technology. *Procedia Computer Science, 48*, 319–24.

Arend, R.J., Sarooghi, H., & Burkemper, A. (2015). Effectuation as ineffectual? Applying the 3E theory-assessment framework to a proposed new theory of entrepreneurship. *Academy of Management Review, 40*(4), 630–51.

Ariely, D., & Jones, S. (2008). *Predictably irrational*. New York, NY: Harper Audio.

Arora, P., Haynie, J.M., & Laurence, G.A. (2013). Counterfactual thinking and entrepreneurial self-efficacy: The moderating role of self-esteem and dispositional affect. *Entrepreneurship Theory and Practice, 37*(2), 359–85.

Ashton, K. (2009). That 'internet of things' thing. *RFID Journal, 22*(7), 97–114.

Aswani, R., Kar, A.K., Ilavarasan, P.V., & Dwivedi, Y.K. (2018). Search engine marketing is not all gold: Insights from Twitter and SEOClerks. *International Journal of Information Management, 38*(1), 107–16.

Aulet, B. (2013). *Disciplined entrepreneurship: 24 steps to a successful startup*. Hoboken, NJ: John Wiley & Sons.

Autio, E., Nambisan, S., Thomas, L.D., & Wright, M. (2018). Digital affordances, spatial affordances, and the genesis of entrepreneurial ecosystems. *Strategic Entrepreneurship Journal, 12*(1), 72–95.

AWS. (2020). *Dropbox migrates 34 PB of data to an Amazon S3 data lake for analytics*. Amazon Web Service. Retrieved November 26, 2021 from https://aws.amazon.com/solutions/case-studies/dropbox-s3/.

Baker, T., & Nelson, R.E. (2005). Creating something from nothing: Resource construction through entrepreneurial bricolage. *Administrative Science Quarterly, 50*(3), 329–66.

Baker, T., Miner, A.S., & Eesley, D.T. (2003). Improvising firms: Bricolage, account giving and improvisational competencies in the founding process. *Research policy, 32*(2), 255–76.

Baller, S., Dutta, S., & Lanvin, B. (2016). *Global information technology report 2016*. Geneva: Ouranos.

Bandura, A. (2012). On the functional properties of perceived self-efficacy revisited. *Journal of Management, 38*(1), 9–44.

Bandura, A., & Locke, E.A. (2003). Negative self-efficacy and goal effects revisited. *Journal of Applied Psychology, 88*(1), 87.

Barad, K. (2003). Posthumanist performativity: Toward an understanding of how matter comes to matter. *Signs: Journal of Women in Culture and Society, 28*(3), 801–31.

Barad, K. (2007). *Meeting the universe halfway: Quantum physics and the entanglement of matter and meaning*. Durham, NC: Duke University Press.

Barney, J. (1991). Firm resources and sustained competitive advantage. *Journal of Management, 17*(1), 99–120.

Barney, J.B., & Clark, D.N. (2007). *Resource-based theory: Creating and sustaining competitive advantage*. Oxford University Press on Demand.

Baron, R.A. (1998). Cognitive mechanisms in entrepreneurship: Why and when entrepreneurs think differently than other people. *Journal of Business Venturing, 13*(4), 275–94.

Baron, R.A. (2000). Counterfactual thinking and venture formation: The potential effects of thinking about "what might have been". *Journal of Business Venturing, 15*(1), 79–91.

Baron, R.A. (2004). The cognitive perspective: A valuable tool for answering entrepreneurship's basic 'why' questions. *Journal of Business Venturing, 19*(2), 221–39.

Baron, R.A., & Ensley, M.D. (2006). Opportunity recognition as the detection of meaningful patterns: Evidence from comparisons of novice and experienced entrepreneurs. *Management Science, 52*(9), 1331–44.

Baron, R.A., & Henry, R.A. (2010). How entrepreneurs acquire the capacity to excel: Insights from research on expert performance. *Strategic Entrepreneurship Journal, 4*(1), 49–65.

Baron, R.A., & Markman, G.D. (2003). Beyond social capital: The role of entrepreneurs' social competence in their financial success. *Journal of Business Venturing, 18*(1), 41–60.

Barreto, H. (1989). *The entrepreneur in micro-economic theory: Disappearance and explanation*. New York, NY: Routledge.

Barrett, M., Davidson, E., Prabhu, J., & Vargo, S.L. (2015). Service innovation in the digital age: Key contributions and future directions. *MIS Quarterly, 39*(1), 135–54.

Baumeister, R.F., & Alquist, J.L. (2009). Self-regulation as a limited resource: Strength model of control and depletion. In J. Forgas, R. Baumeister, & D. Tice (eds) *Psychology of Self-regulation: Cognitive, Affective, and Motivational Processes*, (pp. 21–33). New York, NY: Psychology Press.

Baumol, W.J. (1996). Entrepreneurship: Productive, unproductive, and destructive. *Journal of Business Venturing, 11*(1), 3–22.

Beckman, C., Eisenhardt, K., Kotha, S., Meyer, A., & Rajagopalan, N. (2012). Technology entrepreneurship. *Strategic Entrepreneurship Journal, 6*(2), 89–93. doi: 10.1002/sej.1134.

Bell, J., & Loane, S. (2010). 'New-wave' global firms: Web 2.0 and SME internationalisation. *Journal of Marketing Management, 26*(3–4), 213–29.

Benbya, H., & McKelvey, B. (2006). Toward a complexity theory of information systems development. *Information Technology & People, 19*(1), 12–34.

Benkler, Y. (2008). *The wealth of networks.* Cambridge, MA: Yale University Press.

Benner, M.J., & Tushman, M.L. (2015). Reflections on the 2013 Decade Award – 'Exploitation, Exploration, and Process Management: The Productivity Dilemma Revisited' ten years later. *Academy of Management Review, 40*(4), 497–514.

Bennett, N., & Lemoine, J. (2014). What VUCA really means for you. *Harvard Business Review, 92*(1/2), 27–42.

Berglund, H., Dimov, D., & Wennberg, K. (2018). Beyond bridging rigor and relevance: The three-body problem in entrepreneurship. *Journal of Business Venturing Insights, 9*, 87–91.

Bhave, M.P. (1994). A process model of entrepreneurial venture creation. *Journal of Business Venturing, 9*(3), 223–42.

Blank, S. (2013). Why the lean start-up changes everything. *Harvard Business Review, 91*(5), 63–72.

Blank, S. (2014). *Born global or die local – building a regional startup playbook.* SteveBlank.com, October 31. Retrieved February 4, 2019 from https://bit.ly/2tFl18p.

Blank, S., & Dorf, B. (2012). *The startup owner's manual: The step-by-step guide for building a great company* (Vol. 1). Pescadero, CA: K&S Ranch.

Brinckmann, J., Grichnik, D., & Kapsa, D. (2010). Should entrepreneurs plan or just storm the castle? A meta-analysis on contextual factors impacting the business planning–performance relationship in small firms. *Journal of Business Venturing, 25*(1), 24–40.

Brockhaus, R.H. (1980). Risk taking propensity of entrepreneurs. *Academy of Management Journal, 23*, 509–520.

Brown, M., & Ellis, S. (2017). *Hacking growth: How today's fastest-growing companies drive breakout success.* London: Random House.

Brown, T. (2008). *Design thinking.* Harvard Business Review Press.

Brown, T., & Katz, B. (2011). *Change by design: How design thinking transforms organizations and inspires innovation.* New York, NY: Harper Business.

Bruyat, C., & Julien, P.A. (2001). Defining the field of research in entrepreneurship. *Journal of Business Venturing, 16*(2), 165–80.

Brynjolfsson, E., & McAfee, A. (2014). *The second machine age: Work, progress, and prosperity in a time of brilliant technologies.* New York, NY: W.W. Norton & Company.

Brynjolfsson, E., McAfee, A., Sorell, M., & Zhu, F. (2008). Scale without mass: Business process replication and industry dynamics. *Harvard Business School Technology & Operations Management Unit Research Paper*, 07-016.

Buchanan, R. (1992). Wicked problems in design thinking. *Design Issues, 8*(2), 5–21.

Buckley, A.P., & Nzembayie, K.F. (2016, May). Teacherpreneurs: From vocation to innovation. In *ICIE2016 – Proceedings of the 4th International Conference on Innovation and Entrepreneurship: ICIE2016* (p. 36).

Bughin, J., Windhagen, E., Smit, S., Mischke, J., Sjatil, P.E., & Gürich, B. (2019). *Innovation in Europe. Changing the game to regain a competitive edge.* Discussion Paper. Retrieved November 25, 2021 from https://www. mckinsey. com/~/media/mckinsey/featured% 20insights/innovation/reviving% 20innovation% 20in% 20europe/mgi-innovation-in-europe-discussion-paperoct2019-vf. pdf).

Bygrave, W. (2007). The entrepreneurship paradigm (I) revisited. In H. Neergard & J. Parm Ulhoi (eds), *Handbook of qualitative research methods in entrepreneurship* (pp. 17–48). Cheltenham, UK and Northampton, MA, USA: Edward Elgar Publishing.

Bygstad, B., Munkvold, B.E., & Volkoff, O. (2016). Identifying generative mechanisms through affordances: A framework for critical realist data analysis. *Journal of Information Technology, 31*(1), 83–96.

Cantillon, R. (1732) (Higgs, H. trans. 1931). *Essai Sur la Nature du Commerce en General.* London: Macmillan.

Carrier, C., Raymond, L., & Eltaief, A. (2004). Cyberentrepreneurship: A multiple case study. *International Journal of Entrepreneurial Behavior & Research, 10*(5), 349–63.

Casson, M. (1982). *The entrepreneur: An economic theory.* Lanham, MD: Rowman & Littlefield.

CB Insights. (2019). *Why startups fail: Top 12 reasons | CB insights.* CB Insights Research. Retrieved November 23, 2021 from https://www.cbinsights.com/research/ startup-failure-reasons-top/.

Ceccagnoli, M., Forman, C., Huang, P., & Wu, D.J. (2012). Co-creation of value in a platform ecosystem: The case of enterprise software. *MIS Quarterly, 36*(1), 263–90.

Cecez-Kecmanovic, D., Galliers, R.D., Henfridsson, O., Newell, S., & Vidgen, R. (2014). The sociomateriality of information systems: Current status, future directions. *MIS Quarterly, 38*(3), 809–30.

Cefis, E., & Marsili, O. (2012). Going, going, gone: Exit forms and the innovative capabilities of firms. *Research Policy, 41*(5), 795–807.

Cervone, H.F. (2011). Understanding agile project management methods using Scrum. *OCLC Systems & Services: International Digital Library Perspectives.*

Chaffey, D. (2015). *Digital business and e-commerce management: Strategy implementation and practice.* Harlow, UK: Pearson Education.

Chaffey, D., & Smith, P.R. (2017). *Digital marketing excellence: Planning, optimizing and integrating online marketing.* London: Routledge, Taylor & Francis Group.

Chandler, G.N., & Hanks, S.H. (1994). Founder competence, the environment, and venture performance. *Entrepreneurship Theory and Practice, 18*(3), 77–90.

Chandler, G.N., DeTienne, D.R., McKelvie, A., & Mumford, T.V. (2011). Causation and effectuation processes: A validation study. *Journal of Business Venturing, 26*(3), 375–90.

Chesbrough, H.W. (2006). *Open innovation: The new imperative for creating and profiting from technology.* Cambridge, MA: Harvard Business Press.

Chesbrough, H. (2007). Business model innovation: It's not just about technology anymore. *Strategy & Leadership, 35*(6), 12-17.

Chesbrough, H. (2010). Business model innovation: Opportunities and barriers. *Long Range Planning, 43*(2), 354–63.

Chesbrough, H., & Rosenbloom, R.S. (2002). The role of the business model in capturing value from innovation: Evidence from Xerox Corporation's technology spin-off companies. *Industrial and Corporate Change, 11*(3), 529–55.

Chi, C. (2021, July 26). *Tam Sam Som: What do they mean & how do you calculate them?* HubSpot Blog. Retrieved November 23, 2021 from https://blog.hubspot.com/marketing/tam-sam-som.

Child, J., & McGrath, R.G. (2001). Organizations unfettered: Organizational form in an information-intensive economy. *Academy of Management Journal, 44*(6), 1135–48.

Chrisman, J.J., Bauerschmidt, A., & Hofer, C.W. (1998). The determinants of new venture performance: An extended model. *Entrepreneurship Theory and Practice, 23*(1), 5–29.

Christensen, C.M. (2013). *The innovator's dilemma: When new technologies cause great firms to fail.* Cambridge, MA: Harvard Business Review Press.

Cimpanu, C. (2020). *AWS said it mitigated a 2.3 Tbps DDoS attack, the largest ever.* ZDNet. Retrieved November 26, 2021 from https://www.zdnet.com/article/aws-said-it-mitigated-a-2-3-tbps-ddos-attack-the-largest-ever/.

Coad, A. (2007). Firm growth: A survey. In *Papers on Economics and Evolution 2007–03, Max Planck Institute of Economics, Evolutionary Economics Group.*

Coghlan, D. (2019). *Doing action research in your own organization.* Thousand Oaks, CA: Sage.

Cohen, W.M., & Levinthal, D.A. (1990). Absorptive capacity: A new perspective on learning and innovation. *Administrative Science Quarterly, 35,* 128–52.

Cohen, W.M., & Levinthal, D.A. (1994). Fortune favors the prepared firm. *Management Science, 40*(2), 227–51.

Coleman, J.S. (1988). Social capital in the creation of human capital. *American Journal of Sociology, 94,* S95–S120.

Constantinides, P., Henfridsson, O., & Parker, G.G. (2018). Introduction: Platforms and infrastructures in the digital age. *Information Systems Research, 29*(2), 381–400.

Cooney, T.M. (2005). Editorial: What is an entrepreneurial team? *International Small Business Journal, 23*(3), 226–35. doi:10.1177/0266242605052131.

Coursera. (2019). *2019's most popular courses.* Coursera. Retrieved November 26, 2021 from https://www.coursera.org/collections/popular-courses-2019.

Croll, A., & Yoskovitz, B. (2013). *Lean analytics: Use data to build a better startup faster.* Sebastopol, CA: O'Reilly.

Cumming, D. (2008). Contracts and exits in venture capital finance. *The Review of Financial Studies, 21*(5), 1947–82.

David, T. (2014, December 30). Your elevator pitch needs an elevator pitch. *Harvard Business Reviews Blog,* Dec 30.

Davidson, E., & Vaast, E. (2010, January). Digital entrepreneurship and its sociomaterial enactment. In *hicss* (pp. 1–10). doi:10.1108.HICSS.2010.150.

Davidsson, P. (2003). The domain of entrepreneurship research: Some suggestions. *Advances in Entrepreneurship, Firm Emergence and Growth, 6*(3), 315–72.

Davidsson, P. (2012). The entrepreneurial process . In S. Carter & D. Jones-Evans (eds), *Enterprise and small business: Principles, practice and policy* (pp. 95–119). Harlow, UK: Pearson Education.

Davidsson, P. (2015). Entrepreneurial opportunities and the entrepreneurship nexus: A re-conceptualization. *Journal of Business Venturing, 30*(5), 674–95.

Davidsson, P. (2016). *Researching entrepreneurship: Conceptualization and design* (2nd edn). New York, NY: Springer.

Davidsson, P. (2021). Ditching discovery-creation for unified venture creation research. *Entrepreneurship Theory and Practice,* 10422587211030870.

Davidsson, P., Delmar, F., & Wiklund, J. (2006). Entrepreneurship as growth: Growth as entrepreneurship. In *Entrepreneurship and the growth of firms* (pp. 21–38). Cheltenham, UK and Northampton, MA, USA: Edward Elgar Publishing.

Davidsson, P., Grégoire, D.A., & Lex, M. (2021). Venture Idea Assessment (VIA): Development of a needed concept, measure, and research agenda. *Journal of Business Venturing, 36*(5), 106130.

Davidsson, P., Recker, J., & von Briel, F. (2020). External enablement of new venture creation: A framework. *Academy of Management Perspectives, 34*(3), 311–32.

Davidsson, P., Steffens, P., & Fitzsimmons, J. (2009). Growing profitable or growing from profits: Putting the horse in front of the cart? *Journal of Business Venturing, 24*(4), 388–406.

De Vries, M.K. (1977). The entrepreneurial personality: A person at the cross-roads. *Journal of Management Studies, 14*(1), 34–57.

DeLanda, M. (2006). *A new philosophy of society: Assemblage theory and social complexity.* London and New York, NY: Continuum.

Delmar, F. (2006). The psychology of the entrepreneur. In S. Carter, & D. Jones-Evans (eds), *Enterprise and small business: Principles, practice and policy* (2nd edn, pp. 152–75). Harlow, UK: Pearson Education.

Delmar, F., & Shane, S. (2003). Does business planning facilitate the development of new ventures? *Strategic Management Journal, 24*(12), 1165–85.

Delmar, F., & Wiklund, J. (2008). The effect of small business managers' growth motivation on firm growth: A longitudinal study. *Entrepreneurship Theory and Practice, 32*(3), 437–57.

Delmar, F., & Witte, F.C. (2012). The psychology of the entrepreneur. In S. Carter, & D. Jones-Evans (eds), *Enterprise and small business: Principles, practice and policy* (3rd edn, pp. 152–78). Harlow, UK: Pearson Education.

Delmar, F., Davidsson, P., & Gartner, W.B. (2003). Arriving at the high-growth firm. *Journal of Business Venturing, 18*(2), 189–216.

DeTienne, D.R. (2010). Entrepreneurial exit as a critical component of the entrepreneurial process: Theoretical development. *Journal of Business Venturing, 25*(2), 203–15.

DeTienne, D.R., & Cardon, M.S. (2012). Impact of founder experience on exit intentions. *Small Business Economics, 38*(4), 351–74.

DeTienne, D.R., & Chandler, G.N. (2004). Opportunity identification and its role in the entrepreneurial classroom: A pedagogical approach and empirical test. *Academy of Management Learning & Education, 3*(3), 242–57.

DeTienne, D.R., McKelvie, A., & Chandler, G.N. (2015). Making sense of entrepreneurial exit strategies: A typology and test. *Journal of Business Venturing, 30*(2), 255–72.

DeTienne, D.R., Shepherd, D.A., & De Castro, J.O. (2008). The fallacy of 'only the strong survive': The effects of extrinsic motivation on the persistence decisions for under-performing firms. *Journal of Business Venturing, 23*(5), 528–46.

Dew, N., Read, S., Sarasvathy, S.D., & Wiltbank, R. (2009). Effectual versus predictive logics in entrepreneurial decision-making: Differences between experts and novices. *Journal of Business Venturing 24*(4), 287–309.

Dimov, D. (2007). Beyond the single-person, single-insight attribution in understanding entrepreneurial opportunities. *Entrepreneurship Theory and Practice, 31*(5), 713–31.

Dimov, D. (2011). Grappling with the unbearable elusiveness of entrepreneurial opportunities. *Entrepreneurship Theory and Practice, 35*(1), 57–81.

Dimov, D.P. (2012). Entrepreneurial opportunities. In S. Carter, & D. Jones-Evans (eds), *Enterprise and small business: Principles, practice and policy* (3rd edn, pp. 120–34). Harlow, UK: Pearson Education.

Dobbs, M., & Hamilton, R.T. (2007). Small business growth: Recent evidence and new directions. *International Journal of Entrepreneurial Behavior & Research, 13*(5), 296–322.

Drucker, P.F. (1985). *Innovation and entrepreneurship practices and principles*. New York, NY: Harper & Row.

Duckworth, A.L., & Quinn, P.D. (2009). Development and validation of the Short Grit Scale (GRIT–S). *Journal of Personality Assessment, 91*(2), 166–74.

Dweck, C. (2015). Carol Dweck revisits the growth mindset. *Education Week, 35*(5), 20–4.

Eagly, A.H., & Chaiken, S. (1993). *The psychology of attitudes*. Forth Worth, TX: Harcourt Brace Jovanovich College Publishers.

Eagly, A.H., & Chaiken, S. (2007). The advantages of an inclusive definition of attitude. *Social Cognition, 25*(5), 582.

Eckhardt, J.T., & Shane, S.A. (2003). Opportunities and entrepreneurship. *Journal of Management, 29*(3), 333–49.

Eckhardt, J.T., & Shane, S.A. (2013). Response to the commentaries: The individual-opportunity (IO) nexus integrates objective and subjective aspects of entrepreneurship. *Academy of Management Review, 38*(1), 160–3.

Eisenmann, T.R., Ries, E., & Dillard, S. (2013). *Hypothesis-driven entrepreneurship: The lean startup*. Cambridge, MA: Harvard Business Review Press.

Ekbia, H.R. (2009). Digital artifacts as quasi-objects: Qualification, mediation, and materiality. *Journal of the American Society for Information Science and Technology, 60*(12), 2554–66.

Erikson, T., & Korsgaard, S. (2016). Knowledge as the source of opportunity. *Journal of Business Venturing Insights, 6*, 47–50.

European Commission. (2019). *White Paper on Artificial Intelligence – a European approach to excellence and trust*. European Commission, Brussels.

European Commission. (2020). *Digital Economy and Society Index (Desi) 2020 – human capital*. European Commission, Brussels.

Europol. (2021). *DarkMarket: World's largest illegal dark web marketplace taken down*. Europol. Retrieved November 26, 2021 from https://www.europol.europa.eu/newsroom/news/darkmarket-worlds-largest-illegal-dark-web-marketplace-taken-down.

Evans, P., & Wurster, T.S. (1999). Getting real about virtual commerce. *Harvard Business Review* (Vol. 77, No. 6, pp. 85–94).

Farrell, J., & Klemperer, P. (2007). Coordination and lock-in: Competition with switching costs and network effects. In M. Armstrong & R.H. Porter (eds), *Handbook of industrial organization* (Vol. 3, Chapter 5). Amsterdam: North Holland.

Fauchart, E., & Gruber, M. (2011). Darwinians, communitarians, and missionaries: The role of founder identity in entrepreneurship. *Academy of Management Journal, 54*(5), 935–57.

Faulkner, P., & Runde, J. (2009). On the identity of technological objects and user innovations in function. *Academy of Management Review, 34*(3), 442–62.

Faulkner, P., & Runde, J. (2012). On sociomateriality. In P. Leonardi, B. Nardi, & J. Kallinikos (eds), *Materiality and organizing,* (pp. 49–66). Oxford: Oxford University Press.

Fisher, G. (2012). Effectuation, causation, and bricolage: A behavioral comparison of emerging theories in entrepreneurship research. *Entrepreneurship Theory and Practice, 36*(5), 1019–51.

Fiss, P.C. (2011). Building better causal theories: A fuzzy set approach to typologies in organization research. *Academy of Management Journal, 54*(2), 393–420.

Fixson, S.K., & Rao, J. (2011). Creation logic in innovation: From action learning to expertise. In D. Greenberg, K. McKone-Sweet, & H.J. Wilson (eds), *The new entrepreneurial leader: Developing leaders who create social, environmental, and economic value in an unknowable world*, 43–61. San Fransisco, CA: Berrett-Koehler.

Flavell, J.H. (1979). Metacognition and cognitive monitoring: A new area of cognitive–developmental inquiry. *American Psychologist, 34*(10), 906.

Förderer, J., Kude, T., Schütz, S., & Heinzl, A. (2014). Control versus generativity: A complex adaptive systems perspective on platforms. In *International Conference on Information Systems 2014, December 14–17*.

Forgas, J.P., Scholar, F.E.E., Baumeister, R.F., & Tice, D.M. (eds) (2011). *Psychology of self-regulation: Cognitive, affective, and motivational processes*. New York, NY: Psychology Press.

Furr, N., & Ahlstrom, P. (2011). *Nail it then scale it: The entrepreneur's guide to creating and managing breakthrough innovation* (No. 658.421 FUR. CIMMYT).

Furr, N., & Dyer, J. (2014, December 31). Choose the right innovation method at the right time. *Harvard Business Review, 12*, 1–6.

Gabrielsson, M., & Kirpalani, V.M. (2004). Born globals: How to reach new business space rapidly. *International Business Review, 13*(5), 555–71.

Gaglio, C.M., & Katz, J.A. (2001). The psychological basis of opportunity identification: Entrepreneurial alertness. *Small Business Economics, 16*(2), 95–111.

Galloway, S. (2017). *The four: The hidden DNA of Amazon, Apple, Facebook and Google*. London: Bantam Press.

Gartner, W.B. (1985). A conceptual framework for describing the phenomenon of new venture creation. *Academy of Management Review, 10*(4), 696–706.

Gartner, W.B. (1988). 'Who is an Entrepreneur?' is the wrong question. *American Small Business Journal, 12*(4), 11–31.

Gartner, W.B. (1990). What are we talking about when we talk about entrepreneurship? *Journal of Business Venturing, 5*(1), 15–28.

Gartner, W.B,, & Carter, N. (2003). Entrepreneurial behaviour and firm organizing processes. In Z. Acs & D. Audretsch (eds), *International handbook of entrepreneurship*, (pp. 99–127). New York, NY: Springer.

Gartner. (2019). *The data center is (almost) dead*. Smarter With Gartner. Retrieved November 26, 2021 from https://www.gartner.com/smarterwithgartner/the-data-center-is-almost-dead/.

Gartner. (2021). *Gartner forecasts worldwide public cloud end-user spending to grow 23% in 2021*. Gartner. Retrieved November 26, 2021 from https://gtnr.it/3wOpt38.

Garud, R., & Gehman, J. (2016). Theory evaluation, entrepreneurial processes, and performativity. *Academy of Management Review, 41*(3), 544–9.

Garud, R., & Giuliani, A.P. (2013). A narrative perspective on entrepreneurial opportunities. *Academy of Management Review, 38*(1), 157–60.

Garud, R., & Karnøe, P. (2003). Bricolage versus breakthrough: Distributed and embedded agency in technology entrepreneurship. *Research Policy, 32*(2), 277–300.

Garud, R., Gehman, J., & Giuliani, A.P. (2014). Contextualizing entrepreneurial innovation: A narrative perspective. *Research Policy, 43*(7), 1177–88.

Garud, R., Gehman, J., & Giuliani, A.P. (2018). Why not take a performative approach to entrepreneurship? *Journal of Business Venturing Insights*, *9*, 60–4.

Garud, R., Jain, S., & Tuertscher, P. (2009). Incomplete by design and designing for incompleteness. In K. Lyytinen, P. Loucopoulos, J. Mylopoulos, & B. Robinson (eds), *Design requirements engineering: A ten-year perspective* (Vol. 14, pp. 137–56). Berlin, Heidelberg: Springer.

Garud, R., Kumaraswamy, A., & Karnøe, P. (2010). Path dependence or path creation? *Journal of Management Studies*, *47*(4), 760–74.

Gawer, A., & Cusumano, M.A. (2014). Industry platforms and ecosystem innovation. *Journal of Product Innovation Management*, *31*(3), 417–33.

George, G., & Bock, A.J. (2011). The business model in practice and its implications for entrepreneurship research. *Entrepreneurship Theory and Practice*, *35*(1), 83–111.

Ghezzi, A., & Cavallo, A. (2020). Agile business model innovation in digital entrepreneurship: Lean startup approaches. *Journal of Business Research*, *110*, 519–37.

Gibson, J.J. (1977). The theory of affordances. In R. Shaw, & J. Bransford (eds), *Perceiving, acting, and knowing: toward an ecological psychology* (pp. 67–82). Hillsdale, NJ: Lawrence Erlbaum.

Giones, F., & Brem, A. (2017). Digital technology entrepreneurship: A definition and research agenda. *Technology Innovation Management Review*, *7*(5), 44–51.

Granovetter, M.S. (1973). The strength of weak ties. *American Journal of Sociology*, *78*(6), 1360–80.

Grant, K.A. (2007). Tacit knowledge revisited – we can still learn from Polanyi. *Electronic Journal of Knowledge Management*, *5*(2), 173–80.

Grant, R.M. (1996). Towards a knowledge-based theory of the firm. *Strategic Management Journal*, *17*(S2), 109–22.

Greenberg, D., McKone-Sweet, K., & Wilson, H.J. (2011). *The new entrepreneurial leader: Developing leaders who shape social and economic opportunity*. San Francisco, CA: Berrett-Koehler Publishers.

Grégoire, D.A., & Shepherd, D.A. (2012). Technology-market combinations and the identification of entrepreneurial opportunities: An investigation of the opportunity-individual nexus. *Academy of Management Journal*, *55*(4), 753–85.

Grégoire, D.A., Barr, P.S., & Shepherd, D.A. (2010). Cognitive processes of opportunity recognition: The role of structural alignment. *Organization Science*, *21*(2), 413–31.

Greiner, L. (1972, July–August). Development and transition in an organization's growth. *Harvard Business Review*.

Gross, N. (2009). A pragmatist theory of social mechanisms. *American Sociological Review*, *74*(3), 358–79.

GSMA. (2020). *The mobile economy 2020*. Retrieved April 17, 2021 from https://www.gsma.com/mobileeconomy/.

Gupta, V., MacMillan, I.C., & Surie, G. (2004). Entrepreneurial leadership: Developing and measuring a cross-cultural construct. *Journal of Business Venturing*, *19*(2), 241–60.

Gustafsson, V. (2006). *Entrepreneurial decision-making: Individuals, tasks and cognitions*. Cheltenham, UK and Northampton, MA, USA: Edward Elgar Publishing.

Hagiu, A., & Rothman, S. (2016). Network effects aren't enough. *Harvard Business Review*, *94*(4), 17.

Halligan, B., & Shah, D. (2009). *Inbound marketing: Get found using Google, social media, and blogs*. Hoboken, NJ: John Wiley & Sons.

Harper, D.A. (2008). Towards a theory of entrepreneurial teams. *Journal of Business Venturing*, *23*(6), 613–26.

Harrison, J.S., Hitt, M.A., Hoskisson, R.E., & Ireland, R.D. (2001). Resource complementarity in business combinations: Extending the logic to organizational alliances. *Journal of Management*, *27*(6), 679–90.

Havnes, P.A., & Senneseth, K. (2001). A panel study of firm growth among SMEs in networks. *Small Business Economics*, *16*(4), 293–302.

Hayek, F.A. (1945). The use of knowledge in society. *The American Economic Review*, *35*(4), 519–30.

Haynie, J.M., Shepherd, D., Mosakowski, E., & Earley, P.C. (2010). A situated metacognitive model of the entrepreneurial mindset. *Journal of Business Venturing*, *25*(2), 217–29.

Hazarbassanova, D.B. (2016). The value creation logic and the internationalisation of internet firms. *Review of International Business and Strategy*, *26*(3), 349–70.

Henderson, R.M., & Clark, K.B. (1990). Architectural innovation: The reconfiguration of existing product technologies and the failure of established firms. *Administrative Science Quarterly*, *35*(1), 9–30.

Henfridsson, O., & Bygstad, B. (2013). The generative mechanisms of digital infrastructure evolution. *MIS Quarterly*, *37*(3), 907–31.

Hennart, J.F. (2014). The accidental internationalists: A theory of born globals. *Entrepreneurship Theory and Practice*, *38*(1), 117–35.

Hisrich, R.D., Peters, M.P., & Shepherd, D.A. (2008). *Entrepreneurship* (7th edn). New York, NY: McGraw-Hill.

Hmieleski, K.M., & Baron, R.A. (2008). Regulatory focus and new venture performance: A study of entrepreneurial opportunity exploitation under conditions of risk versus uncertainty. *Strategic Entrepreneurship Journal*, *2*(4), 285–99.

Hmieleski, K.M., & Baron, R.A. (2009). Entrepreneurs' optimism and new venture performance: A social cognitive perspective. *Academy of Management Journal*, *52*(3), 473–88.

Höchstötter, N., & Lewandowski, D. (2009). What users see–Structures in search engine results pages. *Information Sciences*, *179*(12), 1796–1812.

Holiday, R. (2014). *Growth hacker marketing: A primer on the future of PR, marketing, and advertising*. London: Penguin.

HolonIQ. (2020). Global EdTech market to reach $404B by 2025 – 16.3% CAGR. HolonIQ. Retrieved November 26, 2021 from https://www.holoniq.com/notes/global-education-technology-market-to-reach-404b-by-2025/.

Huang, J.C., Henfridsson, O., Liu, M.J., & Newell, S. (2017). Growing on steroids: Rapidly scaling the user base of digital ventures through digital innovation. *MIS Quarterly*, *41*(1), 301–14.

Huffman, J. (2018). *The growth marketer's playbook: A strategic guide to growing a business in today's digital world*. Seattle, WA: Jim Huffman.

Hull, C.E.K., Hung, Y.T.C., Hair, N., Perotti, V., & DeMartino, R. (2007). Taking advantage of digital opportunities: A typology of digital entrepreneurship. *International Journal of Networking and Virtual Organisations*, *4*(3), 290–303.

Hunter, R., Hughes, M., Liu, K., Ethridge, D., & Picard, N. (2018). Global top 100 companies by market capitalisation. *PricewaterhouseCoopers (PwC)*.

IDC. (2020). *IOT growth demands rethink of long-term storage strategies, says IDC*. Retrieved December 15, 2021, from https://www.idc.com/getdoc.jsp?containerId=prAP46737220

Irish Times. (2014). *Cantillon: Why isn't Stripe based in Ireland?* Retrieved 10 June, 2021 from https://www.irishtimes.com/business/technology/cantillon-why-isn-t -stripe-based-in-ireland-1.1689208.

ITU. (2019). *Measuring digital development: Facts and figures 2019*. International Telecommunication Union.

ITU. (2020). *Digital skills insights 2020*. International Telecommunication Union.

Jia, J., Jin, G.Z., & Wagman, L. (2020). GDPR and the localness of venture investment. Available at SSRN 3436535.

Johnson, G., Shriver, S., & Goldberg, S. (2020). Privacy & market concentration: Intended & unintended consequences of the GDPR. https://dx.doi.org/10.2139/ ssrn.3477686.

Kahneman, D. (2011). *Thinking, fast and slow*. New York, NY: Farrar, Straus and Giroux.

Kahneman, D., & Lovallo, D. (1994). Timid choices and bold forecasts: A cognitive perspective on risk taking. *Management Science, 39*(1), 17–31.

Kahneman, D., & Miller, D.T. (1986). Norm theory: Comparing reality to its alternatives. *Psychological Review, 93*(2), 136.

Kahneman, D., Slovic, P., & Tversky, A. (1982). *Judgment under uncertainty: Heuristics and biases*. Cambridge University Press.

Kahneman, D., & Tversky, A. (1979). Prospect theory: An analysis of decision under risk. *Econometrica: Journal of the Econometric Society, 47*(2) 263–92.

Kahneman, D., Knetsch, J.L., & Thaler, R.H. (1991). Anomalies: The endowment effect, loss aversion, and status quo bias. *The Journal of Economic Perspectives, 5*(1), 193–206.

Kallinikos, J., Aaltonen, A., & Marton, A. (2013). The ambivalent ontology of digital artifacts. *MIS Quarterly, 37*(2), 357–70.

Kannan, P., & Li, H. (2017). Digital marketing: A framework, review and research agenda. *International Journal of Research in Marketing, 34*(1), 22–45. Doi:10.1016/ j.ijresmar.2016.11.006.

Katz, M.L., & Shapiro, C. (1986). Technology adoption in the presence of network externalities. *Journal of Political Economy, 94*(4), 822–41.

Kauffman, G.B. (1994). Chaos and order: The complex structure of living systems. *American Scientist, 82*(5), 476–8.

Kazanjian, R.K., & Drazin, R. (1990). A stage-contingent model of design and growth for technology based new ventures. *Journal of Business Venturing, 5*(3), 137–50.

Kelley, T., & Littman, J. (2001). The art of innovation: Success through innovation the IDEO way. New York, NY: Currency.

Kelley, T., & Littman, J. (2005). *The ten faces of innovation*. New York, NY: Currency/ Doubleday.

Kemp, S. (2021). *Digital 2021: Global overview report – deteriorate – global digital insights*. [online] DataReportal – Global Digital Insights. Retrieved May 17, 2021 from https://datareportal.com/reports/digital-2021-global-overview-report.

Kerr, W.R., Nanda, R., & Rhodes-Kropf, M. (2014). Entrepreneurship as experimentation. *The Journal of Economic Perspectives, 28*(3), 25–48.

Khan, M.A., & Salah, K. (2018). IoT security: Review, blockchain solutions, and open challenges. *Future Generation Computer Systems, 82*, 395–411.

Khelil, N. (2016). The many faces of entrepreneurial failure: Insights from an empirical taxonomy. *Journal of Business Venturing, 31*(1), 72–94.

Kidwell, J.J., Vander Linde, K., & Johnson, S.L. (2000). Applying corporate knowledge management practices in higher education. *Educause Quarterly, 23*(4), 28–33.

Kihlstrom, R.E., & Laffont, J.J. (1979). A general equilibrium entrepreneurial theory of firm formation based on risk aversion. *Journal of Political Economy, 87*(4), 719–48.

Kim, P.H., & Aldrich, H.E. (2017). Urban legends or sage guidance: A review of common advice about entrepreneurial teams. In C. Ben-Hafaïedh & T.M. Cooney (eds), *Research handbook on entrepreneurial teams: Theory and practice* (pp. 45–72). Cheltenham, UK and Northampton, MA, USA: Edward Elgar Publishing.

Kirzner, I.M. (1973). *Competition and entrepreneurship*. Chicago, IL: University of Chicago Press.

Kirzner, I.M. (1979). *Perception, opportunity, and profit: Studies in the theory of entrepreneurship*. Chicago, IL: University of Chicago Press.

Kirzner, I.M. (1980). The primacy of entrepreneurial discovery. In A. Seldon (ed), *The prime mover of progress: The entrepreneur in capitalism and socialism* (pp. 1–30). London: The Institute of Economic Affairs.

Kirzner, I.M. (1997). Entrepreneurial discovery and the competitive market process: An Austrian approach. *Journal of Economic Literature, 35*(1), 60–85.

Klein, P.G. (2008). Opportunity discovery, entrepreneurial action, and economic organization. *Strategic Entrepreneurship Journal, 2*(3), 175–90.

Klofsten, M. (1994). Technology-based firms: Critical aspects of their early development. *Journal of Enterprising Culture, 2*(1), 535–57.

Knickrehm, M., Berthon, B., & Daugherty, P. (2016). Digital disruption: The growth multiplier. Optimizing digital investments to realize higher productivity and growth. *Accenture*.

Knight, F.H. (1921). *Risk, uncertainty and profit*. New York, NY: Hart, Schaffner and Marx.

Knight, G.A., & Cavusgil, S.T. (2004). Innovation, organizational capabilities, and the born-global firm. *Journal of International Business Studies, 35*(2), 124–41.

Kolko, J. (2011). *Exposing the magic of design: A practitioner's guide to the methods and theory of synthesis*. New York, NY: Oxford University Press.

Kollmann, T. (2006). What is e-entrepreneurship? Fundamentals of company founding in the net economy. *International Journal of Technology Management, 33*(4), 322–40.

Kolvereid, L., & Bullvag, E. (1996). Growth intentions and actual growth: The impact of entrepreneurial choice. *Journal of Enterprising Culture, 4*(1), 1–17.

Koolman, G. (1971). Say's conception of the role of the entrepreneur. *Economica*, 269–86.

Kotler, P., Kartajaya, H., & Setiawan, I. (2016). *Marketing 4.0: Moving from traditional to digital*. Hoboken, NJ: John Wiley & Sons.

Kraus, S., Palmer, C., Kailer, N., Kallinger, F.L., & Spitzer, J. (2018). Digital entrepreneurship: A research agenda on new business models for the twenty-first century. *International Journal of Entrepreneurial Behavior & Research, 25*(2), 353–75.

Krueger, N.F., Reilly, M.D., & Carsrud, A.L. (2000). Competing models of entrepreneurial intentions. *Journal of Business Venturing, 15*(5), 411–32.

Kunkel, S.W. (2001). Toward a typology of entrepreneurial activities. *Academy of Entrepreneurship Journal, 7*(1), 75–90.

Kuratko, D.F. (2016). *Entrepreneurship: Theory, process, and practice*. Boston, MA: Cengage Learning.

Ladd, T. (2016). The limits of the lean startup method. *Harvard Business Review, 94*(3), 2–3.

Langley, A. (1999). Strategies for theorizing from process data. *Academy of Management Review, 24*(4), 691–710.

Latour, B. (2005). *Reassembling the social: An introduction to actor-network-theory.* Oxford: Oxford University Press.

Laudon, K.C., & Traver, C.G. (2019). *E-commerce 2018: Business, technology, society* (14th edn). Harlow, UK: Pearson.

Layton, M.C., Ostermiller, S.J., & Kynaston, D.J. (2020). *Agile project management for dummies.* Hoboken, NJ: John Wiley & Sons.

Law Library of Congress. (2018). *Regulation of cryptocurrency around the world.* The Law Library of Congress, Global Legal Research Center.

Leitch, C., Hill, F., & Neergaard, H. (2010). Entrepreneurial and business growth and the quest for a 'comprehensive theory': Tilting at windmills? *Entrepreneurship Theory and Practice, 34*(2), 249–60.

Leonardi, P.M. (2011). When flexible routines meet flexible technologies: Affordance, constraint, and the imbrication of human and material agencies. *MIS Quarterly, 35,* 147–67.

Leonardi, P.M. (2012). Materiality, sociomateriality, and socio-technical systems: What do these terms mean? How are they related? Do we need them? In P.M. Leonardi, B.A. Nardi, & J. Kallinikos (eds), *Materiality and Organizing: Social Interaction in a Technological World,* (pp. 25–48). Oxford: Oxford University Press.

Liao, J., Welsch, H., & Tan, W.L. (2005). Venture gestation paths of nascent entrepreneurs: Exploring the temporal patterns. *The Journal of High Technology Management Research, 16*(1), 1–22.

Lichtenstein, B.B., Carter, N.M., Dooley, K.J., & Gartner, W.B. (2007). Complexity dynamics of nascent entrepreneurship. *Journal of Business Venturing, 22*(2), 236–61.

Lichtenthaler, U. (2009). Absorptive capacity, environmental turbulence, and the complementarity of organizational learning processes. *Academy of Management Journal, 52*(4), 822–46.

Lipshitz, R., & Strauss, O. (1997). Coping with uncertainty: A naturalistic decision-making analysis. *Organizational Behavior and Human Decision Processes, 69*(2), 149–63.

Loane, S., McNaughton, R.B., & Bell, J. (2004). The internationalization of internet-enabled entrepreneurial firms: Evidence from Europe and North America. *Canadian Journal of Administrative Sciences/Revue Canadienne des Sciences de l'Administration, 21*(1), 79–96.

Lovallo, D., & Kahneman, D. (2003). Delusions of success. *Harvard Business Review, 81*(7), 56–63.

Low, M.B. (2001). The adolescence of entrepreneurship research: Specification of purpose. *Entrepreneurship Theory and Practice, 25*(4), 17–26.

Low, M.B., & MacMillan, I.C. (1988). Entrepreneurship: Past research and future challenges. *Journal of Management, 14*(2), 139–61.

Lumpkin, G.T., & Dess, G.G. (1996). Clarifying the entrepreneurial orientation construct and linking it to performance. *Academy of Management Review, 21*(1), 135–72.

Lund, S., & Manyika, J. (2017). *Defending digital globalization.* Retrieved November 26, 2021 from https://www.mckinsey.com/mgi/overview/in-the-news/defending -digital-globalization.

Lusch, R.F., & Nambisan, S. (2015). Service innovation: A service-dominant logic perspective. *MIS Quarterly, 39*(1), 155–76.

Lyytinen, K., Yoo, Y., & Boland Jr., R.J. (2016). Digital product innovation within four classes of innovation networks. *Information Systems Journal*, *26*(1), 47–75.

Mahnke, V., & Venzin, M. (2003). The internationalization process of digital information good providers. *Management international review*, *43*(1), 115.

Majchrzak, A., & Markus, M.L. (2012). Technology affordances and constraints theory (of MIS). In E. Kessler (ed.), *Encyclopedia of management theory* (pp. 832–6). Thousand Oaks, CA: Sage.

Manso, G. (2016). Experimentation and the returns to entrepreneurship. *The Review of Financial Studies*, *29*(9), 2319–40.

Manyika, J., Lund, S., Bughin, J., Woetzel, J.R., Stamenov, K., & Dhingra, D. (2016). *Digital globalization: The new era of global flows* (Vol. 4). San Francisco, CA: McKinsey Global Institute.

Markman, K.D., Gavanski, I., Sherman, S.J., & McMullen, M.N. (1993). The mental simulation of better and worse possible worlds. *Journal of Experimental Social Psychology*, *29*(1), 87–109.

Marston, S., Li, Z., Bandyopadhyay, S., Zhang, J., & Ghalsasi, A. (2011). Cloud computing – the business perspective. *Decision Support Systems*, *51*(1), 176–89.

Mason, C.M., & Harrison, R.T. (2006). After the exit: Acquisitions, entrepreneurial recycling and regional economic development. *Regional Studies*, *40*(1), 55–73.

Mason, C., & Harvey, C. (2013). Entrepreneurship: Contexts, opportunities and processes. *Business History*, *55*(1), 1–8.

Masters, B., & Thiel, P. (2014). *Zero to one: Notes on start ups, or how to build the future*. London: Random House.

Matlay, H. (2004). E-entrepreneurship and small e-business development: Towards a comparative research agenda. *Journal of Small Business and Enterprise Development*, *11*(3), 408–14.

Maurya, A. (2012). *Running lean: Iterate from plan A to a plan that works* (2nd edn). Sebastopol, CA: O'Reilly.

Maurya, A. (2016). *Scaling lean: Mastering the key metrics for startup growth*. London: Penguin.

McAfee, A., & Brynjolfsson, E. (2017). *Machine, platform, crowd: Harnessing our digital future*. New York, NY: W.W. Norton & Company.

McClelland, D.C. (1961). *The achievement society*. Princeton, NJ: Von Nostrand.

McCloy, R.A., Campbell, J.P., & Cudeck, R. (1994). A confirmatory test of a model of performance determinants. *Journal of Applied Psychology*, *79*(4), 493.

McClure, D. (2007). *Startup metrics for pirates*. Read October 12, 2016. http:// 500hats .typepad.com/500blogs/2007/09/startup-metrics.html.

McGrath, R.G. (2010). Business models: A discovery driven approach. *Long Range Planning*, *43*(2), 247–61.

McGrath, R.G. (2013). Transient advantage. *Harvard Business Review*, *91*(6), 62–70.

McKelvie, A., & Wiklund, J. (2010). Advancing firm growth research: A focus on growth mode instead of growth rate. *Entrepreneurship Theory and Practice*, *34*(2), 261–88.

McKelvie, A., Haynie, J.M., & Gustafsson, V. (2011). Unpacking the uncertainty construct: Implications for entrepreneurial action. *Journal of Business Venturing*, *26*(3), 273–92.

McKelvey, B., Tanriverdi, H., & Yoo, Y. (2016). Complexity and information systems research in the emerging digital world. *MIS Quarterly*, *6*, 1–3

McKinsey. (2020). *Cybersecurity in a digital era*. McKinsey & Company.

McMullen, J.S. (2017). Are you pivoting away your passion? The hidden danger of assuming customer sovereignty in entrepreneurial value creation. *Business Horizons*, *60*(4), 427–30.

McMullen, J.S., & Dimov, D. (2013). Time and the entrepreneurial journey: The problems and promise of studying entrepreneurship as a process. *Journal of Management Studies*, *50*(8), 1481–512.

McMullen, J.S., & Shepherd, D.A. (2006). Entrepreneurial action and the role of uncertainty in the theory of the entrepreneur. *Academy of Management Review*, *31*(1), 132–52.

Metcalfe, B. (1995). Metcalfe's law: A network becomes more valuable as it reaches more users. *Infoworld*, *17*(40), 53–4.

Miaskiewicz, T., & Kozar, K.A. (2011). Personas and user-centered design: How can personas benefit product design processes? *Design Studies*, *32*(5), 417–30.

Milano, M. (2019). *The digital skills gap is widening fast. Here's how to bridge it.* World Economic Forum. Retrieved November 26, 2021 from https://www.weforum .org/agenda/2019/03/the-digital-skills-gap-is-widening-fast-heres-how-to-bridge-it/ .

Mill, J.S. (1909). *Principles of political economy ... Edited with an Introduction by WJ Ashley*. London: Longmans & Company.

Milliken, F.J. (1987). Three types of perceived uncertainty about the environment: State, effect, and response uncertainty. *Academy of Management Review*, *12*(1), 133–43.

Mohr, L. (1982). *Explaining organizational behavior*. San Francisco, CA: Jossey-Bass.

Moore, G.A. (1999). *Crossing the chasm: Marketing and selling high-tech products to mainstream customers*. New York, NY: Harper Business.

Moroz, P.W., & Hindle, K. (2012). Entrepreneurship as a process: Toward harmonizing multiple perspectives. *Entrepreneurship Theory and Practice*, *36*(4), 781–818.

Moteleb, A.A., & Woodman, M. (2007). Notions of knowledge management systems: A gap analysis. *Electronic Journal of Knowledge Management*, *5*(1), 55–62.

Muller, R.M., & Thoring, K. (2012). Design thinking vs. lean startup: A comparison of two user-driven innovation strategies. *Leading Through Design Proceedings of the DMI 2012 International Research Conference*, August 8-9, Boston, MA.

Murphy, P.J., Liao, J., & Welsch, H. (2005). A conceptual history of entrepreneurial thought. *Academy of Management Annual Meeting Proceedings*, *8*(1), A1–A6. doi: 10.5465/AMBPP.2005.18779543.

Mutch, A. (2013). Sociomateriality – taking the wrong turning? *Information and Organization*, *23*(1), 28–40.

Nambisan, S. (2013). Information technology and product/service innovation: A brief assessment and some suggestions for future research. *Journal of the Association for Information Systems*, *14*(4), 215.

Nambisan, S. (2017). Digital entrepreneurship: Toward a digital technology perspective of entrepreneurship. *Entrepreneurship Theory and Practice*, *41*(6), 1029–55.

Nambisan, S., & Baron, R.A. (2013). Entrepreneurship in innovation ecosystems: Entrepreneurs' self-regulatory processes and their implications for new venture success. *Entrepreneurship Theory and Practice*, *37*(5), 1071–97.

Nambisan, S., & Baron, R.A. (2021). On the costs of digital entrepreneurship: Role conflict, stress, and venture performance in digital platform-based ecosystems. *Journal of Business Research*, *125*(C), 520–32.

Nambisan, S., & Sawhney, M. (2011). Orchestration processes in network-centric innovation: Evidence from the field. *Academy of Management Perspectives*, *25*(3), 40–57.

Nambisan, S., Lyytinen, K., Majchrzak, A., & Song, M. (2017). Digital innovation management: Reinventing innovation management research in a digital world. *MIS Quarterly*, *41*(1), 223–38.

Nambisan, S., Wright, M., & Feldman, M. (2019). The digital transformation of innovation and entrepreneurship: Progress, challenges and key themes. *Research Policy*, *48*(8), 103773.

Nickerson, R.S. (1998). Confirmation bias: A ubiquitous phenomenon in many guises. *Review of General Psychology*, *2*(2), 175.

Nonaka, I., & Takeuchi, H. (1995). *The knowledge-creating company: How Japanese companies create the dynamics of innovation*. New York, NY: Oxford University Press.

Nygren, E., Sitaraman, R.K., & Sun, J. (2010). The akamai network: A platform for high-performance internet applications. *ACM SIGOPS Operating Systems Review*, *44*(3), 2–19.

Nzembayie, K.F. (2019). Mechanisms driving digital new venture creation & performance: an insider action research study of pure digital entrepreneurship in EdTech. Doctoral Thesis, Technological University Dublin. DOI:10.21427/qbz0-5k11.

Nzembayie, K.F., & Buckley, A.P. (2020). Entrepreneurial process studies using insider action research: Opportunities & challenges for entrepreneurship scholarship. *European Management Review*, *17*(3), 803–15.

Nzembayie, K.F., Buckley, A.P., & Cooney, T. (2019). Researching pure digital entrepreneurship – a multimethod insider action research approach. *Journal of Business Venturing Insights*, *11*, e00103.

O'Reilly, T. (2007). What is Web 2.0: Design patterns and business models for the next generation of software. *Communications & Strategies*, No. 1, p. 17, First Quarter 2007. Available at SSRN: https://ssrn.com/abstract=1008839.

O'Reilly, T. (2009). What is Web 2.0: Design patterns and business models for the next generation of software. In H. Donelan, K. Kear, & M. Ramage (eds), *Online communications & collaboration: a reader* (pp. 225–35). London & New York: Routledge

OECD. (2019a). *The missing entrepreneurs 2019: Policies for inclusive entrepreneurship*. Paris: OECD Publishing.

OECD. (2019b). *Regulatory effectiveness in the era of digitalisation*. Paris: OECD Regulatory Policy Division.

OECD. (2020). *OECD digital economy outlook 2020*. Paris: OECD Publishing. https://doi.org/10.1787/bb167041-en.

Oliva, R., Sterman, J.D., & Giese, M. (2003). Limits to growth in the new economy: Exploring the 'get big fast' strategy in e-commerce. *System Dynamics Review*, *19*(2), 83–117.

Orlikowski, W.J. (2007). Sociomaterial practices: Exploring technology at work. *Organization Studies*, *28*(9), 1435–48.

Orlikowski, W.J. (2009). The sociomateriality of organisational life: Considering technology in management research. *Cambridge Journal of Economics*, bep058.

Orlikowski, W.J., & Scott, S.V. (2008). 10 sociomateriality: Challenging the separation of technology, work and organization. *The Academy of Management Annals*, *2*(1), 433–74.

Orlikowski, W.J., & Scott, S.V. (2015). Exploring material-discursive practices. *Journal of Management Studies*, *52*(5), 697–705.

Osterwalder, A., & Pigneur, Y. (2010). *Business model generation: A handbook for visionaries, game changers, and challengers.* Hoboken, NJ: John Wiley & Sons.

Oviatt, B.M., & McDougall, P.P. (2005). Defining international entrepreneurship and modeling the speed of internationalization. *Entrepreneurship Theory and Practice, 29*(5), 537–54.

Parker, G.G., Van Alstyne, M.W., & Choudary, S.P. (2016). *Platform revolution: How networked markets are transforming the economy and how to make them work for you.* New York, NY: W.W. Norton & Company.

Pavlou, P.A., & El Sawy, O.A. (2006). From IT leveraging competence to competitive advantage in turbulent environments: The case of new product development. *Information Systems Research, 17*(3), 198–227.

Penenberg, A.L. (2009). *Viral loop: From Facebook to Twitter, how today's smartest businesses grow themselves.* New York, NY: Hachette Books.

Pennings, J.M., & Harianto, F. (1992). The diffusion of technological innovation in the commercial banking industry. *Strategic Management Journal, 13*(1), 29–46.

Penrose, E.T. (1959). *The theory of the growth of the firm.* Oxford: Oxford University Press.

Perry, J.T., Chandler, G.N., & Markova, G. (2012). Entrepreneurial effectuation: A review and suggestions for future research. *Entrepreneurship Theory and Practice, 36*(4), 837–61.

Phan, P.H. (2004). Entrepreneurship theory: Possibilities and future directions. *Journal of Business Venturing, 19*(5), 617–20. doi:10.1016/j.jbusvent.2003.09.001.

Pickering, A. (2010). *The mangle of practice: Time, agency, and science.* Chicago, IL: University of Chicago Press.

Pittaway, L. (2012). The evolution of entrepreneurship theory. In S. Carter, & D. Jones-Evans, *Enterprise and small business: Principles, practice and policy* (3rd edn, pp. 120–34). Harlow, UK: Pearson Education.

Plattner, H., Meinel, C., & Weinberg, U. (2009). *Design thinking.* Landsberg am Lech: Mi-Fachverlag.

Polanyi, M. (2009). *The tacit dimension.* Chicago, IL: University of Chicago Press.

Porter, M.E. (1980). Industry structure and competitive strategy: Keys to profitability. *Financial Analysts Journal, 36*(4), 30–41.

Porter, M.E. (1985). *Competitive advantage: Creating and sustaining superior performance.* New York, NY: Free Press.

Porter, M.E., & Heppelmann, J.E. (2014). How smart, connected products are transforming competition. *Harvard Business Review, 92*(11), 64–88.

Porter, M.E., & Heppelmann, J.E. (2015). How smart, connected products are transforming companies. *Harvard Business Review, 93*(10), 96–114.

Prasad, A., Venkatesh, R., & Mahajan, V. (2010). Optimal bundling of technological products with network externality. *Management Science, 56*(12), 2224–36.

PricewaterhouseCoopers. (2021, May). Global top 100 companies – March 2021. Retrieved November 23, 2021 from https://www.pwc.com/gx/en/services/audit-assurance/publications/global-top-100-companies.html.

Raelin, J. (2011). From leadership-as-practice to leaderful practice. *Leadership, 7*(2), 195–211.

Raelin, J.A. (2016). Imagine there are no leaders: Reframing leadership as collaborative agency. *Leadership, 12*(2), 131–58.

Ramoglou, S., & Tsang, E.W. (2016). A realist perspective of entrepreneurship: Opportunities as propensities. *Academy of Management Review, 41*(3), 410–34.

Read, S., Sarasvathy, S.D., Dew, N., & Wiltbank, R. (2016). Response to Arend et al: Co-creating effectual entrepreneurship research. *Academy of Management Review, 41*(3), 528–36..

Reed, D.P. (2001). The law of the pack. *Harvard Business Review, 79*(2), 23–154.

Reeves, M., Levin, S., & Ueda, D. (2016). The biology of corporate survival. *Harvard Business Review, 94*(1), 44–55.

Reynolds, P.D., Bygrave, W.D., & Autio, E. (2003). others. 2004. *Global Entrepreneurship Monitor Global 2003 Executive Report.*

Ries, E. (2011). *The lean startup: How today's entrepreneurs use continuous innovation to create radically successful businesses.* New York, NY: Crown Books.

Roberts, N., Galluch, P.S., Dinger, M., & Grover, V. (2012). Absorptive capacity and information systems research: Review, synthesis, and directions for future research. *MIS Quarterly, 36*(2), 625–48.

Roese, N.J. (1994). The functional basis of counterfactual thinking. *Journal of Personality and Social Psychology, 66*(5), 805–818.

Rogers, E.M. (1995). *Diffusion of innovations* (4th edn). New York, NY: Free Press.

Rotter, J.B. (1966). Generalized expectancies for internal versus external control of reinforcement. *Psychological Monographs: General and Applied, 80*(1), 1.

Sarasvathy, S.D. (2001). Causation and effectuation: Toward a theoretical shift from economic inevitability to entrepreneurial contingency. *Academy of Management Review, 26*(2), 243–63.

Sarasvathy, S.D. (2003). Entrepreneurship as a science of the artificial. *Journal of Economic Psychology, 24*(2), 203–20.

Sarasvathy, S.D., Dew, N., Velamuri, S.R., & Venkataraman, S. (2003). Three views of entrepreneurial opportunity. In Z.J. Acs, & D.B. Audretsch (eds), *Handbook of entrepreneurship research* (pp. 141–60). Norwell, MA: Kluwer Academic Publishers.

Say, J.B. (1816). *Catechism of political economy: Or, familiar conversations on the manner in which wealth is produced, distributed, and consumed in society.* London: Sherwood, Neely, and Jones.

Sayes, E. (2014). Actor–Network Theory and methodology: Just what does it mean to say that nonhumans have agency? *Social Studies of Science, 44*(1), 134–49.

Schindehutte, M., & Morris, M.H. (2009). Advancing strategic entrepreneurship research: The role of complexity science in shifting the paradigm. *Entrepreneurship Theory and Practice, 33*(1), 241–76.

Schön, D.A. (1984). *The reflective practitioner: How professionals think in action.* New York, NY: Basic Books.

Schumpeter, J. (1942). Creative destruction. *Capitalism, Socialism and Democracy* (pp. 82–5). London: Routledge.

Schumpeter, J. (1963). *The theory of economic development: An inquiry into profits, capital, credit, interest, and the business cycle* (3rd edn). New York, NY: Oxford University Press.

Schwab, K. (2017). *The fourth industrial revolution.* New York, NY: Currency Books.

Selden, P.D., & Fletcher, D.E. (2015). The entrepreneurial journey as an emergent hierarchical system of artifact-creating processes. *Journal of Business Venturing, 30*(4), 603–15.

Senyard, J.M., Baker, T., & Davidsson, P. (2011). Bricolage as a path to innovation for resource constrained new firms. In *Academy of Management Proceedings* (Vol. 2011, No. 1, pp. 1–5). Academy of Management.

Sexton, D.L., Upton, N.B., Wacholtz, L.E., & McDougall, P.P. (1997). Learning needs of growth-oriented entrepreneurs. *Journal of Business Venturing, 12*(1), 1–8.

Shah, S.K., & Tripsas, M. (2007). The accidental entrepreneur: The emergent and collective process of user entrepreneurship. *Strategic Entrepreneurship Journal, 1*(1–2), 123–40.

Shane, S. (2000). Prior knowledge and the discovery of entrepreneurial opportunities. *Organization Science, 11*(4), 448–69.

Shane, S.A. (2003). *A general theory of entrepreneurship: The individual-opportunity nexus*. Cheltenham, UK and Northampton, MA, USA: Edward Elgar Publishing.

Shane, S., & Venkataraman, S. (2000). The promise of entrepreneurship as a field of research. *Academy of Management Review, 25*(1), 217–26.

Shapero, A. (1975). The displaced, uncomfortable entrepreneur. *Psychology Today, 9*(6), 83–8.

Shapiro, C., & Varian, H.R. (1998). *Information rules: A strategic guide to the network economy*. Cambridge, MA: Harvard Business Press.

Shaver, K.G., & Scott, L.R. (1991). Person, process, choice: The psychology of new venture creation. *Entrepreneurship Theory and Practice, 16*(2), 23–45.

Shelton, C., & Archambault, L. (2018). Discovering how teachers build virtual relationships and develop as professionals through online teacherpreneurship. *Journal of Interactive Learning Research, 29*(4), 579–602.

Shepherd, D.A., & DeTienne, D.R. (2005). Prior knowledge, potential financial reward, and opportunity identification. *Entrepreneurship Theory and Practice, 29*(1), 91–112.

Shepherd, D., & Wiklund, J. (2009). Are we comparing apples with apples or apples with oranges? Appropriateness of knowledge accumulation across growth studies. *Entrepreneurship Theory and Practice, 33*(1), 105–23.

Shepperd, J.A., Ouellette, J.A., & Fernandez, J.K. (1996). Abandoning unrealistic optimism: Performance estimates and the temporal proximity of self-relevant feedback. *Journal of Personality and Social Psychology, 70*(4), 844.

Shih, W. (2018). Why high-tech commoditization is accelerating. *MIT Sloan Management Review, 59*(4), 53–8.

Siebel, T.M. (2019). *Digital transformation: Survive and thrive in an era of mass extinction*. New York, NY: RosettaBooks.

Simon, H.A. (1981). *The sciences of the artificial*. Cambridge, MA: MIT Press.

Simon, H.A. (1996). *The architecture of complexity: Sciences of the artificial* (3rd edn). Cambridge, MA: MIT Press.

Simon, M., Houghton, S.M., & Aquino, K. (2000). Cognitive biases, risk perception, and venture formation: How individuals decide to start companies. *Journal of Business Venturing, 15*(2), 113–34.

Smith, A. (1904). *The wealth of nations. An inquiry into the nature and causes of the wealth of nations* (5th edn). London: Methuen and Co. Ltd.

Song, M., Parry, M.E., & Kawakami, T. (2009). Incorporating network externalities into the technology acceptance model. *Journal of Product Innovation Management, 26*(3), 291–307.

Spender, J.C. (1996). Making knowledge the basis of a dynamic theory of the firm. *Strategic Management Journal, 17*(S2), 45–62.

Srinivasan, A., & Venkatraman, N. (2018). Entrepreneurship in digital platforms: A network centric view. *Strategic Entrepreneurship Journal, 12*(1), 54–71

Stacey, R.D. (1996). *Complexity and creativity in organizations*. San Francisco, CA: Berrett-Koehler Publishers.

Stevenson, H.H., & Jarillo, J.C. (1990). A paradigm of entrepreneurship: Entrepreneurial management. *Strategic Management Journal*, *11*, 17–27.

Storey, D.J., & Greene, F.J. (2010). *Small business and entrepreneurship*. London: Financial Times Prentice Hall.

Tangney, J.P., Baumeister, R.F., & Boone, A.L. (2004). High self-control predicts good adjustment, less pathology, better grades, and interpersonal success. *Journal of Personality*, *72*(2), 271–324.

Tapscott, D. (2014). *The digital economy anniversary edition: Rethinking promise and peril in the age of networked intelligence*. New York, NY: McGraw-Hill Professional.

Teece, D.J. (2010). Business models, business strategy and innovation. *Long Range Planning*, *43*(2), 172–94.

Teece, D.J. (2012). Dynamic capabilities: Routines versus entrepreneurial action. *Journal of Management Studies*, *49*(8), 1395–401.

Thaler, R.H. (2015). *Misbehaving: The making of behavioral economics* (1st edn). New York, NY: W.W. Norton & Company.

Thompson, E.R. (2009). Individual entrepreneurial intent: Construct clarification and development of an internationally reliable metric. *Entrepreneurship Theory and Practice*, *33*(3), 669–94.

Thrift, N. (1999). The place of complexity. *Theory, Culture & Society*, *16*(3), 31–69.

Tice, D.M. (2009). How emotions affect self-regulation. In J.P. Forgas, R.H. Baumeister, & D.M. Tice (eds), *Psychology of Self-regulation*, (pp. 201–16). New York, NY: Psychology Press.

Tilson, D., Lyytinen, K., & Sørensen, C. (2010). Research commentary – digital infra-structures: The missing IS research agenda. *Information Systems Research*, *21*(4), 748–59.

Tiwana, A., Konsynski, B., & Bush, A.A. (2010). Research commentary – platform evolution: Coevolution of platform architecture, governance, and environmental dynamics. *Information Systems Research*, *21*(4), 675–87.

Tredinnick, L. (2009). Complexity theory and the web. *Journal of Documentation*, *65*(5), 797–816.

Tufekci, Z. (2015). Algorithmic harms beyond Facebook and Google: Emergent chal-lenges of computational agency. *Colorado Technology Law Journal*, *13*, 203.

Ulrich, K.T., & Eppinger, S.D. (2011). *Product design and development*. New York, NY: McGraw-Hill.

UNCTAD. (2019). *Digital economy report 2019. Value creation and capture: Implications for developing countries*. United Nations.

UNCTAD. (2021). *Global e-commerce jumps to $26.7 trillion, COVID-19 boosts online sales*. United Nations Conference on Trade and Development. Retrieved November 26, 2021 from https://unctad.org/news/global-e-commerce-jumps-267 -trillion-covid-19-boosts-online-sales.

United Nations. (2021). *With almost half of world's population still offline, digital divide risks becoming 'new face of inequality', Deputy Secretary-General warns General Assembly | Meetings Coverage and Press Releases*. United Nations. Retrieved November 26, 2021 from https://www.un.org/press/en/2021/dsgsm1579 .doc.htm.

Utterback, J. (1994). Mastering the dynamics of innovation: How companies can seize opportunities in the face of technological change. *University of Illinois at Urbana-Champaign's Academy for Entrepreneurial Leadership Historical Research Reference in Entrepreneurship*.

Van de Ven, A.H., & Engleman, R.M. (2004). Event-and outcome-driven explanations of entrepreneurship. *Journal of Business Venturing, 19*(3), 343–58.

Vargo, S.L., & Lusch, R.F. (2017). Service-dominant logic 2025. *International Journal of Research in Marketing, 34*(1), 46–67.

Venkataraman, S. (1997). The distinctive domain of entrepreneurship research. *Advances in Entrepreneurship, Firm Emergence and Growth, 3*(1), 119–38.

Venkataraman, S., Sarasvathy, S.D., Dew, N., & Forster, W.R. (2012). Reflections on the 2010 AMR decade award: Whither the promise? Moving forward with entrepreneurship as a science of the artificial. *Academy of Management Review, 37*(1), 21–33.

Von Briel, F., Recker, J., & Davidsson, P. (2018). Not all digital venture ideas are created equal: Implications for venture creation processes. *The Journal of Strategic Information Systems, 27*(4), 278–95.

Von Briel, F., Recker, J.C., Selander, L. et al. (2020). Researching digital entrepreneurship: Current issues and suggestions for future directions. *Communications of the Association for Information Systems: CAIS.*

Von Hippel, E., & Von Krogh, G. (2015). Crossroads – identifying viable 'need–solution pairs': Problem solving without problem formulation. *Organization Science, 27*(1), 207–21.

Vopson, M. (2021). *The world's data explained: How much we're producing and where it's all stored.* World Economic Forum. Retrieved November 26, 2021 from https://www.weforum.org/agenda/2021/05/world-data-produced-stored-global-gb -tb-zb/.

Walker, H. (2006). The virtual organisation: A new organisational form? *International Journal of Networking and Virtual Organisations, 3*(1), 25–41.

Watson, J. (2007). Modeling the relationship between networking and firm performance. *Journal of Business Venturing, 22*(6), 852–74.

Weick, K.E. (1995). *Sensemaking in organizations* (Vol. 3). Thousand Oaks, CA: Sage.

Weinberg, G & Mares, J (2014). *Traction: A startup guide to getting customers.* S-curves Publishing, USA.

Weinberg, G., & Mares, J. (2015). *Traction: How any startup can achieve explosive customer growth.* London: Penguin.

Welsum, D.V. (2016). *Enabling digital entrepreneurs.* WDR 2016 Background Paper. Washington, DC: World Bank. Washington, DC. Retrieved November 26, 2021 from https://openknowledge.worldbank.org/handle/10986/23646 License: CC BY 3.0 IGO.

Welter, F. (2011). Contextualizing entrepreneurship – conceptual challenges and ways forward. *Entrepreneurship Theory and Practice, 35*(1), 165–84.

Wennberg, K., & DeTienne, D.R. (2014). What do we really mean when we talk about 'exit'? A critical review of research on entrepreneurial exit. *International Small Business Journal, 32*(1), 4–16.

Wennberg, K., Wiklund, J., DeTienne, D.R., & Cardon, M.S. (2010). Reconceptualizing entrepreneurial exit: Divergent exit routes and their drivers. *Journal of Business Venturing, 25*(4), 361–75.

Wiklund, J., & Shepherd, D. (2003). Knowledge-based resources, entrepreneurial orientation, and the performance of small and medium-sized businesses. *Strategic Management Journal, 24*(13), 1307–14.

Wiklund, J., Davidsson, P., Audretsch, D.B., & Karlsson, C. (2011). The future of entrepreneurship research. *Entrepreneurship Theory and Practice, 35*(1), 1–9.

Wiklund, J., Davidsson, P., & Delmar, F. (2003). What do they think and feel about growth? An expectancy=value approach to small business managers' attitudes toward growth. *Entrepreneurship Theory and Practice, 27*(3), 247–70.

Winborg, J., & Landström, H. (2001). Financial bootstrapping in small businesses: Examining small business managers' resource acquisition behaviors. *Journal of Business Venturing, 16*(3), 235–54.

Wood, R., & Bandura, A. (1989). Social cognitive theory of organizational management. *Academy of Management Review, 14*(3), 361–84.

World Bank. (2021). *GDP (current US$) | Data*. World Bank Data. Retrieved November 25, 2021 from https://data.worldbank.org/indicator/NY.GDP.MKTP.CD.

World Bank Group. (2016). *World development report 2016: Digital dividends*. World Bank Publications.

World Economic Forum (2016a), *New Vision for education: Fostering social and emotional learning through technology*. Geneva: World Economic Forum.

World Economic Forum. (2016b). *Introducing the digital transformation initiative*. Digital Transformation, World Economic Forum. Retrieved November 26, 2021 from https://reports.weforum.org/digital-transformation/introducing-the-digital -transformation-initiative/.

World Economic Forum. (2019). *Digitizing entrepreneurship for impact*. Geneva: World Economic Forum. Retrieved November 26, 2021 from http://www3.weforum .org/docs/WEF_Digitizing_Entrepreneurship_for_Impact_Report.pdf.

World Economic Forum. (2021). *The global risks report 2021* (16th edn) [online]. Geneva: World Economic Forum. Retrieved November 25, 2021 from https://www3 .weforum.org/docs/WEF_The_Global_Risks_Report_2021.pdf.

Ylikoski, P. (2018). Mechanism-based theorizing and generalization from case studies. *Studies in History and Philosophy of Science Part A, 78*, 14–22.

Yoo, Y. (2010). Computing in everyday life: A call for research on experiential computing. *MIS Quarterly, 34*(2), 213–31.

Yoo, Y. (2012). Digital materiality and the emergence of an evolutionary science of the artificial. In P.M. Leonardi, B. Nardi, & J. Kallinikos (eds), *Materiality and organizing: Social interaction in a technological world* (pp. 134–54). Oxford: Oxford University Press.

Yoo, Y., Boland Jr., R.J., Lyytinen, K., & Majchrzak, A. (2012). Organizing for innovation in the digitized world. *Organization Science, 23*(5), 1398–408.

Yoo, Y., Henfridsson, O., & Lyytinen, K. (2010). Research commentary – the new organizing logic of digital innovation: An agenda for information systems research. *Information Systems Research, 21*(4), 724–35.

Zahra, S.A., & Nambisan, S. (2011). Entrepreneurship in global innovation ecosystems. *AMS Review, 1*(1), 4–17.

Zahra, S.A., & Nambisan, S. (2012). Entrepreneurship and strategic thinking in business ecosystems. *Business Horizons, 55*(3), 219–29.

Zahra, S.A., & Wright, M. (2011). Entrepreneurship's next act. *Academy of Management Perspectives, 25*(4), 67–83.

Zahra, S.A., Sapienza, H.J., & Davidsson, P. (2006). Entrepreneurship and dynamic capabilities: A review, model and research agenda. *Journal of Management Studies, 43*(4), 917–55.

Zervas, G., Proserpio, D., & Byers, J.W. (2017). The rise of the sharing economy: Estimating the impact of Airbnb on the hotel industry. *Journal of Marketing Research, 54*(5), 687–70.

Zhang, J., Lichtenstein, Y., & Gander, J. (2015). Designing scalable digital business models. *Advances in Strategic Management, 33*, 241–277.

Zittrain, J.L. (2006). The generative internet. *Harvard Law Review, 119*(7), 1974–2040.

Zittrain, J. (2008). *The future of the internet – and how to stop it.* Cambridge, MA: Yale University Press.

Zott, C., Amit, R., & Massa, L. (2011). The business model: Recent developments and future research. *Journal of Management, 37*(4), 1019–42.

Index

absorptive capacity (ACAP) 85–6
achievement context models 23
actionable metric 67
actor-derived social mechanisms 16
actor-independent mechanisms 15, 96, 157–8
actor knowledge and means 96
adaptability 119
ad-based multisided models 70
Adobe Flash-based content 130–1
Advanced RISC Machines (ARM) 104
affiliate marketing 93
affordances 52–4
age of pervasive digitization 46–7
agile affordances 54
agile planning 28, 148
AI-aided decision-making 123
Airbnb 3, 53, 121
Ajzen, I. 23
algorithmic harm 123–4
Amazon 3, 45, 87, 121, 131
Amazon Web Services (AWS) 60, 102–3
Amit, R. 91
anthropocentrism of entrepreneurship theories 73–4
anti-competitive practices 121
anti-trust regulations 121
Apple 3–4
Application Programming Interface (API) 53
applications layer and external enablers 103–4
Artificial Intelligence (AI) 2, 45–6, 98, 114, 159
Asana 60, 148
Awareness, Acquisition, Activation, Revenue, Retention, and Referral (AAARRR) 146–7

Baron, R.A. 24, 79

barriers and potential solutions, digital entrepreneurship 159–60
  cybersecurity threats 125–9
  digital credit access 119–21
  digital divides and skills gap 117–19
  digital technology fragmentation 130–2
  regulatory uncertainty and international policy fragmentation 121–5
basic intelligence and interest 23–4
Baumol, W.J. 21, 128
beachhead market 147–8
behavioral economics 31
behavioral psychologists 24
Benbya, H. 75–6
Benner, M.J. 3, 65
Berners-Lee, T. 99
Big data 45–6, 112–14, 159
bird-in-hand principle 28–9, 31
Bitcoin 103
Blank, S. 68, 89
blockchain technology 128–9
BMI *see* business model innovation (BMI)
bounce rate 95, 152
brainstorming 71
Brinckmann, J. 28
browser wars 130
Bruyat, C. 37
build-measure-learn 67
Build-Measure-Learn feedback loop 68
business growth 23
business model (BM) 62
Business Model Canvas (BMC) 62, 67, 139
business model innovation (BMI) 63
Business-to-Business (B2B) negotiation 141–2
Business-to-Consumer (B2C) model 140

Printed and bound by CPI Group (UK) Ltd, Croydon, CR0 4YY

16/04/2025

14658489-0002